FOOTBALL'S
GREAT HEROES AND
ENTERTAINERS

JIMMY
GREAVES

With Norman Giller

HODDER &
STOUGHTON

First published in Great Britain in 2007 by Hodder & Stoughton
An Hachette Livre UK company

1

Copyright © Jimmy Greaves 2007

A CIP catalogue record for this title is available from the British Library

ISBN 978 0 340 96030 1

Typeset in Plantin Light by Palimpsest Book Production Limited,
Grangemouth, Stirlingshire

Printed and bound in Great Britain by
Clays Ltd, St Ives plc

Hodder & Stoughton policy is to use papers that are natural, renewable and
recyclable products and made from wood grown in sustainable forests.
The logging and manufacturing processes are expected to conform to the
environmental regulations of the country of origin.

Hodder & Stoughton Ltd
A division of Hodder Headline
338 Euston Road
London NW1 3BH

www.hodder.co.uk

To the memory of Bobby Moore.
A hero, entertainer and good friend

CONTENTS

(in order of birth)

ACKNOWLEDGEMENTS

Jimmy Greaves and Norman Giller wish to thank Hodder's legendary Roddy Bloomfield for commissioning the book. He is our entertaining hero of publishing. Marion Paull has performed her usual thorough and conscientious editing role on our behalf, and we thank Mark Read for his perfectly tailored jacket, and Hannah Knowles for her expert go-between work. In particular we are indebted to sports factician Mike Giller for his safety-net work on the many facts and stats that have put flesh on Jimmy's strong, expert opinions. Thanks, too, to Kezia Storr of PA Photos for her help on picture research. The biggest thanks of all go to the footballers featured in the following pages, heroes and entertainers every one of them.

Photographic Acknowledgements

The authors and publisher would like to thank PA Photos for permission to reproduce all photographs in this book.

Introduction

THE RULES OF A VERY SELECT GAME

WHEN my editor and good friend of many years, Roddy Bloomfield, asked me to select the fifty greatest footballers of my lifetime I thought, 'What a nice easy earner.' Wrong! It has been sheer torture, not so much deciding which players to pick as those that I have to leave out.

This book is going to make me enemies because of the footballers I have failed to shoehorn into my list. At one stage I could not even find a place for David 'Golden Balls' Beckham until Roddy relented and allowed me fifty-one players!

What, no Gary Lineker? There will be people pointing the finger and saying that this is jealousy on my part because he overtook me as the second highest goalscorer for England.

Let me kick that one into touch straight away. The selection rules are that I can only have a certain number of players from each era, and crisp finisher that he was, Gary in my opinion rates just behind Michael Owen, Ian Rush, Alan Shearer and the new kid on the block, Wayne Rooney.

What, no Peter Shilton? Without question, a great goalkeeper but I have Gordon Banks and Pat Jennings pipping Shilts by a fingertip, and I was only allowed so many goalkeepers. There was no way I was going to leave the legendary Lev Yashin out, and you will know why when you read my assessment of the great 'Man in Black'.

What, no Ossie Ardiles, Ruud van Nistelrooy, Jurgen Klinsmann and a cluster of other great foreign imports? Again, I had to ditch many of those I have admired because my selection of foreign players was restricted. I stuck to all-time greats Pelé, Puskas, Di Stefano, Maradona, Cruyff and Co. I could not ignore modern masters like Eric Cantona, Thierry Henry, Gianfranco Zola and Dennis Bergkamp.

I know my selections will start more arguments than they will solve, but opinion makes the football world go round and I hope this book will give you ammunition for good enjoyable debate with your mates.

The fifty-one players are set out in the order that they were born, and I finish with a chapter in which I rate the top ten post-war managers.

The way I worked with my long-time writing partner Norman Giller (whom I have known and tried to avoid for coming up fifty years) was that he provided all the statistical facts and figures, leaving me to supply the opinions, gut reactions and any anec-dotes that I think will bring you closer to my heroes. In short, the facts of the books are Norman's, while the feelings are mine.

Norman could not resist pointing out that we produce books the way I used to play the game. 'You get somebody to do all the running around for you,' he said, 'and then provide the finishing touch and take all the glory.' Nasty – but true!

I hope when you have finished reading the book you will feel that you know the greatest players of my lifetime better than you did before, and understand just why I consider them to be *Heroes and Entertainers*.

Enjoy!

Jimmy Greaves

1

Stanley Matthews

Born: Hanley, Stoke-on-Trent, Staffs, 1 February 1915

Died: Newcastle-under-Lyme, Staffs, 23 February 2000, aged 85

Career span: 1932–65

Clubs: Stoke City 1932–47 (295 league games, 51 goals); Blackpool 1947–61 (379 league games, 17 goals); Stoke City 1961–65 (59 league games, 3 goals)

England: 54 caps, plus 29 wartime international appearances; 3 goals plus 8 in wartime

Club honours: 2 Second Division championships (Stoke), 1 FA Cup (Blackpool)

Oldest footballer to play First Division football, aged 50 years and 5 days

Footballer of the Year 1948 and 1963

First European Footballer of the Year 1956

First footballer knighted 1965

EVEN more than sixty years on I can still hear the voice in my head: 'Shackleton passes to Finney, who goes past one man, two men and slips the ball out to Matthews. He dribbles around the full-back as if he's not there and centres for Lawton to volley in a brilliant goal for England . . .'

The voice belonged to me. It was the commentary I was making up as I ran along the pavement with a tennis ball at my feet, impersonating my heroes. I was imagining myself in their boots, not even dreaming that one day I would play with the greatest of them all – Sir Stanley Matthews.

This was in the immediate post-war years of ration books, petrol coupons, no television just wireless, Old Labour in power nationalising everything in sight, and my football gods earning a maximum twelve quid a week.

Who would have thought that some eighteen years later I would be partnering my idol Stanley Matthews – by then, Sir Stanley – in his farewell testimonial game . . . and then, seven years on, playing with him again in the last competitive game of his life when he was 57. That was at one and the same time the funniest and saddest match in which I ever played.

I will come to those two games after going through the life and footballing times of possibly the finest footballer who ever breathed; certainly the most famous Englishman ever to lace up a pair of boots. You could go anywhere in the world, from Argentina to Zanzibar, and they would have heard of the 'Wizard of Dribble'.

Stanley's dad, Jack Matthews, was a professional featherweight boxer known as 'the Fighting Barber of Hanley'. He was by all accounts a very clever boxer, feinting with one hand and hitting with the other, and adopting now-you-see-me-now-you-don't tactics to avoid being hit by counter punches.

Well, that was also the way Stanley played the game, only he feinted with his feet rather than his fists, and he perfected a unique dropping-of-the-shoulder technique that confused and bemused a legion of full-backs. They used to say that when Stanley sold a dummy, half the spectators had to pay to get back into the ground.

I have this theory that the best forwards, those who can drift through defences as if they're not there, are the best liars. They spend their careers 'conning' defenders into thinking they are going to do one thing while all the time having something else in mind.

Nobody was a better liar than Our Stanley. He told some whop-pers to deceive defenders. He used to convince full-backs that he was going to go on their inside, and then, with a sudden shuffle and a subtle change of pace, he would dramatically nip past on the outside, leaving his marker to tackle his shadow.

His ball control was mesmerising. It was as if he had the ball on a piece of invisible elastic. He would shuffle towards the full-back, tip tapping it from one foot to the other; then with the deftness of a juggler he would flick the ball past the defender and with jet-pace acceleration, race to collect it and bring it back under his command.

Put Stanley in a 100 yards race and he would finish down the field, but over ten yards with a ball to sniff he was whippet-quick.

Stanley loved proving the critics wrong. Time and again they predicted he would hang up his boots, but he kept playing and featured in a First Division match at the ridiculous age of 50 years and five days old.

I got out of the game at the top aged 31 because I was feeling knackered (yes, it was premature and I later regretted it). Stanley played for another twenty years, and was still reluctant to retire when most people were looking forward to their old-age pension.

The reason he was able to play on and on is because of the lifestyle instilled into him by his dad. Almost as soon as he could walk, Stanley would follow exercises set for him by his father, a fitness fanatic who demanded that his three sons follow in his nimble footsteps.

When most fathers and sons were still thinking about getting out of bed, Stanley and his brothers would be early-morning road running with their dad as he prepared for his next fight (he lost just a handful of more than 300 contests and was the nine-stone champion of the Potteries).

Stanley maintained this fitness regime throughout his life, and I remember him taking lots of vitamins and doing vigorous exercises when we used to keep company on the celebrity football circuit late in his career.

I've got a lovely trivia question for you. Who was the only player to score a hat-trick for England at White Hart Lane, my old hunting ground?

It was, of course, Our Stanley. Throughout his career he was more concerned with making than taking goals, but in a match against Czechoslovakia at Tottenham in 1937 he moved inside from the wing because England had been reduced by injury to ten men in those pre-substitute days.

He completed the only international hat-trick of his career in the very last minute. During one of our trips abroad, I asked the lovely old boy what had been his most memorable goal and it was the hat-trick that came immediately to his mind. He told me:

It was an amazing game, and I bet even you didn't play in one like it during all your years at Tottenham. The score stood at 4–4 with seconds to go. I dashed into the penalty area to meet a cross from the left and steered the ball into the net from close range. I don't think anybody, including me, could believe that Stanley Matthews had completed a hat-trick. There are few other goals that stand out in my mind, because I could never be classed as a goalscoring winger like Tom Finney or little Johnny Hancocks. Mind you, I recall once running three-quarters of the length of the field to score England's eighth goal in a wartime international in Manchester. It was my first goal for five years!

The game for which Stanley is most remembered, of course, is the 1953 FA Cup final at Wembley, which became known as 'the Matthews Final'. I watched it in black and white on a Pye television with a nine-inch screen, but could not have been more excited had it been in blazing colour on a panoramic cinema screen.

Blackpool, trailing 3–1 to Bolton with just twenty minutes to go, looked dead and buried. Enter stage right, the Maestro, who was 37 years old and trying to win at Wembley after twice being a runner-up with the Seasiders in 1948 and 1951.

He turned the game – and Bolton's defence – inside out with a dazzling display of right-wing wizardry, inspiring a miraculous comeback and laying on a last-minute winner for South African outside-left Bill Perry.

This was the match in which the magnificent Stan Mortensen became the one and only player to score an FA Cup final hat-trick at Wembley. In fairness, it should not be remembered as the 'Matthews Final', more the 'Stanleys Final'.

Stanley Matthews' value in today's transfer market? Let the bidding begin at £50 million. When it looked as if Stoke were prepared to sell him for £10,000 in 1938, thousands of fans took to the streets in protest. He was finally allowed to move to Blackpool for £11,500 in 1947 because, at 32, Stoke felt he had little petrol left in the tank. He was still motoring down the wing eighteen years later!

England foolishly left him out of the 1950 World Cup finals match against the United States, and were beaten 1–0 in what remains one of the biggest shock results in the history of the game. He was left watching helplessly from the bench. It was like leaving Montgomery on the touchline at El Alamein.

Stanley played in the 1954 finals at the age of 39, by which time the Wizard was losing some of his magic, but he rediscovered his Midas touch in a 1956 international against the soon-to-be-crowned world champions Brazil at Wembley. He was marked by Nilton Santos, one of the greatest ever left-backs. Stanley gave Santos such a run-around on the way to England's 4–2 victory that, when the Brazilian shook his hand at the end, he said, 'Mr Matthews, you are the King.'

Move the calendar forward nine years, and I found myself privileged and honoured to be partnering Stanley in the forward line for his farewell testimonial match against an all-star World XI at Stoke City. We were up against players of the calibre of Di Stefano, Puskas and Masopust. Lev Yashin was in goal. I think I managed to pop in a couple of goals in a 6–4 victory, but this is about Stanley Matthews not me, and we carried him off shoulder-high at the end towards his glorious sunset.

Little did I realise that seven years later I would play with him again in what was to prove his final competitive match.

It was the summer of 1972, the year after I had bowed out of league football, and Stanley and I were playing together in Kuwait for a 'golden oldies' team as ambassadors for British Petroleum. As well as the two of us, our side included Johnny Haynes, John Charles, George Cohen, Ron Springett and the bearded wonder, Jimmy Hill. The temperature was a roasting 110 degrees Fahrenheit and most of us were shattered by the walk from the dressing room to the pitch. Stanley, being Stanley, refused to consider taking a breather, and exhausted himself with a series of his twinkle-toed dribbles.

Our captain Johnny Haynes had no mercy, and kept hitting those trademark 40-yard through balls for Stanley to chase. No chance! The great man made it clear he wanted the ball to his feet, and I fell about laughing as I watched Haynsie, hands on hips, glaring at the Grand Old Wizard of football because he would not try to get on the end of his passes.

It would never have entered proud Stanley's head to allow himself to be substituted, and when he saw our manager Dave Underwood waving for him to come off – with us losing 4–1 against the full Kuwaiti international team – he immediately walked out of earshot and moved across to the left wing.

Dave was one of the great characters of football. He had been a good-class goalkeeper with Liverpool and Fulham, and had bravely dived at the feet of so many forwards that his nose was spread across his face. Fulham manager Vic Buckingham used to introduce him to everybody as 'my chauffeur Appleyard'.

He later became chairman of Barnet and kindly gave me a lifeline by letting me play during my days battling with the bottle. Now here he was in far-off Kuwait wondering how he could get the world's most famous footballer off the pitch without embarrassing him.

Dave thought quickly and walked right the way around the perimeter of the field. Then, with the game in full flow, he walked on to the pitch holding up his arms as if parting the Red Sea. He cupped his hands to his mouth and shouted at the top of his voice, 'Gentlemen, it is my privilege to accompany the great Sir Stanley Matthews off the pitch. Please accord him the ovation he deserves.'

First of all the Kuwaiti players started to applaud, and then the capacity crowd took it up and cheered Stanley – escorted by Dave Underwood almost in a butlering role – as the Maestro made a reluctant exit.

That was the only time in his life he was substituted and it was hilarious to watch, yet also desperately sad. The curtain was coming down on the King on a corner of a foreign field, when his farewell deserved a Wembley setting.

The relatively young Cliff Jones, my former Tottenham teammate, replaced the old master and, with his fresh legs, we pulled back to force a 4–4 draw.

So I was there at the end of one of the greatest football careers ever. It had lasted forty years from his first kicks as a professional back in 1932.

As long as the ball is round, there will never be another quite like him. Sir Stanley Matthews, Wizard of Dribble.

2

Tom Finney

Born: Preston, Lancashire, 5 April 1922
Career span: 1946–59
Club: Preston (433 league games, 187 goals). Played one European
Cup-tie with Lisburn Distillery in 1963–64 (a 3–3 draw with Benfica)
England: 76 caps, 30 goals
Club honours: 1 Second Division championship, FA Cup runner-up
Footballer of the Year 1954 and 1957
Knighted 1998

IT seems almost sacrilegious to say, but according to a huge body of opinion within the game, Tom Finney was a better player than Stanley Matthews. While Stanley was the people's favourite, Finney is the one who often comes out top with the professionals.

Whenever I meet an old pro who was a contemporary of the wing masters, they invariably make the point that while Matthews took the eye with his devastating dribbling, Finney gave something extra to the team effort and was the more productive all-round player.

Our careers crossed briefly. Mine was just kicking off with Chelsea in 1957 when Tom was coming to the close of his extraordinary devotion to Preston. I got lucky and managed to bang in five goals against the North Enders, and Tom was kind enough to tell the newspapers, 'This kid is the most natural goalscorer since Dixie Dean.'

Let me return the compliment all these years later by saying that Tom Finney is the man I hold up as an example of the perfect professional. He gave all he had to the game without asking for anything in return. He was modesty personified, and a master of all the footballing skills.

And now I am going to contradict myself by pointing out that, astonishingly, Tom was never ever a full-time professional. Throughout his career he worked as an electrician and plumber, building up a nice little business in the trade he always insisted on having as a safety net in case he got kicked out of football. Imagine answering a knock at the front door today and finding Wayne Rooney standing there in blue boiler suit with a bag of plumbing tools in his hand, saying, 'You want your pipes fixing, missus?' That was how it was with Tom. Every weekday after training he would go on his rounds as a plumber.

What you have to remember is that the most Tom ever earned in his career from football was £20 a week. He had hung up his boots by the time the maximum wage was kicked out in 1961.

He made a one-match comeback with Lisburn Distillery, doing a favour for their manager George Eastham Senior, and played in the 3–3 draw against Benfica in a European Cup-tie in 1963–64. He did not play in the second, away leg because he could not afford the time off from his plumbing business. Distillery were hammered 5–0.

Tom's loyalty to Preston is legendary. He is still heavily involved with the club as president more than sixty-seven years since joining them, and a beautiful statue of him at Deepdale is there to remind future generations of the Finney legacy of class mixed with outstanding sportsmanship.

Amazingly, Preston turned him down when he first applied to join the club on leaving school in 1936. He was told he was too small and scrawny. Tom went away and began an apprenticeship as an electrician with his father's electrical firm, while in his spare time working out in the gymnasium.

He showed his determination to become a two-footed player by wearing a slipper on his strongest left foot to encourage himself to use the right. Preston suddenly realised they had a diamond in their midst, but Tom's dad refused to let him sign professional forms until he qualified as a plumber/electrician.

Then the little matter of the war intervened. He played for Preston in the 1940–41 Wartime League Cup final when Arsenal were beaten 2–1 in a replay at Ewood Park, but it was 1946 before his career really got under way.

He was such a versatile player that he won his 76 England caps in three different positions – outside-right (40), outside-left (33) and centre-forward (three) – and he also played much of one game as an emergency inside-forward. His 30 goals was then a record for an England player.

Injury cost Finney another dozen caps, and he would have won even more but for the selectors dithering over whether to play both him and Stanley Matthews in the same attack. When they finally played together in Portugal in 1947, England won 10–0! They scored a goal each, and between them laid on four each for Tommy Lawton and Stan Mortensen.

Gentleman Tom was never booked, and was respected throughout the game for his sportsmanship. When the lira-laden Italians came hunting him in the late 1950s he was very tempted because it would have set him up financially for life, but the Preston chairman told them where to stick their offer. 'Tom Finney plays for no club but Preston,' he said. Tom wasn't even given the chance to talk to them. These were the 'soccer slave' days when players did what they were told by their clubs.

Tom experienced some downs as well as ups during his England career. He was in the England team humbled by the United States at the 1950 World Cup finals – 'It was a complete freak result,' he said. 'We played them off the park for much of the game but it was one of those days when the ball just wouldn't go into the net.'

He sat in the Wembley press box nursing an injury when England were beaten 6–3 by Hungary in 1953. 'I remember the Hungarians coming out on to the pitch ten minutes earlier than usual, and doing all sorts of juggling tricks as they warmed up,' he recalled. 'My companion in the press box said, "It's easy to do that with nobody marking you." But we recognised they were as good as they looked when they rattled into a 4–1 lead inside the first twenty minutes. That was as good an international team as I ever saw.'

Tom played in the second game against the Hungarians in Budapest the following year. England were thumped 7–1, the biggest defeat in their history.

'We all realised then that there was a different way to play the game,' he said. 'It was the start of a complete re-think. Suddenly it dawned on us that we were not as good as we thought we were.'

Tom's next boast will be his first, and so I turned to his former Preston team-mate Tommy Docherty for an assessment of Finney the player: 'Quite simply, the best English player of all time. He could have worn a heavy overcoat and still gone past defenders. He had pace, ball control, was two footed, as brave as they come. It was a privilege to play on the same planet let alone the same pitch as him.'

And what about the supposed bitter rivalry between Tom and Stanley Matthews? I asked Stanley about it during our many conversations, and he told me, 'It was something built up by the press. Tom and I never ever had a cross word. He was a great, great footballer and one of the most versatile players ever to grace a football field. It was a joy to play with him.'

I shall leave the last word to Bill Shankly, who handed his No. 4 Preston shirt to Tommy Doc. Shanks once overheard a football reporter saying that Tony Currie – after a particularly good game – was in the class of Finney. 'Aye, you're right,' said Shanks, mischievously. 'But you have to remember that Tom is now in his sixties.'

3

Len Shackleton

Born: Bradford, Yorkshire, 3 May 1922
Died: Grange-over-Sands, Cumbria, 28 November 2000, aged 78
Career span: 1938–57
Clubs: Arsenal 1938 (as an amateur); Bradford Park Avenue 1940–46 (wartime football); Newcastle United 1946–48 (57 league games, 26 goals); Sunderland 1948–57 (320 league games, 98 goals)
England: 5 caps, 1 goal

NEVER in the field of football politics has one man made such a big impact by saying so little. Len Shackleton, my *favourite* footballer when I was a kid in short trousers, made the 'Old Boy' network spit blood when he published an autobiography in which he devoted a chapter to 'The Average Club Director's Knowledge of Football'. It was completely blank.

I just wish I'd thought of it first! It was a well-aimed and fully justified kick in the egos of the little men who ran (I almost said ruined) football in those immediate post-war years when

Shackleton was the Clown Prince. He was the most gifted player of his generation, able to make the ball almost sit up and talk. His extraordinary talent was rewarded with just five England caps. The establishment was terrified of his individualism and showmanship.

One short-sighted England selector said, 'We do not select Mr Shackleton because the England team plays at Wembley *not* the London Palladium.'

Shack was a legend in the football planet that he created for himself. He used to play one-twos with the corner flag, and he would sit on the ball in the middle of a game and challenge opponents to try to get it away from him. It was nothing for him to kick a ball with such bottom spin that it would travel 15 yards and then come back to him as if he had it under some sort of hypnotic control.

He was like a more disciplined Gazza, intelligent enough to take up a distinguished new career as a football journalist after collecting an ankle injury in a First Division match at Arsenal in August 1957. On that same day I was making my debut for Chelsea. The player who had captured my imagination more than any other was hanging up his boots just as I was starting out on my adventure. In fact, I was so taken by him that I copied his pipe-smoking habit, and acknowledged him many years later when I became 'Pipe Smoker of the Year'.

Long after he had stopped playing, I had the pleasure of bumping into Shack on the after-dinner circuit, where he was as entertaining as he had been on the pitch. He told me hair-raising tales of what it was like to be a top-flight footballer in the 1940s and 1950s.

'You have to remember,' he said, 'that we came into post-war football on a conveyor belt of being robots. To win the war we had to be regimented, disciplined and do what we were told. That was fair enough, but then this was carried over into peacetime, and there were people running football who expected players to kow-tow to them and do their bidding without questioning anything. Those players who tried thinking for themselves were quickly jumped on.'

Shack was convinced that anybody playing north of Watford had less chance of gaining international recognition than London-based players. 'Selectors used to get nose bleeds if they came up to the North East,' he said, with typical bluntness mixed with biting humour. 'I told Walter Winterbottom that he could get to the North East without a passport. There were loads of talented players up there who never got a look-in for an England cap.'

Winterbottom was the man who had the responsibility of managing the England football team for the first sixteen years after the war, but none of the power. He was the puppet of amateur selectors, those football club directors who Shack cut off at the knees. In my opinion Walter was never given the recognition he deserved for his service to English football. He set up a nation-wide coaching network, and was always dignified and gentlemanly in the face of fierce criticism from the Fleet Street hatchet men. Mind you, he could go on a bit with his tactical talks.

Shack once sat patiently listening to a typically long-winded lecture from ex-schoolteacher Walter on how he wanted Shack, Stanley Matthews and Stan Mortensen to work their way through the opposition defence with a series of wall passes. Once Walter had talked them into the penalty area, Shack raised his hand and asked, 'Into which corner of the net would you like us to put the ball?'

No wonder the establishment was frightened stiff of Shackleton's waspish wit. He put action where his mouth was, joking on the pitch as much as off it. Once, playing for Sunderland at Highbury and with the Wearsiders 2–1 in the lead, he dribbled the ball into the Gunners' penalty area. He then deliberately placed his foot on the ball like a little Napoleon, and pretended to comb his hair while miming looking into a mirror.

He might easily have been performing his clowning tricks for Arsenal. He started his career with them as an amateur immediately after leaving school in 1938. But the Highbury hierarchy considered him too small to make the grade, and they let him go home to Yorkshire, where he played for Bradford Park Avenue while serving as a 'Bevin Boy' down the mines.

In five years of wartime league football with Bradford he scored 160 goals, and was hooked by Newcastle in 1946 for what was then a huge transfer fee of £13,000.

It is an understatement to say that his debut for the Magpies was sensational. He scored six goals in the 13–0 demolition of Newport County, including a first-half hat-trick in two and a half minutes.

Within two years he had fallen out with the directors at Newcastle, and moved on to Sunderland for a British record-equalling £20,000. He told me, 'People said that from then on I was biased towards Newcastle. That's nonsense. I didn't care which team beat them.'

Shack was a man of many moods and odd interests. He owned a barber's shop on Wearside. 'There would have been too many temptations if I'd run a pub like most other players,' he said. 'I could not become addicted to having my hair cut!'

He also found time to become a qualified boxing referee. 'I know a few football refs I'd liked to have counted out,' he joked.

It was an open secret throughout football that he and his Sunderland centre-forward partner Trevor Ford detested each other. 'I wouldn't say I disliked him, Jim,' he told me. 'He liked himself enough for both of us.'

During one game Shack worked his way deep into the opposition penalty area, dummied his way around the goalkeeper and then – ignoring an open goal – pushed the ball back into Ford's path. 'There,' he shouted, 'don't say that I never pass the ball to you.'

A whole crowd of exceptional inside-forwards – schemers in modern jargon – took the eye in the forties and fifties, including pass masters of the calibre of Raich Carter, Wilf Mannion, Ivan (Ivor) Broadis, Eddie Baily, Jackie Sewell and Jimmy Hagan. But it was the rebel-without-a-pause Shackleton who gave goosebumps to a young schoolkid in the streets of Dagenham, dreaming of one day emulating his heroes.

Not many players could claim to have got the rules of the game changed. Shack did. He was trying to waste time in the last moments of a match but realised, when taking a corner, that if the ball was pumped back upfield, it could perhaps fetch an equalising goal for the opposition. So from the corner he kicked it deliberately straight into touch, and by the time the ball had been retrieved and the throw-in taken the ninety minutes were up. The powers-that-be quickly got together and outlawed that little bit of gamesmanship.

Let's finish this portrait of the inimitable Shack with a memory of one of the great England goals. Playing against world champions West Germany at Wembley in December 1954, he waited for the goalkeeper to come racing off his line and then impudently chipped the ball over his head and into the net.

He was never picked for England again. What a way to treat a genius.

4

Billy Wright

Born: Ironbridge, Shropshire, 6 February 1924
Died: Whetstone, North London, 3 September 1994, aged 70
Career span: 1938–59
Club: Wolves 1938–59 (490 league games, 13 goals; 541 games, 19 goals, in total)
England: 105 caps, 3 goals. First footballer in the world to win 100 caps. Captain 90 times, a record later equalled by Bobby Moore
Club honours: 3 league championships, 1 FA Cup (captain)
Footballer of the Year 1952
Awarded a CBE 1959

WILLIAM Ambrose Wright is a name that fills me with nostalgia, not only for my lost youth when I idolised him as a player, but for the memorable moments when our careers crossed both on the pitch and in the world of the media.

Billy was the heart-of-oak captain of Wolves and England when I was first starting my long love affair with football, acting out my schoolboy fantasies on the playing fields – and in the streets – of Dagenham.

I once ran on to the Tottenham pitch as a short-trousered schoolboy after being dared by my mates Johnny Sugarman and Dave Emerick to get the great man's autograph. Bill was walking off at the end of the game when I shoved the penny one-sheet programme under his nose and said, 'Give us yer autograph please, Mr Wright.' Billy, being Billy, obliged. Can you imagine that happening with today's prima donnas?

The next time Billy and I came face to face on the pitch was at Stamford Bridge in August 1958 at the start of my second season as a professional with Chelsea. We gave defending league champions Wolves such a run-around that Billy decided there and then that he would hang up his boots at the end of the season. I just happened to be on fire that day and notched five of our six goals. The newspapers unkindly said that I had embarrassed Billy and made him look like a dinosaur, while in actual fact he was not marking me.

At the back end of that season I played in the last three matches of Billy's magnificent 105-cap international career, and found him to be a lovely bloke who went out of his way to make me feel comfortable as a newcomer to the England squad. We remained good pals for the rest of our lives.

When I was growing up in the 1950s, Wolves were equal with Manchester United as the outstanding club side. They pioneered European football with a series of thrilling floodlit friendlies at Molineux, beating top continental teams including the Di Stefano-dominated Real Madrid and Puskas-propelled Honved. Billy was the heart and soul of the team in what was literally the golden age for Wolves. They even played in luminous old gold and black shirts that glowed in those early days of floodlit football.

He was a driving right-half for much of his career, but then switched with phenomenal success to centre-half after the cool and cultivated Neil Franklin had walked out of English football to play in the outlawed Colombian league.

There was no way Billy should have been a success in the middle of the defence. At 5ft 10in he was not tall enough to take on players such as Lofthouse, Lawton and Tommy Taylor. He had never shown himself to be particularly strong in the air when playing in the No. 4 shirt. Yet by sheer determination and willpower he turned himself into a formidable centre-half who could match the best of them in the air. In the dressing room we used to joke that it was the most amazing transformation since April Ashley became a woman (a headline-hitting sex change of the time).

After giving blood, sweat and tears to club and country, Billy switched to management with Arsenal, following a brief fling in charge of the England Under-23s. The understanding was that he would eventually succeed Walter Winterbottom, so if he had not taken the Highbury bait, Alf Ramsey would never have got a sniff of the England manager's job for the 1966 World Cup!

By then Billy had married his lovely Joy of the Beverley Sisters singing trio. They were like Posh and Becks in black and white.

His move into management was a disaster. It was like watching a non-swimmer trying to cross the Channel as he struggled to keep his head above water at Arsenal. Despite bringing in top-flight players including George Eastham, Frank McLintock and Joe Baker, he just could not find a winning formula. He was simply too nice to succeed in the managing business, and it did him a favour when he was sacked on the eve of the World Cup in the summer of 1966.

He moved into television as Head of Sport at what was then ATV in the Midlands, later Central. That was where our paths crossed again after I had first of all hung up my boots and then got a personal drink problem under control.

Billy was my boss and we got on famously, even though I was in on some of the terrible pranks that we used to play on him. He never ever lost his temper on the football pitch, but I remember him once racing around the ATV offices, soaking wet, trying to catch Chris Tarrant, who had caught Billy with a bucket-of-water-gag that we had earlier used on the *Tiswas* show.

Once when I was on air in the Birmingham studio, doing a

late-night analysis of a Midlands match, I got a message to take an urgent call. I went to the phone during the commercial break and found Billy on the line. He had left three hours earlier to drive to his North London home.

'Jim, I'm in desperate trouble and need you to help me out,' he said.

I wondered what the hell was wrong. 'Anything for you, Bill,' I said.

'I've left my joint in the fridge,' he said.

'Do what?' I replied, wondering if my ears were deceiving me. I knew Billy had started drinking but to my knowledge he never ever touched drugs.

'My joint,' he said. 'It's a leg of beef and we've got people coming to dinner tomorrow night. It's in the studio fridge. Bring it with you and drop it in on the way home.'

So it was that at two o'clock in the morning I made a detour to North London and as I turned into Billy's road there he was in his dressing-gown and striped pyjamas, waving his arms like a traffic cop. I pulled up and handed him his joint of beef.

'Sorry about this,' he said. 'I didn't want you waking Joy. She'd have gone mad if she knew I'd forgotten the meat. She keeps telling me I'm getting forgetful.'

Famously a teetotaller throughout his playing career, Billy made up for it when he moved into the world of television, where alcohol flows like black gold from a Texas oilfield. But, with the loving support of Joy and their girls, he had the character to beat what became something of a monster. Some of the happiest years of his life followed, after he retired from television and became a director of his beloved Wolves. I wonder how different his life might have been had he stayed there at the end of his playing days to be groomed as successor to Stan Cullis?

Billy and I had hours of discussion about the highs and lows of his career. Two matches stand out, starting with the first defeat by a foreign team at Wembley when England were taken apart 6–3 in November 1953 by Ferenc Puskas and the Magical Magyars:

It was as if the Hungarians had stepped off another planet. I was never allowed to forget how Puskas controlled the ball with the sole of his left boot on the right side of the penalty area. As I made a challenge, he pulled the ball back like a marksman reloading a rifle and fired it into the net all in one sweet movement. I was left tackling thin air. It was their third of four goals scored in the first-half. Geoffrey Green, the doyen of football writers, described it beautifully in The Times. *He wrote that I went flying into the tackle like a fire engine going in the wrong direction for the blaze.*

It was typical of the always self-effacing Billy that he would tell this story against himself. In contrast, another memory that he shared was of England's 10–0 annihilation of Portugal in Lisbon in 1947. England paralysed the Portuguese with two goals inside the first two minutes through Stan Mortensen – making his England debut – and Tommy Lawton. It was the first time the selectors dared play Matthews and Finney in the same forward line, and they ran riot. They scored a goal each and both Lawton and Mortensen helped themselves to four goals. Billy recalled:

'I can honestly say that this was the closest thing I ever saw to perfection on the football field. Everything we tried came off, and Portugal just didn't know what had hit them. There was a dispute before the game over which ball should be used. Walter Winterbottom demanded the usual full-size ball that was common to most international matches, but the Portuguese coach wanted a size four ball, the type used in our youth and schools football. The referee ordered that we should play with the full-size ball, and we had it in the back of their net within twenty seconds of the kick-off. It seemed to take the goalkeeper an age to retrieve the ball, and he was fiddling

around on his knees appearing to be trying to disentangle it from the corner of the netting. We were in possession within moments of the restart and quickly realised that the goalkeeper had switched the ball for the smaller one. A minute later he was also fishing that one out of the back of the net! I doubt if there has ever been a more sensational debut than Stan Mortensen's. A goal inside the first minute and four in all! Incredible. Stan was a real miracle man. Only two years earlier he had been dragged unconscious from the wreckage of a crashed bomber that he had been piloting. He had head injuries that threatened to end his life, let alone his football career. He and his Blackpool team-mate Stanley Matthews – the Two Stans – were brilliant together. This was the match in which Tommy Lawton jokingly complained to Matthews that the lace was facing the wrong way when he centred it.'

It was my privilege to have known Billy Wright as an opponent, team-mate, boss and – best of all – friend for more than thirty years. It was fitting that he was born in Ironbridge, the small Shropshire town that was the starting point for the industrial revolution. He was always industrious and a man of iron will. They threw away the mould when they made him.

5

Nat Lofthouse

Born: Bolton, Lancashire, 27 August 1925
Career span: 1942–60
Club: Bolton 1942–60 (452 league games, 255 goals)
England: 33 caps, 30 goals
Club honours: 1 FA Cup (captain)
Footballer of the Year 1953
Awarded an OBE 1994

I T was sheer torture having to decide between Nat Lofthouse and Tommy Lawton as the centre-forward to represent my early love of the game. In the end I came down for the Lion because my selections are based on players from my lifetime. Tommy 'the Headmaster' Lawton touched the summit of his success before and during the war.

I think Lofty would agree that if they were matched at their peak, Tommy would win by a head, with Dixie Dean challenging them both as the greatest England No. 9 from the old school.

A quick true Tommy Lawton story before I move on. While I was working at TVam in the 1980s, Tommy and his wife came into the studio from their Nottingham home and I did a nostalgia piece with Tommy. After the interview finished, Bruce Gyngell – the larger than life Australian boss of TVam – came bounding into

25

the hospitality room and warmly shook Tommy by the hand. 'You're a legend, mate,' he said. 'Thanks so much for coming in. I suppose you and your wife are going to spend a couple of days in London?'

Embarrassed, Tommy – then in his sixties – replied, 'No, we're going straight back to Nottingham. Can't afford London prices.'

Bruce's mouth dropped open. 'You mean you can't even afford the price of a meal for you and your lovely wife?'

Tommy, one of the all-time greats of English football, shook his head, obviously feeling self-conscious. 'No, we're catching the midday train back to Nottingham. Might get a bite on the rattler.'

Bruce took me to one side and said, 'Go up to accounts, get five hundred pounds in readies on my say-so, put it in an envelope and give it to Tommy with TVam's compliments.'

After I had done the business and a grateful Mr and Mrs Lawton had left the studio, Bruce gave me a real bollocking. 'You lot should be ashamed of yourselves,' he said. 'We know how to treat our sporting heroes in Australia.'

'Hold on, Bruce,' I said. 'I'm only working here at the crack of dawn every day because I was not exactly rolling in it when I came out of the game. Tommy I'm afraid is typical of the old-school footballers. They were appallingly treated by the people who ran the game, and kept on slave-labour wages.'

But Bruce had made Tommy's day, and I didn't know whether to laugh or cry.

Another challenger for the crown of No. 1 centre-forward of the immediate post-war years was another Tommy – Taylor, the Barnsley boy who made his name at Old Trafford and then perished with the Busby Babes in the 1958 Munich air disaster. I had the unforgettable experience of sharing a room with Tommy when he made his final England appearance. Walter Winterbottom called me up when I was 17 to get some experience of the international atmosphere, and he put me under Tommy's wing.

He was a smashing bloke, full of good humour, sound advice and an in-depth knowledge of centre-forward tactical play. A few weeks later he died at Munich, and I looked at that short time we spent together as something very special.

Lofthouse edges out Lawton and Taylor in my list simply because he was one of the strongest and most competitive attack leaders I ever saw making his presence felt on a football pitch.

His link with Bolton is every bit as strong as Tom Finney's ties with Preston.

Nathaniel Lofthouse was the youngest of four sons of the head horsekeeper of Bolton Corporation, and he attended the same Castle Hill School as his predecessor in the England No. 9 shirt, Tommy Lawton.

Lofty has served Bolton for more than sixty years, first as player, later as coach, scout, briefly manager and more recently as the club president. He scored a club record 255 goals in 452 league matches for the Wanderers, and had an exceptional striking rate at international level with 30 goals in 33 games.

It was somehow fitting that Rocky Marciano was reigning as world heavyweight champion when Nat was at his mightiest. Nat was the Marciano of football, playing with clenched fists and crashing through defences with brute force and little concern for his or anybody else's physical welfare. Like the never-beaten Marciano, Nat would never accept defeat. And, like the Rock, Lofthouse – away from the sporting arena – was a gentle person who was never ever boastful or arrogant.

I've told Nat that I come out in bruises any time I see him or one of his team-mates from that Bolton team of the 1950s. I arrived as a Chelsea professional at the back end of Lofty's career, but saw enough from close up to know that he had a shrewd tactical brain to go with his raw power.

Those Bolton lads could have taught the Aussie cricketers a thing or three about sledging. Nat would greet us as we ran out on to the Burnden Park pitch with a shouted aside, 'Here come the Southern Softies.'

That would start off a round of only half-joking comments from the hardest defence I ever played against. Tommy Banks, their England international full-back with a tackle like a clap of thunder, would say to our winger Peter Brabrook, 'If thou tries to go past me, lad, thou'll get gravel rash . . .'

And a favourite comment from their iron-hard right-half Derek Hennin, shouted loudly to his defensive colleagues just before the first whistle, was, 'If my inside-forward [which was me, incidentally] 'appens to come through, chip him back to me . . .'

There was not a schoolboy in the land who did not worship Lofty overnight when he became the legendary Lion of Vienna. It was May 1952, and I was 12 years old and at my most impressionable. Some forty or so years on I sat alongside Lofty at a dinner in Bolton, and we got to talking about the match with which he will forever be linked. He told me:

To be honest I have only a blurred recollection of that game in Vienna. It was deadlocked at 2–2 with about eight minutes to go when I raced half the length of the pitch with the ball at my feet and a pack of Austrian defenders at my heels. Goalkeeper Gil Merrick had thrown the ball out following a corner, and Tom Finney pushed it ahead of me and I set off for goal. The Austrian goalkeeper was in two minds and hesitated about coming out. He was a split-second too late to stop me shooting as he finally raced off his line. We collided head on and I went out like a light. Our trainer Jimmy Trotter brought me around with the magic cold sponge, and it was Jimmy who told me that I had scored. I had a splitting headache but it was well worth it.

It seems to have been forgotten that it was Lofthouse who scored the first Bolton goal in the 1953 'Matthews FA Cup final' after just ninety seconds, but what he has never been allowed to forget is the second of his two goals that clinched the FA Cup for Wanderers against Manchester United in 1958.

In each of the finals Wanderers were up against the sympathy vote. Everybody outside Bolton wanted Stanley Matthews to break his FA Cup duck with Blackpool in 1953, and the entire nation was together in wanting Manchester United to win in 1958 in the wake of the terrible Munich air disaster that decimated the Busby Babes.

Sentiment was a winner in 1953 when Matthews at last got his winner's medal, but Lofthouse had no intention of being sunk in a sea of sympathy again five years later. He led the Bolton team like a man inspired, continually flourishing his fist and demanding greater effort from his team-mates. Here's another one for your trivia knowledge: that Bolton side cost exactly £110 to put together. I shall repeat that, £110 . . . not £110,000. Each player was discovered locally and purchased by the Lancashire club for the statutory £10 signing-on fee.

It was Nat's second goal against United that had him vilified everywhere outside Bolton. He put goalkeeper Harry Gregg and the ball into the net with a good old-fashioned shoulder-charge. It was a physical gesture that summed up his approach to the game – 'Get out of the way . . . Nat Lofthouse is here!'

Today, of course, he would have got an instant red card, but it was a different game then and physical contact was encouraged rather than outlawed.

Many years later Nat told me, 'In those days it was every man for himself, and it made for a great spectacle. Goalkeepers were fair game, and they used to give as well as receive. I had great shoulder-to-shoulder battles with some outstanding keepers, including Swiftie, Bert Trautmann and Bert Williams. It was all part and parcel of the game. Nobody would have complained if our goalkeeper Eddie Hopkinson had been barged into the net at the other end.'

The Lion is still in his den at the Reebok ground, where they have named a stand after him. He was one of the bravest men ever to pull on an England shirt. They talk about the Three Lions . . . this one stood out all on his own.

6

Danny Blanchflower

Born: Belfast, 10 February 1926

Died: London, 9 December 1993, aged 67

Career span: 1943–1963

Clubs: Glentoran 1943–49; Barnsley 1949–51 (68 league games, 2 goals); Aston Villa 1951–54 (148 league games, 10 goals); Tottenham 1954–63 (337 league games, 15 goals)

Northern Ireland: 56 caps, 2 goals

Club honours: 1 league championship, 2 FA Cups (captain), 1 European Cup-Winners' Cup (captain), Skipper of the historic double-winning team in 1960–61

Footballer of the Year 1958 and 1961

I WAS fortunate enough to play with some of the finest footballers ever to cross the white line, but nobody had quite the same impact and influence on me as Danny Blanchflower. He always talked such good sense that I used to feel as if I was sitting at his feet taking it all in. We named our eldest son after him, and Danny was his godfather. That's how close I was to the Irish genius.

Danny was the poet of the sixties' 'Super Spurs'. He gave the team style and panache, and was a captain in every sense of the word, inspiring the players around him with his almost arrogant performances while lifting them with words of wisdom. His contribution to the team was every bit as important as that of our outstanding manager Bill Nicholson.

His influence went much farther and deeper than his displays on the pitch. He was the dressing-room tactician, the training-ground theorist, the man who spoke up for players during moments of crisis and misunderstanding.

Danny rivalled even my England team-mate Johnny Haynes for firing a pass through the heart of a defence, and to see him playing in tandem for Northern Ireland with the midfield maestro Jimmy McIlroy was truly poetry in motion.

Apart perhaps from Bobby Moore, I did not play with a better reader of the game than Danny. He seemed to know what opponents and team-mates were going to do before they did, and he had the courage and intelligence to make tactical decisions in the heat of battle that most people are happy to sort out in the dressing-room inquest when it is too late.

He could lift and motivate players before vital matches with Churchillian-class rallying speeches, and he had a wit that was as sharp as a razorblade. It broke the hearts of those of us who knew him well to see him suffering from Alzheimer's disease later in his life.

I prefer my memories of him in his golden days when there was no better captain or more creative and authoritative wing-half in the game.

A classic example of how he could turn things around came just before we played Atletico Madrid in Rotterdam in the 1963 European Cup-Winners' Cup final, when we were bidding to become the first team to take a major European trophy back to Britain.

Our 'indestructible' Dave Mackay failed a fitness test shortly before the final, and this really shook manager Bill Nicholson, who like everybody else believed in the miracle that was Mackay. He was thoroughly miserable at the pre-match team-talk and built Atletico Madrid up as the greatest team he had ever seen. The impression he gave us was that their defenders were as big as mountains and would crush any forward silly enough to go near them. He made their attack sound as if they had five forwards with the skill of Di Stefano and the shooting power of Puskas. I knew that Bill Nick (one of the all-time great managers, of course) was trying to avoid any complacency among us, but he overplayed it and frightened us to death!

As Bill Nick finished his dismal pre-match talk, Danny stood up and said, as if he was a lawyer, 'If you don't mind, Boss, I'd like to say a word in our defence!' He then did a magnificent job of repairing our shattered confidence. I wish I'd got what he said down on a tape-recorder because it was the most inspiring rallying speech I had ever heard. It would have served as a lesson to all managers and coaches on how to lift and motivate a team before a vital match.

He told us to put ourselves in the place of the Atletico players and to imagine what *they* were thinking about *us*. We had the repu-tation of being one of the greatest club teams in the world and Danny, a master of the word game, convinced us that Atletico would be petrified. We won 5–1, and for once I was pleased to see Bill Nick proved hopelessly wrong with his analysis of a team.

This was all a million miles away from Danny's start in foot-ball, playing for Glentoran in his native Belfast while holding down a job as an apprentice electrician at Gallachers' cigarette factory. 'I could see my life going up in smoke,' he said with typical humour.

He lied about his age to get into the RAF during the war and became a navigator. Perhaps this training helped him because in later years he definitely showed an exceptional navigational sense on the pitch.

Danny made a belated entry into the Football League when Barnsley paid Glentoran £6,000 for him in 1949, and he at last got the stage his skill deserved when he moved to Aston Villa for £15,000 in 1951. He told me he became disillusioned at Villa because 'they were living in the dark ages, training by lapping the pitch rather than being in the middle of the park with a football at their feet'.

It was his ten years at Tottenham that lifted him into the land of legend, captaining, encouraging and cajoling the first team of the twentieth century to win the League and FA Cup double. Three years earlier he suffered the anguish of hearing that his brother Jackie, Manchester United centre-half, had been so seriously injured in the Munich air crash that he never played again. They had been a formidable pair for Northern Ireland, and a bit of the sparkle went out of Danny after that family tragedy.

I joined Tottenham the season after the double year, following my Italian 'holiday', and we won the FA Cup by beating Burnley at Wembley in 1962 and then lifted the Cup-Winners' Cup with that historic victory in Rotterdam.

A knee injury brought a premature end to Danny's career, and he switched to writing a column in the *Sunday Express* that was always piercing and perceptive.

I thought he should have been groomed as successor to Bill Nick and become manager at White Hart Lane, but when he did try his hand at management (with the Northern Ireland team and, briefly, with Chelsea) he suddenly seemed for the first time in his career to be lacking ideas and inspiration.

I had a chuckle to myself when Danny became the first person to tell Eamonn Andrews where to stuff his *This Is Your Life* book. 'The programme is an invasion of privacy and cheap entertainment for a voyeuristic public,' he said. I also happened to know that he was involved in a little romance on the side at the time, and did not want to risk this becoming public property.

He was always candid with his views and would never say things just for the sake of saying them, as CBS of America discovered in 1967. Soccer was trying to get off the ground in the States and CBS hired Danny as a commentator, but he was quickly sent packing when he continually told viewers the truth about the rubbish they were being served up. Most of the players were either past their sell-by date or were novices who could never have dreamed of playing football Blanchflower-style.

Danny used to have us in fits with his off-the-cuff cracks, Irishisms that he used to offer tongue in cheek. A lot of it was blarney, but he would say, 'Blarney, yes, but never baloney.' Let's end with just a handful of his witty sayings in memory of not only one of the best but also the brightest of all footballers . . .

- *'Our objective is to equalise before the other team score.'*
- *'It's not winning that matters as much as* wanting *to win.'*
- *'Everything in our favour was against us.'*
- *'Have you noticed that ideas don't work unless you do?'*
- *'If we don't know what we're going to do, how can the other side? We will confuse them with our confusion.'*
- *'Football is so simple. While* we *have the ball* they *can't score.'*
- *'It's important to get our retaliation in first.'*
- *'There's a move on to get bigger, wider goals. Surely it would be more economical to pick small, narrower goalkeepers.'*
- *'I have come up with an idea how to slow the game down, because it has become far too helter-skelter. Let's play with square rather than round balls.'*
- *'This idea of deciding drawn matches by penalties is so good that they should* start *the game with a penalty shoot-out and then play a match if the teams are tied.'*

I was alongside Danny when a veteran Spurs director, who had been on the wrong end of Danny's cutting tongue, said, 'The trouble with you is that you think you know all the answers.'

Danny put an arm around his shoulder to soften the blow of his counter – 'Ah, God bless you, sir, but your problem is that you don't even know the questions.'

I confess to a tear in the eye as I think of him – the king of blarney and one helluva footballer, Danny Blanchflower.

7

Alfredo Di Stefano

Born: Buenos Aires, 4 July 1926

Career span: 1943–1966

Clubs: River Plate 1943–45 (11 games, no goals); Huracán on loan 1946–47 (25 games, 10 goals); River Plate 1947–49 (65 games, 49 goals); Millonarios 1949–53 (294 games, 267 goals); Real Madrid 1953–64 (282 games, 216 goals); Espanyol 1964–66 (21 games, 9 goals)

International caps: Argentina – 6 games, 6 goals; Colombia – 4 games, 0 goals, not recognised by Fifa; Spain – 31 games, 23 goals

Club honours: 2 Argentinian league championships; 4 Colombian league championships; 8 Spanish league championships; 1 Spanish Cup; 5 European Cups (1956–60)

European Footballer of the Year 1957 and 1959

ONLY the élite players are featured in this selection of the top fifty-one players of my lifetime, and if there was a vote for the most *complete* forward among them, then Alfredo Di Stefano would surely top the poll. He wore a No. 9 on his back, but patrolled wherever he felt he could best serve his team. Most of his time was spent strolling around in midfield, but suddenly he would glide into the penalty area for a vital goal or pop up as a support to his defence.

I was honoured to be on the same pitch as Alfredo the Great in about half a dozen games, including one international, two jubilee matches and several testimonials, including the Stanley Matthews farewell celebration in 1965 and England against the Rest of the World two years earlier.

Watching him from the sidelines, I used to think he was a strolling player, but out on the pitch I found out otherwise. He could be like greased lightning when it really mattered, and would click through the gears as if driving a high-performance Ferrari.

There was a touch of typical Argentinian arrogance about him. That is not meant as a criticism. The best players from the land of the tango seem to have a natural rhythm about their play and need a *machismo* mood to motivate them. I'm thinking of such players as Maradona, Antonio Rattin, Omar Sivori, Mario Kempes and Gabriel Batistuta.

Nicknamed (before he lost his hair) *Saeta Rubia* (Blond Arrow), he had a marathon runner's stamina, and technical ability that was second to none. His instant control of the ball and his passing accuracy were things of beauty that made other pros purr.

Here's a trivia question that will have most people stumped. What did I have in common with Alfredo apart from the fact that we were both footballers? It might amaze you to know that we both had Irish grandmothers! Mine was called Katie O'Reilly, while Alfredo's maternal grandmum was born in Ireland. Could this be why he tied defences in granny knots? (Sorry!) Alfredo's dad was an Italian immigrant, and young Alfredo grew up with dual Argentinan/Italian nationality and finished up as a naturalised Spaniard.

His career was rarely far from a controversy or two. When the Argentinian league players went on strike in 1949, he packed his boots and headed off to play in the outlawed Colombian league (the same territory where Neil Franklin virtually torpedoed his career).

Di Stefano's arrival in Spain in 1953 almost caused an international incident as well as bringing two of the world's greatest club rivals close to civil war. River Plate of Argentina and Millonarios of Colombia both claimed he was registered with them, and meantime Barcelona announced they had signed him following what was described as his 'defection' from Colombia.

While the three clubs were slogging it out over which of them 'owned' one of the world's outstanding players, Real Madrid suddenly entered stage right and insisted they had Di Stefano's signature on a contract.

The Spanish Federation then decided that Di Stefano would play half a season for Real and the other half for Barcelona, a crazy call that led to the resignation of the official who had come up with the brainwave. You could almost hear John Cleese: 'What do you expect – he's from Barcelona.'

Finally, Di Stefano started his now legendary career with Real and Barcelona bitterly complained that no less a person than General Franco had poked his nose in and persuaded Alfredo to join his favourite club. This was one dictator influencing another, because Alfredo was the Great Dictator of the football field.

Barcelona officials and fans made no secret of their disgust at Di Stefano's change of mind. They insulted him at every turn, openly mocking him after his less than impressive performances in his early games with Real, but when he played against Barcelona, he scored a hat-trick. From then on there was no turning back for

Alfredo, who was – along with Ferenc Puskas – the main motivator of Real's five successive European Cup triumphs.

The sad thing is that Di Stefano never got to play on the World
Cup finals stage. If the world had seen the way he could play the
game, he would have been considered the king of football, up there
with Pelé and Maradona instead of just a step or two behind them.

Asked how he compared with Maradona, Di Stefano said,
'Technically, he is far superior to me in what he can do with a
ball; my ability to cover an entire field and versatility is what I hold
over him, though with the right training he could easily do the
same. I have a very high regard for him as a footballer, and I would
have enjoyed playing alongside him.'

Maradona, always looking for a chance to take a crack at Pelé,
commented, 'The arguments continue about whether I was a better
player than Pelé, but what is beyond dispute is that Di Stefano
was superior to Pelé. I am proud to have people compare me with
him. He was The Master.'

The Dutch may claim to have invented 'Total' football, but I
suggest that Alfredo was ahead of them in being able to play the
game to a high standard on any part of the pitch.

What a journey he had made from a farm in Argentina, where
he and his two brothers used to kick a stuffed cow's bladder around.
I once heard him described as 'a Nureyev on grass', but Rudolf
could not back-heel a ball like him. It was just one of the great
skills that he perfected. And could Nureyev have performed the
Nutcracker if somebody had been trying to kick him up the arse?

The only thing that disappointed me about Alfredo was that
he was cold and aloof off the pitch. A lot of people considered
him an arrogant prima donna, but I like to give him the benefit
of the doubt and put it down to innate shyness. Even when, as
manager, he guided Valencia to the *La Liga* title and Spanish Cup,
he was still reticent about coming out of his shell to give illumin-
ating interviews. Late in his life he became Real Madrid's honorary

president, but still kept himself to himself as he battled with heart-related illnesses.

He used to come alive in the only place that mattered to him, the football ground. That was his stage, and in his days as a strolling player he was a showman who knew every trick in the book.

Di Stefano gave one of the most perfect performances ever witnessed in the 1960 European Cup final when Real beat Eintracht Frankfurt 7–3 at Hampden Park. Not only Glasgow but the world belonged to him that night.

A bit of name dropping here. I was discussing the game with Sean Connery, as you do. A football nut, Sean was in the crowd that night, one of those who gave the two teams a fifteen-minute standing ovation at the end of their classic contest.

'They played football that made the hair on the back of my neck stand on end,' said Sean, who was shaken *and* stirred by the game. 'I have never seen anything like it in my life. Di Stefano was like an emperor, strutting around the pitch and pointing to where he wanted the ball and then, when he had got it, pointing again to where he was going to play it, and he always landed it precisely in the right place to do most damage to the Eintracht defence. It was a mesmerising performance, and I felt privileged to be there as a spectator.'

Di Stefano helped himself to a hat-trick on that memorable night, and he inspired his partner to score four goals. I refer, of course, to the Magical Magyar Ferenc Puskas. And, presenting my choices in the order in which they were born, he just happens to be next on my list. Di Stefano and Puskas together . . . just the way it should be.

8

Ferenc Puskas

Born: Budapest, 2 April 1927

Died: Budapest, 17 November 2006, aged 79

Career span: 1943–1967

Clubs: Kispest/Honved 1943–56 (349 league games, 357 goals); Espanyol (guest player, 1957); Real Madrid 1958–67 (179 league games, 155 goals)

International caps: Hungary – 85 games, 84 goals; Spain – 4 games, no goals

Club honours: 5 Hungarian league championships; 5 Spanish league championships; 2 European Cups

Olympic gold medal 1952

World Cup runner-up 1954

W<small>HEN</small> I first played against Ferenc Puskas, my mate Bobby Moore and I had a private laugh as the Hungarian legend prepared to come on to the pitch. This was during England's game against the Rest of the World, arranged to celebrate the FA's centenary at Wembley in 1963. 'It's going to get easier for you now,' I shouted to Mooro. Eusebio, the master Bobby had been marking, was called off and substituting for him was Puskas!

By then, Puskas was on the downhill run of his astonishing career and losing a battle with increasing weight. But the most famous left foot in football was still in good working order, and I felt privileged to get a close-up view of it.

That left foot was a magic wand of a weapon with which Puskas took apart the best defences in the world. We first became aware of it in England in 1953 when Puskas led Hungary's waltz to a 6–3 victory at Wembley, a game I spotlighted in the Billy Wright chapter.

This was all in the first phase of a Puskas career that fell into two distinct halves. In part one he was the captain and chief executioner of the club side Honved and of the Hungarian national team, which were almost one and the same thing.

Honved were originally known as Kispest, a Budapest-based club for which Ferenc's father had been an outstanding player. He followed his dad into the team and had just established himself as the star striker when the government decided they wanted a club to be represented by the Hungarian Army.

Kispest was merged with another club, and the best footballers in the country were transferred to what was now the Army team. All the players were given a rank, and Puskas, as captain, was created a Major. Forever after he was known as the Galloping Major, yet funnily enough he never ever galloped on a football pitch. He used to glide over the turf, always extremely light on his feet for – how can I say this politely – a rotund gentleman. Oh sod it, let's get real. He was a fatso.

The Hungarian team he skippered was sensational, first coming to world prominence when they won the Olympic title in 1952. Amateurs? Shamateurs more like. They didn't do a day's work in their lives, and were full-time footballers. It made a mockery of what was then an amateur competition before the word was rightly scrubbed from the sporting vocabulary.

On the way to the 1954 World Cup finals Hungary put together a sequence of 29 unbeaten matches over four years, including the 6–3 and then 7–1 victory over the 'Old Masters' of England. They eventually fell at the heartbreak hurdle of the World Cup final. Puskas went into the game carrying an injury picked up during an 8–3 first-round victory over a deliberately under-strength West Germany. It was the German first-team they met in the final, and Puskas scored the opening goal as Hungary went into a 2–0 lead inside ten minutes.

But the gamble of playing a half-fit Puskas failed. Germany hit back to win 3–2. Puskas started to celebrate what he considered a late equaliser until English referee Bill Ling controversially ruled it offside after consulting Welsh linesman Mervyn Griffiths.

I discussed that match with Ferenc after we played in the Stanley Matthews farewell game in 1965. What I discovered about Puskas that night was that he liked a good laugh and, even more, a good drink. A lot of pints went into making his famous belly. While still sober, he told me:

The Germans deliberately kicked me in the first match so that I would not be fit for the final. It was the most miserable time of my life, because I knew in my heart we were the best team in the finals. I have never been so disappointed as when Mr Ling ruled my goal offside. It should have been allowed, then we would have gone into extra-time, and who knows what might have happened.

The second part of Ferenc's two-pronged career followed the Hungarian Revolution against Russian occupancy in 1956. Honved were on a football tour at the time, and most of the players decided to seek exile rather than go back to live under the Red thumb.

Puskas settled in Spain after Italian clubs had decided he was past it and overweight, and he became a key member of the Real Madrid team from 1958 until 1966. His prolific partnership with Alfredo Di Stefano was famed and feared throughout the game. They did not hit it off straight away because the introverted Di Stefano – a complete contrast as a character to the always joking, heavy-drinking Puskas – was clearly jealous that his empire was being invaded by what he first thought was a fat clown.

They were neck-and-neck in the first season at the top of the Spanish goalscoring league, and in the last game Puskas had the chance to become the outright leader as he raced towards an empty goal. But instead of shooting he unselfishly squared a pass for Di Stefano to score, and from then on they were the best of mates.

The dynamic duo reached their peak together with that 7–3 drubbing of Eintracht Frankfurt in the 1960 European Cup final. 'The greatest night of my life,' was how four-goal Puskas summed it up.

It's remarkable to think that Puskas was 31 before he joined Real, the age at which I got off the football roundabout. His goals output for Hungary had been nothing short of astonishing – 84 in 85 games – and he scored another 357 goals in 349 Hungarian league games. This was better than a goal a game, almost unheard of at any level of football.

The old left foot was still working its magic in Spain, and he netted 155 goals in 179 *La Liga* matches.

Football remained his life after he hung up his shooting boots. He coached in Spain and Canada before taking the reins of Greek club, Panathinaikos. Against all odds he inspired them to reach the final of the European Cup in 1971, losing 2–0 to Johan Cruyff's Ajax.

Two Greek championships followed before Puskas – by then as big as a baby hippo – took to travelling the world. He coached in Chile, Saudi Arabia, Spain, Greece, Egypt, Paraguay and Australia, improving teams wherever he went and winning the Australian championship with Hellas in 1990–91. He feared returning to his homeland because of the poison spread against him by the Communist regime when he defected after the 1956 uprising. Messages were sent to him making it clear that as a Major in the Hungarian Army he was being treated as a deserter, and his punishment would have been execution by firing squad.

He was granted a full pardon by the Magyar government after the Berlin wall came tumbling down, and arguably the most famous of all Hungarians returned home to spend his declining years in Budapest. He put in a spell as caretaker coach of the national team in 1992 before accepting a role in youth development.

Puskas had been so poor when he was a kid that he and his brother shared the same clothes and shoes. Tragically, he finished up where he had begun, with so little money that Fifa and Real Madrid were persuaded to pay for his health care when he became another victim of Alzheimer's. There was a scandal over a sell-out testimonial match arranged to raise money for him when only a small percentage of the profits found their way into Puskas' pocket.

Following his death in 2006 at the age of 79, his former partner Alfredo Di Stefano made a rare public statement. 'Ferenc was first and foremost a wonderful human being, who loved life,' he said. 'He was also the best of footballers, who loved playing. I considered it a privilege to have him as a friend and as a partner on the football pitch.'

The Hungarian Football Association named their national stadium after him. Ferenc had definitely come home.

9

Lev Yashin

Born: Moscow, 22 October 1929
Died: Moscow, 20 March 1990, aged 60
Career span: 1949–1970
Club: Moscow Dynamo (326 league games)
Russian caps: 78. Club honours: 5 Soviet Union league championships,
   3 Soviet Union Cups
European Footballer of the Year 1963
European Nations Cup 1960
Olympic gold medal 1956

LEV YASHIN is the legendary goalkeeper who once almost broke my heart on a football pitch. I promise I am not exaggerating when I say that but for him I would have scored four first-half goals for England against the Rest of the World at Wembley in 1963.

Just to confirm that I am not dreaming this, I looked up a report of the game by the distinguished *Times* reporter Geoffrey Green:

The first half provided a match within a match, Russia's legendary 'Man in Black' goalkeeper Lev Yashin against England's finest goal-poacher Jimmy Greaves. Four times Greaves, the Artful Dodger of the penalty area, worked his way into goalscoring positions. Four times we were convinced he was going to score, and four times the human spider that is Yashin denied him with saves that were at one and the same time spectacular yet made to look simple by this master custodian. Sporting Greaves led the applause when Yashin was called off to be substituted by Yugoslavian goalkeeper Soskic. Secretly, the Tottenham goal machine must have been praising the football Gods that the 'Iron Curtain' that Yashin had dropped on his goal had been removed . . . It was Greaves who fittingly snatched the late winning goal for England when he beat Soskic with a typical rapier finish after a thunderbolt shot from Bobby Charlton had been beaten out just moments after the Tottenham executioner had struck a shot against the post. You can bet all the vodka in Russia that Yashin, reduced to a spectator on the touchline bench, would have saved the Greaves goal.

Yes, that was the way it was, and perfectly described by the doyen of football writers, who became a personal friend of mine and told me in later years that Yashin that day at Wembley had been 'out of this world'. One of the more lurid newspaper headlines read: 'Yashin leaves Greaves Gnashing'.

I am not telling this story to pat myself on the back, but to illustrate the incredible goalkeeping ability and agility of the Russian giant. Standing 6ft 3in and with telescopic arms that seemed as long as his legs, he used to cover the goal like a huge black octopus.

I remember that one shot of mine in the first half was, so I thought, a certainty for the back of the net until Yashin raised a mighty Russian fist and punched it away with all the power of Henry Cooper landing a hook on Cassius Clay's jaw (as he had in the same Wembley Stadium four months earlier!).

It was Lev's performance at Wembley – with the cream of European soccer reporters looking on – that clinched for him the title of European Footballer of the Year. He remains the only goalkeeper ever to have won the award.

After that match, Yashin and I often bumped into each other

in testimonial games (the Stanley Matthews farewell stands out in my memory, yet again!) and he always greeted me with a huge Russian bear hug. This was all during the supposed Cold War, but there was nobody as warm with his greeting and feelings as the towering Lev Yashin.

Amazingly, football was his second-string sport and he was ready to give up the game in 1953 because he could not see a way to progress at club and country level. The goalkeeping job at Moscow Dynamo and with Russia (or the Soviet Union as they were then known) was in the safe hands of Alexei 'Tiger' Khomich, who was as big an idol as Yashin was to become.

Lev was about to switch full-time to his first love, ice hockey, after helping his Moscow team win the Russian championship, when Khomich announced his retirement. The Olympic title was as much prized for 'Iron Curtain' countries as the World Cup, and Yashin was made a 'Russian Hero of Sport' after a succession of stunning performances to clinch the gold medal at Melbourne in 1956. While all this was going on, Ferenc Puskas and his Hungarian team-mates were defecting because of the Russian invasion of Budapest. It's a funny old world.

For the next three World Cup campaigns, Yashin was the undisputed number one No. 1 and he was a major force in helping Russia through to the finals of 1958, 1962 and 1966. He travelled as a distinguished reserve to the 1970 finals in Mexico. Russia reached three World Cup quarter-finals with Yashin as their last line of defence, but the nearest they got to winning the tournament was in England in 1966. Yashin and his team-mates were beaten 2–1 by West Germany in the semi-final, and lost the third-place play-off to Portugal 2–1.

Lev performed heroics between the posts in the semi-final at Goodison Park after Russia had been reduced to nine men, with one player sent off and another hobbling off in what was more of a war than a football match.

Thanks largely to Yashin's goalkeeping brilliance, the Soviet Union had been the first winners of the European Nations' Cup in 1960 (a tournament that took two years to complete, and is now better known as the European Championship). Russia beat Yugoslavia 2–1 after extra time in the final in Paris, and it was Yashin who was first to get his huge hands on the trophy.

How about this for anybody who collects trivial statistics – during his 22-year career Yashin saved no fewer than 151 penalties! In his 78 international matches he conceded just 70 goals.

With facts and figures like that, how could I fail to have him in my list ahead of exceptional foreign-born goalkeepers of the calibre of Bert Trautmann, Peter Schmeichel, Fabian Barthez and Petr Cech. Please remember when criticising my judgement that I was restricted in the number of overseas players I was allowed.

Once asked the secret of his success, Yashin said, 'The trick is to have a smoke to calm your nerves, then toss back a strong drink to tone your muscles.' It was advice he was later asked not to repeat because it sent out the wrong message to young footballers.

On his retirement, Yashin became the national goalkeeping coach. He was employed by the Sports Ministry and given the honorary title of Colonel. He was also briefly team manager, but did not enjoy the responsibility. 'Goalkeeping is the only thing I know,' he said.

Like so many old pros, he was so lost without the day-to-day regime of training that he turned to the bottle and became hooked on vodka. His last years were torturous. He had just managed to beat his alcoholism when he had to have a leg amputated following complications to an old knee injury. Lev finally succumbed to cancer in 1990, aged just 60, and was given a State funeral as a Russian 'Master of Sport'. He had been awarded the Order of Lenin, Russia's top medal, which usually went to cosmonauts and army generals. In an unofficial poll he came second only to spaceman Yuri Gagarin as 'the greatest Russian hero'. He beat

Gordon Banks by a fingertip in the Fifa-organised vote for the 'Goalkeeper of the Twentieth Century' accolade. A bronze statue was unveiled in his memory outside the Moscow Dynamo stadium.

The last time I saw Lev was just a year before he died, when he came to London as a surprise final guest on Billy Wright's *This Is Your Life* tribute programme. He was the colour of parchment and obviously seriously ill, but he was determined not to miss a final meeting with Billy, his old adversary from the days of the floodlit thrillers at Molineux, when Moscow Dynamo were among Wolves' victims.

Asked about his proudest moment in football, Lev picked out that match at Wembley when he made four stupendous saves against me. I too will always recall that game with pride, because I know I came second to one of the greatest goalkeepers ever to take his place between the posts.

10

John Charles

Born: Swansea, 27 December 1931
Died: Wakefield, 21 February 2004, aged 72
Career span: 1946–1974
Clubs: Swansea 1946–48 (apprentice); Leeds United 1948–57 (297 league games, 150 goals); Juventus 1957–62 (150 league games, 93

goals); Leeds 1962 (11 league games, 3 goals); Roma 1962–63 (10 games, 4 goals); Cardiff City 1963–66 (69 league games, 18 goals); player-manager Hereford United 1966–71; player-manager Merthyr Tydfil 1972–74

Wales: 38 caps, 15 goals

Club honours: 3 Italian league championships, 2 Italian Cups

Italian Player of the Year 1958

BIG John Charles – *Il Buono Gigante*, the Gentle Giant – makes it comfortably on to my list, and if the selection were confined to just ten players he would *still* be on it. Those of a certain age lucky enough to have seen John play will confirm that he was arguably the greatest British-born footballer of them all. A case could be made out for him to be placed ahead of George Best, Bobby Moore, Stanley Matthews and Tom Finney.

The reason he gets left out of so many 'Who's the greatest?' debates is that he spent his peak years playing in *Serie A* with Juventus, where he was worshipped as a footballing god.

I got a ringside view of how John had captured Italian hearts during my brief stay with AC Milan in 1961. In a way he threw a huge shadow over the rest of us – Denis Law, Joe Baker and me – as we tried to fit into the Italian manner of doing things. John took to it like a duck to *acqua*, and the Italian fans expected us to follow suit. But the three of us could not get close to his total commitment, which was matched only by Gerry Hitchens with Inter Milan.

Whether playing at centre-forward or centre-half, John was a world-class performer. He was built like a heavyweight boxer, standing 6ft 2in and weighing in at around 14 stone. Yet he was as light on his feet as a gymnast, and prided himself on playing the game with fairness and sportsmanship. No wonder he was known as the Gentle Giant.

He could have become a star in any sport. During his National

Service in the early 1950s he represented his regiment with distinction at rugby, boxing, cricket, quarter of a mile running, basketball and, of course, football. If they had stuck a pair of thick-rimmed glasses on him he could have passed as Clark Kent.

Despite petitions from Leeds fans, John never got the knighthood he deserved. He had to make do with a CBE and the Freedom of his hometown of Swansea, where he started his career as a youth player before being snapped up by Leeds. His brother Mel had a similar physique but was not quite in the same class. Mel didn't set the earth on fire with his move to Arsenal, where he was handicapped by a recurring knee injury.

John was equally effective in defence or attack for Leeds, and the emergence of young centre-half Jack Charlton allowed him to switch to the No. 9 shirt. I asked John once whether he preferred to play centre-half or centre-forward, and he told me in his booming bass voice – which earned him decent rewards as a recording star – 'Jimbo Boyo [he always called me that], you know better than anybody that nobody gives a damn about the guy working his bollocks off to clear the ball off the line. It's the goalscorers like you who get all the glory, so obviously I enjoyed it most when I was putting the ball into the net.'

We travelled the football world together for exhibition matches late in our careers and always shared a hotel room. He used to insist on me getting the duty-free fags, and by the end of our trips he would have smoked two thirds of the 400 cigarettes that we were allowed. I was tremendously fond of Big John and could never bring myself to tell him that perhaps occasionally *he* should buy the ciggies. He was much too big to argue with!

No wonder he was a god in Italy. He scored an astonishing 93 goals in 150 *Serie A* matches for Juventus in an era of suffocating *catenaccio*, which translates as 'door-bolt'. No forward was marked by fewer than two players, and I have miserable memories of being accompanied by three defenders whenever I stepped anywhere near the opposition half. I always half expected them to follow me into the loo.

John was a buddy of mine, so I can be accused of bias in my assessment of him. Let me support my case with some facts. In his opening season in Italy he was voted Italian Footballer of the Year after shooting Juventus to their first championship, and in an independent poll was voted the most valuable player in Europe. A certain Alfredo Di Stefano was in second place.

Recollections of his powerhouse performances for Juventus never faded, and in 1997 on the occasion of the club's centenary he was voted the best foreign player ever to have worn the black and white stripes of Juve. Michel Platini, three times European Footballer of the Year, was second in the public poll.

He was often almost a one-man team at Leeds, and his 150 goals in 297 league games – many of them played as a centre-half – was testimony to his finishing power. It was his all-round genius that attracted the record £65,000 bid that took him to Juventus. His value today would have been enough to clear the Elland Road debts in one swoop. He had a hammer of a shot in either foot, and I have never seen a player to match his supremacy in the air, in either penalty area.

His domestic life became a bit of a mess and he returned briefly to Leeds in 1962 – 'the biggest mistake I ever made, Jimbo Boyo, was leaving Juventus'.

He tried to rekindle his old Italian glories with Roma, but a succession of injuries reduced him, by his sky-scraping standards, to just an ordinary player.

John got a welcome home to the Valleys in 1963, taking his final shots with Cardiff City before going through the motions as player-manager at non-league Hereford and then Merthyr Tydfil. He wandered around like a lost man when briefly managing Hamilton Steelers in far-off Canada.

Like so many players of his generation, he paid the price for all the heading of the old leather ball. He suffered Alzheimer's, which turned him into a shambling stranger with little memory of his glory days.

A quick word about the weight of the ball may be appropriate. At the kick-off of a game it would weigh exactly the same as today's match ball. But unlike the modern ball, it was made of leather, which was not water resistant, and on a wet, muddy day it could sometimes weigh twice as much during the late stages of a game. I was one of the shrewd ones who preferred the ball played to me on the ground, and I headed it as rarely as possible.

On the international stage, John played 38 times for Wales. It would have been double that but for Juventus being reluctant to release him for friendlies. He made an impressive impact with the Wales team in the 1958 World Cup but injury prevented him from taking part in their quarter-final against Brazil (1–0 winners thanks to a debut World Cup goal from a 17-year-old unknown kid called Pelé).

I had many conversations with John before the Alzheimer's took hold, and he told me that he would have loved to play in the modern game. 'They can't kick you up in the air like they used to with us, Jimbo Boyo,' he said. 'It's now ridiculous the amount of protection the players are given by the referee. It's taken a lot of the excitement out of football.'

When I think of how knighthoods are tossed around like confetti, it is nothing short of disgraceful that Big John – and Billy Wright – did not get a look in.

As far as the Italians are concerned he was like an English knight on a white charger (OK, Welsh knight!), and he will always be remembered as the Gentle Giant who left a huge footprint on Italian football folklore.

I was proud to call him a friend, and will always argue the case for him to be recognised as one of the all-time great British-born footballers. Well done, John Boyo.

11

Francisco 'Paco' Gento López

Born: Guarnizo, Cantabria, 21 October 1933

Career span: 1952–1971

Clubs: Racing Santander 1952–53 (10 games, 2 goals); Real Madrid
1953–71 (761 league and cup games, 253 goals)

Spain: 43 caps, 5 goals

Club honours: 12 *La Liga* titles, 2 Spanish Cups, a record 6 European
Cups

I F all the players featured in this book were matched in a race
over 100 metres there would be only one winner, Francisco 'Paco'
Gento (with dear old Bobby Moore somewhere near the back of
the field!).

Gento was the fastest thing on two feet, whooshing down the
left touchline for the great Real Madrid team as if jet-propelled.
He was once clocked over 100 metres at 10.9 seconds. Pretty fast,
yes? I should add that this was with a ball at his feet! No wonder
he became known throughout Spain as '*El Supersonico*'.

He was a key player in every one of Real's historic five successive European Cup final victories from 1956 to 1960, and was the
only one of the Famous Five (Kopa, del Sol, Di Stefano, Puskas,

Gento) to go on to a full house of a record six European Cup final victories with Real in 1966. He was also a runner-up in 1962 and 1964. It's hard to imagine anybody ever beating his record of six winning European Cup finals (AC Milan's Paolo Maldini is the only challenger to his consistency with five wins and three defeats).

As late as 1971 he was still chasing silverware, helping Real reach the European Cup-Winners' Cup final where they were beaten in a replay by a Peter Osgood goal for Chelsea.

Known to all as Paco – the common abbreviation of Francisco – he developed his speed while chasing birds on his family's small-holding. We have a saying in football that fleet-footed players 'are fast enough to catch pigeons'. Well, Gento could!

Santander spotted Gento playing local football and signed him for a season before Real came swooping in for him in 1953, when he was 20.

At first Gento was treated as something of a novelty act at Real as he raced past full-backs and continued racing into the crowd. His ball control and tactical awareness were appalling. But once the Real coaches got him to balance his natural speed with knowing what to do with the ball he became an enormous asset to the team. He not only perfected his crossing technique but added the dimension of a whiplash left-foot shot that brought him a shoal of goals.

The first time I became aware of Gento was in the mid-fifties, just after I had joined the Stamford Bridge groundstaff. Chelsea right-back Peter Sillett came back from a trip to Spain where England drew 1–1 in front of a 125,000 crowd in Madrid, and he said in his Hampshire burr, 'I marked a player who's so fast that I got burned by his exhaust!' That was my introduction to the legend that is Gento.

I got my first look at Paco the Paceman in the flesh when I played for England at the Bernabeu Stadium on 15 May 1960, when all the rain in Spain that day was mainly on the pitch. We played in a quagmire, but Gento managed to show pace and precision to create their first goal as we took a 3–0 pasting. Jimmy Armfield marked him as well as any full-back in the world could have done. I think Gento was surprised to find a defender as quick as Our Jim, who started out as a rugby wing three-quarter and could really motor.

What I remember most about that Sunday game was Alfredo Di Stefano continually going to the touchline to demand that he be substituted. The great man wanted to save himself for the European Cup final against Eintracht Frankfurt at Hampden Park three days later.

If you want to see evidence of just how good a player Gento was, beg, steal or borrow a video/DVD of that classic Real–Eintracht final. He set up one of the four goals for Ferenc Puskas with a darting 50-metre run in which he went past three German defenders as if they were statues.

There were few more idolised players in Spain than Gento. That phenomenal Real Madrid side of the late 1950s relied heavily on overseas talent and Gento was one of the outstanding home-grown players. He was made captain of a young Spanish international team, which became known as 'Yeah, Yeah' after The Beatles, and the crowd would sing 'We Love You Yeah Yeah Yeah' whenever they scored a goal.

Paco did not dribble like a Matthews or a Finney. He used to go straight for the jugular, sprinting towards the defence with the ball at his feet and using body mimes to trick his way past opposing players.

My next view of Gento was at Wembley on 26 October 1960, when Spain arrived with all their big guns. The forward line read: Enrique Mateos, Luis Del Sol, Alfredo Di Stefano, Luis Suarez and Gento. That's as good as it gets.

But with Jimmy Armfield managing to keep Gento under lock and key for most of the match, we put together one of our most satisfying performances to beat them 4–2 after they had twice battled back to equalise on another rain-saturated pitch.

I played in a couple more friendly internationals against Spain and Gento, and he was in the Rest of the World team that took on England in the centenary celebrations at Wembley in 1963. We were also on opposing sides in several testimonial matches. In every game I was impressed not only by his speed and skill, but also his sportsmanship. He was a great ambassador for Spain, and it was fitting that after he had hung up his boots he was appointed an official travelling ambassador for Real Madrid, the club for which he gave one hundred per cent at all times.

He was such a modest, retiring man that he rarely gave interviews, but I found the following quote from him, which sums up the way he approached the game:

I was always a believer that football should be first and last a team game. Once the side has the necessary togetherness, then individual players can be allowed to surface. At Real we were lucky in having exceptional individual masters like my dear friends Alfredo Di Stefano and Ferenc Puskas. But each of them accepted that the team should come first. You do not win five successive European Cup finals unless you are all playing for each other. People always talked about my speed, and while I was proud of being able to sprint I also liked to think I had adequate skills on the ball. Mind you, it made my life much easier knowing the quality of the players I had around me. I don't like to live in the past, but I will be surprised if there is ever a better team performance than the one Real produced against Eintracht Frankfurt in the 1960 European Cup final in Glasgow. That was as close as you will ever see to sheer perfection.

Paco Gento is a man of few words. He let his feet do the talking and they left behind the message that he was one of the finest – and certainly one of the fastest – left-wingers of any era.

12

Garrincha (Manoel Francisco dos Santos)

Born: Pau Grande, Brazil, 28 October 1933
Died: Rio de Janeiro, 20 January 1983, aged 49
Career span: 1953–1972
Clubs: Botafogo 1953–65 (581 games, 232 goals); Corinthians 1966 (10 games, 2 goals); Atletico Junior 1968 (1 game); Flamengo 1968–69 (15 games, 4 goals); Olaria 1972 (10 games, 1 goal)
Brazil: 50 caps, 12 goals (42 wins, 7 draws)
Club honours: 5 equivalent of Brazilian league titles
World Cup 1958 and 1962

Y OU are not going to believe half the things I am about to tell you about the mad man (or the miracle man, if you prefer) who was Garrincha, but I assure you they are all true – except perhaps the claim that he lost his virginity to a goat.

There has definitely never been another footballer quite like Garrincha, a nickname meaning little bird. His team-mates used to call him Mané, which in Brazil can be interpreted as 'fool' or 'half wit'. He was close to being the village idiot in the small mountain retreat of Pau Grande, where he grew up close to poverty with his thirteen brothers and sisters. The only thing that saved him from total ridicule was his ability to play the game of football better than almost anybody who ever breathed. There is a school of opinion in Brazil that he was even better than Pelé.

He was a cripple at birth in 1933, and doctors feared he would never be able to walk properly. An operation left one leg shorter than the other, and both legs were so bowed you could have run a pig through them without him knowing. He wore two left boots, which confused a procession of full-backs trying to fathom which way he was going to go next. His biographer Ruy Castro traced his ancestry to an Indian tribe in Brazil among whom bowed legs were common.

Garrincha showed little interest in following a career in football until he was virtually dragged to Botafogo for a trial by a former professional who had seen him playing in a kick-around in Pau Grande. In the trial match he was marked by Nilton Santos, one of the most accomplished full-backs of all time. During one run Garrincha took the ball up to Santos, feinted left, feinted right and then stuck the ball through his legs and was past him in a flash to collect it and race away to score. 'It might be a good idea to sign this kid,' Santos muttered after the match. 'The way he can dribble the ball it's better we have him with us than against us.'

With a ball at his feet Garrincha could be the most bewitching, bewildering and stunning winger who ever pulled a defence apart. He was such an individualist that even Brazilian coaches, with their preaching of freedom of expression, were petrified of his independent spirit. It was only after a deputation of his team-mates had pleaded on his behalf that he was reluctantly included in the 1958 World Cup match against Russia following a stuttering goalless draw with England.

He and 17-year-old Pelé made their World Cup debuts together, transforming Brazil into an unbeatable side. Amazingly, they were never on the losing side together. Garrincha's contribution to the 1958 and 1962 World Cup triumphs of Brazil were greater than anybody's. He tried to motivate the Brazilians again in 1966, but a cartilage operation and injuries received in a car smash had robbed him of much of his unique magic.

Garrincha won 50 caps while playing for Botafogo, Corinthians and Flamengo, but his glittering career was overshadowed by a series of domestic squabbles and scandals. He left his wife and eight daughters to marry a vivacious nightclub singer whom he had got pregnant at the same time as his wife.

Incidentally, the singer introduced herself to Garrincha while he was standing naked in the shower after the 1962 World Cup final. I am reliably informed that he was hung like a donkey, and it gave a new meaning to love at first sight. It was the start of a fifteen-year headline-hitting romance. And that is only the half of it.

Garrincha never ever seemed to grow up, and was considered a man-child. His grasp of what was going on around him was that of a vacant person. For instance, when his Brazilian team-mates were jumping around in celebration of their fantastic World Cup final victory against Sweden in 1958 he wondered what all the fuss was about. He honestly thought the World Cup tournament was being contested on a league basis, and that they still had to play all the other teams in the tournament.

I was in the England World Cup team that Garrincha destroyed with his amazing skill in the 1962 quarter-finals in Chile. The man was a footballing genius. Full stop. He beat our goalkeeper Ron Springett twice, first with a thumping header and then with a viciously swerving 20-yard shot that spun into the net like a Shane Warne leg-break. It was the first time we had heard the phrase 'the banana shot'. A local newspaper headline the next morning read: 'FROM WHICH PLANET DOES GARRINCHA COME?'

When I think of Garrincha I recall a stray dog that invaded the pitch during that quarter-final. It led a posse of ball boys and players a dance before I went down on all fours to capture it. The four-legged intruder seemed very relieved as I handed him to an official. So relieved, in fact, that he rewarded me by pissing all the way down the front of my England shirt and shorts. In those days there were no second kits provided, so I could not change at half-time and ponged all through the game. Garrincha, an animal-loving country boy who kept, among other things, fifty birds in his village home, fell in love with the stray. He saw the dog as a lucky omen because of the unbelievable game he – Garrincha, not the dog! – had against us, and took it home to Brazil with him. It was reported in the English newspapers that he said he was going to name the dog after me, 'Yimmy Greaves'. He was barking mad.

In 1964 I took part with England in a 'Little World Cup' tournament in Rio, and during a day off we sat on the sidelines and watched Brazil play Argentina. Apart from the naked violence running through the game, I particularly remember Garrincha dummying Argentine defender Vairo so many times that he didn't know whether he was on his arse or his elbow. At one stage during a run, with Vairo trying to close-mark him, Garrincha deliberately left the ball behind and poor Vairo kept chasing after him not realising that the ball was sitting unattended ten yards away.

In another game, just before the World Cup in 1958, he waltzed past three defenders and took the ball to the goal-line with an empty net facing him. He then ran back towards the defenders he had just tormented, beat them again and then walked the ball into the net before hooking it up under his arm and casually walking back towards the centre-circle. The watching manager of Brazil warned him that if he did not stop this sort of clowning, he would never play for Brazil.

Garrincha's off-the-pitch behaviour made George Best seem like a sober monk. He was continually boozed, and was involved in several horrendous car crashes. In 1969 he drove into a lorry, killing his mother-in-law and badly injuring himself. Ten years earlier he had been at the wheel of his car when he ran over his own father,

Amaro. He drove off without stopping, and when a chasing mob caught up with him they found that he was so drunk he had no idea what he had done. Police took no further action when they discovered that his injured father, an alcoholic, was also drunk.

In all, Garrincha fathered fourteen children, including an illegitimate one while on a two-week tour of Sweden with his club Botafogo.

He had an amazing international record – 50 caps, 42 victories, seven draws. The only time he experienced defeat was in the final match of his career with Brazil. That was the 1966 World Cup game against Hungary at Goodison, by which time Pelé had been kicked out of the tournament. 'Without Mané,' said Pelé, 'I would never have been a three-times World Cup winner.'

Garrincha played football like a towering intellectual, but was as simple as an illiterate child off the pitch. He had no understanding of the tax system, and throughout his retirement was hounded by the Brazilian authorities for unpaid back tax. Thousands of dollars collected on trips around the world were found rotting in his house when he was investigated by inland-revenue officials.

It was not only the taxman who was chasing him, but a procession of debtors, including his ex-wife and former lovers seeking alimony and child maintenance payments. A vigilante mob came looking for him one day, and Garrincha wisely decided he was best off out of the country. He and his nightclub singer dashed off to Rome, where she continued her career while he – having failed to attract the interest of any Italian clubs – drank himself towards oblivion.

The Roman 'holiday' lasted two years before Garrincha headed back home. He received a hero's welcome and was given pride of place on a float at one of Brazil's biggest carnivals. The crowds thronging the streets and millions watching on television could not believe what had happened to their idol. Dressed in his Brazilian kit, he just sat staring into space, unaware of what was going on around him.

He seemed to have elected to lose himself in the bottle despite numerous warnings about what he was doing to his liver. When he died in 1983, he was just 49, and Brazil – the whole football world – mourned the passing of a true giant of the game.

In death, he was as loved as he had been in his peak playing days because he was considered a man of the people. On his modest headstone his epilogue reads: 'Here rests in peace one who brought Joy to the People.'

Garrincha was as mad as a hatter, but what a player!

13

Johnny Haynes

Born: Kentish Town, London, 17 October 1934
Died: Edinburgh, 18 October 2005, aged 71
Career span: 1950–70
Clubs: Fulham 1950–70 (594 league games, 146 goals); Durban City 1970
England: 56 caps, 18 goals (22 games as captain)

OF all the hundreds of team-mates I had during my playing career, Johnny Haynes was the one I most enjoyed playing with. We could read each other like a book (a much better book than this one), and we knew exactly where to be on the pitch to get the best from our performances and cause most damage to the opposition defence.

There will always be a debate about whether Johnny or David Beckham – one of his successors as England captain – had the better ball delivery from long range. Well my vote would go to Haynsie, who could pass just as accurately as Becks but with either foot.

I was always on at John to come and join me at Tottenham, the club he should have signed for direct from school as he only lived down the road at Edmonton. But the silly sod chose Fulham, just because his best mate Tosh Chamberlain had settled in there.

Fulham, of course, treated him royally, making him the game's first £100-a-week footballer after the lifting of the maximum wage in 1961. He rewarded them with undying loyalty, but at the expense of never winning a meaningful medal throughout his club career. Had he been with us at Tottenham, or with Arsenal – a club that always coveted him – he would surely have won a stack of medals.

Johnny was *the* pass master, and my favourite England playing partner (at club level, Bobby Smith and the highly skilled Alan Gilzean were the sidekicks who brought the best out of me).

Haynsie used to serve the ball on a plate, and I owed him plenty of my 44 international goals. He could have doubled his goals output if he had put his mind to it, but he preferred to concentrate on his main role as a creator.

I remember John giving me terrible stick after I had failed to score against Lev Yashin at Wembley. He took every opportunity to remind me that he once scored a hat-trick against Russia at Wembley in 1958, with Lev Yashin in goal!

There have been few, if any, to touch him for long-distance passing, and his brilliantly disguised reverse pass time and again dismantled defences.

If he had a fault it was that he expected everybody around him to match his sky-high standards, and he used to give withering looks to anybody who dropped a pass short or was not in the right position at the right time to run on to one of his pin-pointed through balls. That perfectionist's attitude did not always endear him to his team-mates, and there were plenty of fans – particularly north of Watford – who tagged on to his nickname, 'Big Head'.

He used to have some blistering rows on the pitch with his mate Tosh Chamberlain, who was as Cockney and as cheeky as they come. Tosh was always ready with a mouthful when John stood, hands on hips, giving him his 'what the f*** was that' look. A true story: Tosh was once sent off for using the c*** word. The referee was fairly certain he was aiming the description at him, but Tosh spread his arms wide in despair and said, 'But, ref, I wasn't talking to you. I was talking to Haynsie. I'm allowed to swear at him 'cos he's on my side, and he *is* a c***.'

While there was a touch of arrogance about Johnny on the pitch, away from football he was marvellous and witty company. Throughout much of his career he had a big interest in a family bookmaking business, and often used to talk the jargon of the race-track.

There was a lot of jealousy of John because of his big wages, which were supplemented by clever management by his agent Bagenal Harvey, who also looked after me. It was Bagenal who set up the famous Brylcreem sponsorship deal for Denis Compton and then passed the contract on to Haynsie. For some reason, he didn't think I was cut out for the Brylcreem image.

In 1964 I almost persuaded Bagenal to talk John into joining Tottenham after Bill Nicholson made it clear that he wanted Haynes as the replacement in midfield for the retired Danny Blanchflower and the tragically killed John White, who was struck by lightning on a golf course. It would have been the perfect buy, but instead we finished up with Terry Venables from Chelsea and another

Fulham stalwart, Alan Mullery. Both were outstanding players, but I am sure each would admit they were not in Johnny's class for passing accuracy.

People have often been sympathetic to me because I missed out on the 1966 World Cup final (believe me, I was not looking for sympathy). But how about Johnny Haynes? He had been one of England's finest players for the five years before Alf Ramsey took over, but did not get a sniff of a place in the England squad once the Walter Winterbottom regime had finished.

Alf saw Johnny as representing the old guard, and was determined to do things his way. Mind you, it might have been different if Haynsie had not got badly injured in a car smash on the way to Blackpool in the summer of 1962 after skippering England in the World Cup finals. He had a beautiful girl by his side, which was the lifestyle Johnny enjoyed as one of sport's most eligible bachelors. He was never quite the same formidable force after that crash, but still – in my opinion – worth his place in the England team. But when did Alf Ramsey and I ever agree on a team selection?

I know this will sound like sour grapes, but the finest England team in my lifetime was *not* the 1966 World Cup-winning side but the team that were undefeated in a six-game sequence in 1960–61. We rattled in 40 goals while conceding just eight. For the record the team (in 4-2-4 formation) was: Ron Springett; Jimmy Armfield, Peter Swan, Ron Flowers, Mick McNeil; Bobby Robson, Haynsie; Bryan Douglas, Little Me, Bobby Smith and Bobby Charlton.

The run included the small matter of a 9–3 victory over Scotland at Wembley. That was Johnny's finest hour. He was magnificent that day, helping me to a hat-trick, scoring two goals himself and totally dictating the game from start to finish with passes that continually paralysed the Scottish defence. We carried him off shoulder high at the final whistle.

It was a performance that made the world sit up, and the Italians, led by Inter Milan, came banging on the door at Craven Cottage. But the Fulham chairman, comedian Tommy Trinder, was determined not to let Haynsie go (not that he wanted to make the trek to Italy), and came out with his funniest line: 'We are going to make Johnny Haynes football's first £100-a-week footballer.'

In this day and age of the £100,000-a-week footballer this sounds like chickenfeed. But remember that no player had earned more than £20 a week before Trinder made that statement, and the average national earnings were around £11 a week.

Sadly, we had gone off the boil by the time we got to Chile for the 1962 World Cup finals, but we might have squeezed through to the final had we not been drawn against Brazil in the quarter-final. They were light-years better than us, and that little git Garrincha destroyed us on his own.

That was the last time Johnny pulled on an England shirt. By the time he had recovered from his car-crash injuries he was looked on as yesterday's man, discarded at the age of 26. What a way to treat a player who had touched peaks of perfection for his country.

He was content to hold his passing-out parade with Fulham, even briefly managing them in an emergency after a tearful Bobby Robson had been sacked in 1968. But he hated that sort of responsibility and quickly handed over the reins to Bill Dodgin.

After a wind-down season playing for Durban City (and helping them win the Springbok championship) he returned from South Africa with his second wife, Avril, and stunned us all by choosing to go to live among the 'auld enemy' in Scotland. He had done very nicely out of his betting shops, and he helped Avril run a dry-cleaning business.

Not long before his tragic death in 2005 I got together with him to talk about old times. For various reasons the interview was never broadcast, but I thought I would share it with you:

JG: *What the hell are you doing living among the Jocks, Haynsie? I thought you hated them.*

JH: Not at all, James. I thought players like Dave Mackay, Denis Law, Jim Baxter and even your old sparring partner Ian St John were among the best footballers in the business. Scots are good people at heart, and have made Avril and I feel very at home in Edinburgh.

JG: *Do you resent the sort of wages the top players are getting today? Blimey, some of them earn more in a week than I picked up throughout my career.*

JH: You are talking to the man who got lots of stick when it became public knowledge that I was on £100 a week. I am delighted to see players getting paid well for what, let's face it, is a very short career at the top. I was more resentful, Jim, when we used to get a maximum twenty quid a week, and clubs were packing the crowds in. Where on earth did all that money go that they took at the gates?

JG: *Straight into the bins of the chairmen and directors, I bet. Nowadays, you can hardly find a player in the Premiership who can speak English.*

JH: Football is an international language that everybody understands. The overseas players are only doing what you did, Jim, when you buggered off to Milan. It's all about earning as much as you can while you can. It's a worry that not enough home-grown talent is coming through, but the standards are so high that I think we will find a new generation of youngsters eventually forcing their way into the first-team squads because of the way they have been inspired by what they see.

JG: *Is there any one British player you would fork out loadsamoney to buy if you were a club chairman with limitless funds?*

JH: My personal favourite is Paul Scholes at Manchester United. He reads the game well, goes where he is needed on the pitch, never ducks responsibility, passes well, and has a little bit of devil about him. What a pity he's called it a day with England. They need his drive in midfield.

JG: *What about David Beckham?*

JH: A very good player with a dream of a right boot. But you know what I'm going to say, James. He's too one-footed and so therefore a bit predictable. It's easy for any team to work out what to do to nullify him when he's playing for England. Just stop the ball getting to him, and suddenly the team is half as effective. And he hasn't got a Jimmy Greaves to pass to.

JG: *And there's nobody around of your class who can put the ball on a handkerchief from forty yards with either foot. But that's enough of that, Haynsie. People will start talking about us. Of all the games we played together, which one stands out above all the others?*

JH: It has to be the 9–3 against Scotland. But if we're honest, Jim, we were lucky that day to find them with a very dodgy goalkeeper.

JG: *Poor old Frank Haffey. The Scots took the piss out of him so much over that game that he emigrated to New Zealand. They used to say: 'What's the time? Nine past Haffey.'*

JH: Tell you what, Jim, I remember us having a bloody good night after that win. There was you, Bobby Smith and me, and I have hazy memories of a nightclub. Sorry, perhaps I shouldn't talk about a boozing night.

JG: *Leave off, John. I never regret memories of those celebration nights after matches . . . or even when we were beaten and drowned our sorrows. Smithy and I got legless after that Scottish win. Blimey, it's not every day you put nine past the Jocks! People are always asking me what it was like to miss out on the 1966 World Cup final.*

JH: Well, what was it like?

JG: *It hurt like hell, if you want to know. But I would have done the same thing in Alf's shoes. The rest of the boys were magnificent against Argentina and Portugal, and there's that old saying, 'Never* *change a winning team.' It must have been bad for you, too. I thought you'd be a cert to lead us.*

JH: No, that car crash did for me, Jim. I damaged my cruciate ligament, and I was never quite the same after that. Alf Ramsey was always asking George Cohen how I was doing, and being the honest bloke he is, George told him that I was not quite ready to play for England again. And that was the truth. Obviously, I would have given anything to lead England out in the final, but Bobby Moore made quite a good job of it! What a player! One of the few truly world-class defenders we've ever produced.

JG: *If you had to pick one England international from our era who would have made it as a big star in today's game, which one would you select?*

JH: Not just because you're facing me, James, but it would be you. Goodness knows how many goals you would score now that they can't tackle from behind.

JG: *Behave yourself, John. I mean a player not here in this room!*

JH: It's a tough one. Just one player. It's got to be Tom Finney. I partnered him on the left wing in my early days with England. He was something special, and was comfortable in any position in the forward line. Stanley Matthews was a magician, but not my personal taste. For me, it would have to be Finney. Can you imagine what he would be worth in today's transfer market? He would cost as much as the Crown Jewels. After Tom, I would choose Bobby Charlton. I suppose he played the role in the 1966 World Cup finals that would have been mine if I had been able to extend my England run. He was a beautifully balanced player, and his shots from outside the box were spectacular. Oh yes, and we mustn't forget Duncan Edwards. He would have been a great player in any era. I cried my eyes out when he died following the Munich air disaster. He was going to become a world star, no doubt about it.

JG: *Finally, Johnny old friend, a very personal question. Did you look after all that dough you made as a £100-a-week player?*

JH: You know me, James. I never exactly threw my money around. The best thing I did was invest my earnings in the betting shops. We sold our chain to the Tote in 1976 and made a tidy profit. The only luxury I allowed myself when Fulham suddenly turned me into a relatively well-off footballer was a brand new Jaguar sports car. Cost just over three grand, and that was the car I smashed up in 1962, wrecking my career. Like you say, James, 'It's a funny old game'.

Just a few months after that interview Johnny died in hospital in Edinburgh following a car crash the day after his 71st birthday. I had lost a great friend. Football had lost a great servant.

14

Dave Mackay

Born: Edinburgh, 14 November 1934

Career span: 1953–72

Clubs: Hearts 1953–59 (135 games, 25 goals); Tottenham 1959–68 (268 league games, 42 goals); Derby County 1968–71 (122 league games, 5 goals); Swindon Town 1971–72 (26 league games, 1 goal)

Scotland: 22 caps, 4 goals

Club honours: 1 Scottish league championship, 1 Scottish Cup (both with Hearts); 1 league championship, 3 FA Cups, 1 European Cup-Winners' Cup – a medal was awarded even though he missed the final through injury (all with Tottenham); 1 Second Division championship (Derby)

Footballer of the Year 1969 (shared with Manchester City's Tony Book)

WHILE Danny Blanchflower was the silky smooth poet of the outstanding Tottenham team of the sixties, Dave Mackay was the swashbuckling pirate – Danny the brains, Dave the heart. He matched Blanchflower's passing and surpassed his passion. Never throughout my career did I play with a more inspirational team-mate. One look at his clenched fist, and I felt I had been transported to the battlefield of Bannockburn. You could almost hear the bagpipes skirling when the magnificent Mackay was in full cry.

Waxing lyrical? Yes, well that is the effect the marvellous memories of Dave Mackay have on me. You know when you were a kid in the playground and used to pick teams at random? Dave would always have been my first choice because he had a bit of everything. There was the skilful left foot, the ability to drill a 40-yard pass with accuracy, the never-give-up competitive spirit, and a tackle that was like the scythe of a claymore.

For all the baubles he won in the game, both as a player and manager, his greatest victory was over adversity. He twice made comebacks after breaking a leg. Not for nothing was he known as the 'Miracle Man' of football.

If somebody put a gun to my head and insisted that I name the *greatest* player in that marvellous 'Super Spurs' side, it would have to be Dave Mackay. He had just about everything in his arsenal (oops, poor choice of word . . . let's say in his locker). He had power, skill, drive, stamina, and showed the sort of heroism that would have won medals in wartime.

Nobody from my generation will need reminding about that unforgettable photograph snapped by legendary *Daily Mirror* photographer Monte Fresco of Dave holding Leeds United's bullying Billy Bremner by the shirt collar and frightening the shite out of him with a brandished fist. This was after Wild Billy had been foolish enough to try to challenge Dave in a tackling contest at White Hart Lane. This was the Master putting the apprentice in his place.

'Billy was a pal of mine,' said Dave. 'But like a lot of that Leeds team, he could be a nasty bugger on the pitch, and he went into a tackle against me that could have led to me breaking my leg again. I just let him know what I thought of him, and warned what would happen if he tried it again. That picture served to haunt me because it's the one people always ask me to sign, and it gives the impression that I was a bully of a player. I like to think I was fair. Firm but fair. OK, *very* firm, but fair.'

Dave had infectious enthusiasm, and I often offered up a silent prayer that he was with me and not against me. I have shuddered at some of his tackles on rival players, and he used to go in just as hard after those two broken leg set-backs. The first time he broke his leg, the right one, it enraged everybody in the Tottenham team. Manchester United skipper Noel Cantwell went roaring into a 50-50 tackle with no intention of playing the ball, and his boot thudded into Dave's shin. This was in the second-leg of a European Cup-Winners' Cup match at Old Trafford, and the crack of breaking bone could be heard around the ground. Dave was understandably bitter about that, and from then on he always called Cantwell 'Cant', making it sound as close as possible to the c*** word. They made it up after both had retired, but for the rest of his playing career he was planning a revenge hit on 'Cant'.

I am doing him an injustice in presenting Dave as all power and passion, and playing on the edge of violence. His tackling was always fair, and he was never ever sent off. Bill Nicholson would not have entertained or encouraged any play that was dirty or cynical. Dave had delicate skills to go with his natural strength. Bobby Moore is one of the few defenders I can think of who could rival him for ball control in a tight situation. The swaggering Scot was the king of the first-time pass, drilling the ball through to a team-mate as accurately and as casually as if in a training stint, despite being under pressure from an opponent.

Dave took over from Danny as Spurs captain, and I can safely say that I played under the two of the greatest club skippers who ever carried a ball on to the pitch.

He didn't suffer fools off the pitch, and could be blunt to the point of rudeness with anybody who poked their nose in where he didn't think it belonged. Football writers either became very close friends with him (particularly if they got in the first round), or were barred enemies. He could be just as lacking in tolerance with any team-mates who stepped out of line, and I recall him putting Terry Venables swiftly in his place when he was a bit too cocky for Dave's taste on his arrival at Tottenham from Chelsea.

He liked to be the top man in training as well as during a game, and I recall a trick he had that made us all respectful of his ability. He would continually volley the ball against the wall from 12 yards in our indoor gymnasium at White Hart Lane. It sounds easy, but just try it. Remember, it has to be a succession of shots without the ball touching the ground. Another fond memory I have is of following Dave as he led us out on to the pitch. As he crossed the white line he would go through his pre-match ritual of kicking the ball high in the air and then catching it on his instep. It was just a little reminder to the opposition players and fans that he could play a bit.

Here's a little statistic that I offer to help add to the legend of Mackay: he played in more than forty cup finals at all levels during his career, and was never once on the losing side! That illustrates what I mean about his competitive spirit. He just hated to lose, and would sink into a depression if ever we lost a game, particularly at home at White Hart Lane. Whether he was playing snooker, darts, tiddlywinks or cards, he would pour every ounce of his concentration into trying to win.

It's amazing now to think that Bill Nicholson bought him from Hearts for £32,000 more by accident than design. He had been chasing Mel Charles at Swansea, and only switched to Mackay after losing out to Arsenal in the race to sign the Welsh giant.

People always got a surprise when they met Dave for the first time away from the football field. The impression given was that he was some sort of colossus, a picture in the mind helped by the fact that he had a barrel chest that he always stuck out with pride when leading his troops into battle.

Yet he stood a sliver under 5ft 8in (despite what the record books might say) and weighed around 12 stone. But he made his mark on every game with such fire and fury that there were times when he frightened me to death, and I was on *his* side.

Dave will always carry two scars hidden away for private moments of grief. He was in the Scottish schoolboys team beaten 8–2 at Wembley by an England team captained by 15-year-old Johnny Haynes. Nine years later he was in the Scotland team decimated 9–3 at Wembley by an England team captained by 24-year-old Johnny Haynes. If you valued your life, you didn't mention those two results in Dave's hearing. Like I say, he was not the best of losers and those two defeats will have cost him lots of sleep.

I remember when Dave was persuaded to join Derby County at the back end of his career. Brian Clough, who knew better than anybody that Dave had a passion for playing that money could not buy, locked him in an office at White Hart Lane and browbeat him until he agreed to sign a contract.

Later, Dave was close to tears when he told me he did not really want to go to Derby because his heart was still at Tottenham. He hated the thought of leaving all his mates – he was the king of our drinking school at the White Hart – and he had a lucrative club-tie manufacturing company that he ran with his business partner Jimmy Burton. Dave was not only a great warrior but something of a worrier, too, and he went through agonies over his decision to finally lay down his shield at Spurs and follow the then relatively inexperienced manager Clough on the road to what he considered the football outpost of Derby.

He thought Bill Nicholson should have given him another two seasons at Spurs, but Bill knew the Mackay engine was running out and did not feel Dave could sustain his midfield-marauding style – and waiting in the wings was the bright young, full-of-energy Steve Perryman to fill Dave's boots.

What Bill Nick didn't realise was that Cloughie had no intention of playing Dave in his old midfield motivating role. In a tactical move that showed Cloughie's genius as a manager, he switched Dave to the heart of the Derby defence. Here he was able to stroll rather than sprint alongside a promising young centre-half called Roy McFarland, and he could conserve energy while others did the running, the chasing and the feuding. It was a masterstroke by Clough, and in the sunset of his career Dave led Derby to the Second Division championship.

He was at last elected Footballer of the Year in 1969, yet it came with the slight of having to share it with Manchester City skipper Tony Book. Dave Mackay was out on his own.

Dave could not get football out of his bones, and in an eventful managing career he steered Derby to the First Division championship in 1974–75 after taking over in controversial circumstances from his former boss Brian Clough. He also managed Swindon Town, Nottingham Forest, Walsall, Doncaster Rovers and Birmingham City, and had a successful coaching career in the Middle East.

Whenever I see Dave, as the pair of us go into the autumn of our years, we always give each other a hug like the old friends that we are, and I regale anybody within earshot that he was one of the all-time greats.

The Scottish selectors rewarded him with just twenty-two caps back in the days when they tended to sneer at exiles. Had he been born an Englishman, he would have followed Billy Wright into the 100-cap category.

But had he been born on our side of the border, he might have lacked the passion of the Real Mackay.

15

Duncan Edwards

Born: Dudley, West Midlands, 1 October 1936
Died: Munich, 21 February 1958
Career span: 1953–58
Club: Manchester United (151 league games, 20 goals; FA Cup 12 games, 1 goal)
England: 18 caps, 5 goals
Club honours: 2 league championships, 1 FA Cup runner-up, 3 FA Youth Cups

CAN a player whose career spanned little more than five years justifiably be included in my list of greatest footballers? When his name is Duncan Edwards – a legend in his short lifetime – the answer is a resounding 'yes'.

His death in Munich from injuries received in the Manchester United air disaster came as I was celebrating my 18th birthday, and I don't mind admitting that I wept at the news of his passing.

The entire nation had been hoping against hope that he would survive, but he finally lost his battle for life fifteen days after the crash. He was 21 and already considered potentially the finest all-round footballer England had ever produced.

I often hear people say that if it had not been for the Munich tragedy, Bobby Moore would never have won an England cap. That is utter nonsense. A place would have been found for Mooro *and* Edwards, which would have meant two of the greatest English footballing heroes playing in the same team. The mind boggles.

I recently read an article describing how I had played for Chelsea against Manchester United in an FA Youth Cup semi-final, and had been completely overshadowed and overpowered by big Dunc, who even in his teens was just over 6ft tall and weighed close to 13 stone.

The match report told how Duncan had started in defence and, when United fell a goal down, moved up to centre-forward, scored two goals and then returned to his defensive duties. This I can believe. He was that good, that versatile. But what's a load of codswallop is my part in the story. I never ever got to play in youth football with Duncan because he was three and a half years older than I was.

He was such an outstanding prospect that he was trusted with First Division football at the age of 16 with the Busby Babes, and he became the then youngest England international at 18 years and 183 days. This was against Scotland at Wembley on 2 April 1955. England won 7–2, and Wolves striker Dennis Wilshaw scored four goals. Duncan played alongside one of his heroes, Wolves and England skipper Billy Wright, who told him, 'With that accent, Dunc, you should be with us at Molineux.'

Billy told me that Duncan gave him a rueful smile and said in his thick Black Country voice, 'Aye, Mr Wright, but Mr Busby called at my house before Mr Cullis.'

Yes, he was that respectful. 'Mr Wright.'

Duncan was just coming towards the end of his two years' National Service when I first met him at an England get-together before what was to prove his final international. I found him to be a lovely, almost innocent character, who did not have a trace of conceit and showed wide-eyed interest in just about every subject there was for conversation. He used to mimic my Cockney voice, not in a pee-taking way but because it fascinated him that we could be talking the same language but with such different accents.

I remember that Tommy Taylor was experimenting with a pipe, and sitting in the hotel lounge after dinner, he was turning almost purple as he tried to puff life into it. Only after he realised that a lot of stifled laughter was coming from the other players did he discover that Duncan had stuffed some pipe cleaner just inside the stem. Big Dunc could be quite a rascal, but he was able to take as well as give in the joking stakes.

He famously used to ride to Old Trafford on a bicycle, and he would faithfully send home two-thirds of his £15-a-week wages to his mum. 'A perfect model for any young footballer,' was how Matt Busby described him.

Sir Bobby Charlton, a Munich survivor who knew Duncan better than most, provides this memory that captures the awe in which Edwards was held:

Duncan was the complete player – good with both feet, strong in the tackle, commanding in the air, had a powerful shot and was an accurate passer of the ball no matter what the distance. He could play in any position and had the ability to dictate and dominate any match.

I remember one particular game when I was playing with

Duncan for the Army against the RAF during our National Service. Duncan received the ball from our goalkeeper deep in our half, passed it to the full-back and took the return pass. Then he exchanged passes with me, stroked the ball to another forward, quickly demanded it back and unleashed the hardest shot you're ever likely to see from the edge of the box.

The ball rocketed towards the goalkeeper's head. He ducked out of the way and the ball crashed into the net.

Quite a few years later I was walking down a street in Cambridge when a chap stopped me. 'You don't remember me, do you, Bobby?' he said. 'I played against you some time back when you were in the Army team.'

The game came back to me, and I asked him which position he played.

'Goalie,' he said.

When I reminded him how he had ducked out of the way of Duncan's shot, he replied, 'Yes, that was the proudest moment of my life.'

I am trying to think of a modern footballer who plays in similar style, so that I can convey to the younger generation just how good he was. Let's say he was a cross between Roy Keane and Steven Gerrard, with their sort of total commitment and determination. But he had a harder shot than either of them, and was so versatile that he could play as a defender, midfield motivator or out-and-out striker.

Billy Wright used to rave about a goal Duncan scored against West Germany in Berlin in 1956. 'Three German defenders just bounced off him as he surged forward from midfield to shoot from twenty-five yards,' he recalled. 'The ball went into the net like a guided missile. It was one of the most spectacular goals I ever saw.'

In his short career he played a key role in Manchester United's back-to-back league championships, and they were going for the hat-trick at the time of the Munich disaster.

There is, of course, no telling how good he might have become. But it's fair to surmise that he would have been right at his peak at the time of the 1966 World Cup in England. He and Mooro together would have been the perfect combination, with Bobby concentrating on defence and big Duncan on prompting the attack. There would have been plenty of room in the team for both of them, so let's put to sleep forever the notion that Bobby Moore would never have played for England but for Munich.

How about this for a statistic: in the 1956–57 season Duncan played a total of 94 – I shall repeat, 94 – competitive games, not including unit matches because he was still in the Army at the time. He just loved to play the game, and could run all day and thrive on it.

He is buried with his sister Carol Anne, who died in 1947 at the age of fourteen weeks. His tombstone reads simply: 'A Day of Memory, Sad to recall, Without Farewell He left us All'. In the nearby parish church of St Francis, in Duncan's hometown of Dudley, there is a striking stained glass window showing him in action, a unique memorial to his brief life. And in the town centre stands a statue in memory of not only an exceptional footballer but also a young man who made an enormous impact on everybody with whom he came in contact. As Billy Wright said, 'He was a smashing lad.'

The last word goes to his old pal Bobby Charlton: 'Duncan was the only player who made me feel inferior. If I had to choose one footballer to play for my life of all those I have seen and played with, it would have to be Duncan. Yes, he was *that* special.'

And so was Bobby Charlton, who just happens to be the next in my birth-order list.

16

Bobby Charlton

Born: Ashington, Northumberland, 11 October 1937

Career span: 1954–74

Clubs: Manchester United 1954–73 (606 league games, 199 goals; 757 games, 249 goals, in total); Preston player-manager 1974–75 (38 games, 8 goals)

England: 106 caps, 49 goals

Club honours: 3 league championships, 1 FA Cup, 1 European Cup

World Cup 1966

Footballer of the Year 1966

European Footballer of the Year 1966

Knighted 1994

FOR many years, Bobby Charlton was the most famous Englishman in the world. I played 46 of my 57 England matches in the same team as Bobby and travelled thousands of miles with him. He was a household name in every country we visited, and was a great ambassador for the game of football and for England.

The sad thing is that all his success – 106 caps, European Footballer of the Year, honours galore and a knighthood – does not seem to have made him very happy. It's easier to get a rebate from the taxman than a laugh from Bobby.

Perhaps I would also be a miserable git if I had survived that terrible Munich air crash. Goodness knows what it must have done to him psychologically, knowing that so many of his mates had perished in the wreckage from which he was thrown clear.

His distinguished England career did not start until two months after Munich, and on his way to plundering a record 49 international goals I rarely saw him with a smile on his face. What a contrast with his big brother, Jack, who was always looking for chances to tell the latest joke and laughed like a drain at many leg-pulling pranks.

From his sensational two-goal debut for Manchester United against Charlton Athletic at the age of 18 it was always obvious that Bobby was destined for great things.

He was equally at home in all forward positions, driving in from the wing, leading the attack, playing a conventional inside-forward role or – as in his later years – dictating the pace and pattern of a match from a deep-lying centre-forward position.

Few could hit a ball as hard and as cleanly as Bobby, and many of his goals were of the spectacular variety that remain etched in the memory.

I played with Bobby through all his hairstyles – from the wavy blond, through the comb-over and then to the distinguished baldness. I got a close-up view of his sportsmanship and his gentlemanly approach, but I was never sucked into that PR image of him being a goody two-shoes. You don't become a winner like Bobby Charlton unless you have a competitive edge, and he could battle with the best of them when it really mattered.

In my view he was at his most exciting and adventurous in his early days with the Busby Babes, and during the five years after Munich when he was making bombing raids down the left wing. He had more influence on matches when he switched to his scheming job, but my favourite memories of him are of his devastating displays in the No. 11 shirt.

I always feel that Bobby saved me and a few boozy England team-mates from at least a temporary suspension from international selection.

It was the eve of England's departure for a match against Portugal in Lisbon in May 1964, and we had just checked in to the Lancaster Gate Hotel under the watchful eye of manager Alf Ramsey, who had been in the job for just a year and was still feeling his way.

Behind Alf's back, Bobby Moore and I called for volunteers to join us for an evening's stroll into London's tempting West End. With thirsty men such as Mooro, Budgie Byrne and me leading the expedition it was odds on the stroll becoming something of a stagger before the night was through. Gordon Banks, George Eastham, Ray Wilson and, surprisingly, Bobby Charlton, chose to tag along.

We stopped off at a favourite drinking oasis called The Beachcomber, and it was fairly late – close to midnight – when we got back to the hotel just a little the worse for wear – merry rather than drunk.

When we went up to our rooms each of us realised our absence-without-leave had been noticed when we found our passports lying on our beds.

This was Alf's subtle way of letting us know he was not pleased. He left it until the end of our final training session for the match before mentioning our little escapade. 'OK, gentlemen,' he said, in that clipped, precise way of his. 'You can all go and get showered and changed now apart from the seven players who, I believe, would like to stay and see me.'

Sheepishly, we stood gathered around Alf while the rest of the squad went back to the dressing room, with quizzical looks over their shoulders.

Alf was short, sharp and to the point. 'You are all lucky to be here,' he said. 'If there had been enough players in the squad I would have left you behind in London. All I hope is that you've learned your lesson and will not do anything silly again.'

I am convinced that if 'Saint' Bobby Charlton had not been with us, Alf would have taken much stronger action. As it was, he named all seven of us in the team and we repaid him by beating Portugal 4–3 in an epic match. Two of the AWOL men – Budgie Byrne and Our Bobby – scored the goals. Budgie helped himself to the sweetest of hat-tricks. Alf allowed himself quite a few G-and-Ts that night.

Alf already had a vision in his head of an England team playing in a revolutionary 4-3-3 formation, the system he had introduced at Ipswich Town with startling effect. He desperately needed a midfield general who could spray passes around with accuracy and authority. Bobby, a slower and more thoughtful player than in his early days when powering down the wing, suited the job down to the ground.

He established himself as a deep-lying centre-forward who played with flair and imagination, and his long-range rocket shots with left or right foot became an eye-catching feature of his play.

Of all Bobby's outstanding performances for England I rated his display against Portugal in the 1966 World Cup semi-final his best. He was the complete master that night, gliding across the Wembley pitch as if he owned it. He scored two cracking goals, and gave such a devastating show that it frightened the watching West Germans into sacrificing Franz Beckenbauer's creative talent in the final. They put him on to marking Bobby and that tactical error played a big part in their eventual defeat. The two most creative players on the pitch cancelled each other out.

Four years later in Mexico Alf made a rare cock-up when he called off Bobby with England leading 2–0 and well in control against West Germany in the 1970 World Cup quarter-final. England had never squandered a two-goal lead during the Ramsey reign. Alf, usually the most cautious of men, thought he had the match won and wanted to rest Bobby for the semi-final. Oops.

It gave the Germans a huge psychological boost to see the retreat of the player they feared the most, and they came roaring back to win 3–2.

It was sad-faced Bobby's 106th and final game for England. Bobby said later, 'I saw Colin Bell warming up and I wondered if one of our players had got a knock. I didn't dream that Alf was going to call me off. I couldn't believe it when my number was held up. It was so disappointing because I felt fantastic, and we had a stranglehold on the game. I felt full of running, and while I understood what Alf was thinking I did not want to come off.' Typically, Bobby came off with dignity, not showing that he was furious.

It was a heart-breaking way to end one of the greatest of all England careers. Both Bobby and his big brother Jack let Alf know on the flight home that they no longer wanted to be considered for international selection. Between them they had played 141 games for England, and had helped take the team to the top of Everest. They deserved a better exit than the suicidal defeat against the Germans.

Bobby packed it in with Manchester United in 1973, and I was astonished when he announced he was going to become player-manager of Preston. I always considered that he had United red blood, and just could not imagine him in another club's colours.

As I guessed, he was not cut out for management and he soon retired to concentrate on business interests that included a travel agency and a soccer school. He flirted briefly with Wigan Athletic before returning 'home' to Old Trafford as a club director, adored by the fans and respected by all his old team-mates.

Since being knighted in 1994, he has become a roving ambassador for English football in general and Manchester United in particular. Our game could not be represented by anyone more

Busby Babe Duncan Edwards is flanked by two legends of the game, Stanley Matthews (*left*) and Billy Wright, before England's Home International against Scotland at Wembley in April 1957.

The Spin Doctor. Len Shackleton makes the ball look misshapen as he puts his spell on it. He could almost make the ball sit up and talk.

The Plumber and the Lion. Tom Finney and Nat Lofthouse on a training run at Stamford Bridge before England's 1955 international against Spain.

Russian Spiderman Lev Yashin denies me a goal at Wembley, one of four first-half saves he made against me during England's match against a Rest of the World team in 1963.

Captain Marvel Danny Blanchflower (*third from left*) parades the FA Cup after Tottenham's 1962 defeat of Burnley at Wembley. Joining in the lap of honour (*left to right*) are Bill Brown, little old me, Dave Mackay, John White and Cliff Jones. This was as good as it gets.

Former 'Partners in Paradise', Ferenc Puskas (*left*) and Alfredo Di Stefano come face to face as rivals in a 1964 Spanish League match between Real Madrid and Español. They were poetry in motion when playing together for Real.

Gentle Giant John Charles became an idol in Italy after establishing himself as the complete all-rounder with Leeds United.

Paco Gento was the fastest thing on two feet as a left winger with Real Madrid, where he was known as *El Supersonico*. He was on the winning side with Real in a record six European Cup finals.

Garrincha (*left*) and Pelé both made their debuts for Brazil in the 1958 World Cup finals and were never on a losing side together on the international stage. Garrincha named a dog after me, 'Yimmy Greaves'. He was barking mad.

Eusebio heads towards the England goal for Portugal in the 1966 World Cup semi-final, with his constant shadow Nobby Stiles valiantly defending. The Toothless Tiger always got the better of the Black Panther.

Re-United in 1995, the 'Holy Trinity' of Old Trafford – Denis Law, Bobby Charlton and George Best. All three were former European Footballers of the Year and were 'Simply the Best'.

Jim Baxter (*left*) and Gianni Rivera (*right*) were both masters of ball control. On retirement, Slim Jim became a publican, and Golden Boy Gianni a politician. Jim pulled pints, Gianni polled votes. Both were elected to my list of the élite of the élite footballers.

Sean Connery and Yul Brynner are shaken but not stirred as Bobby Moore and I treat them to some East London humour during a Pinewood Studios visit after the opening game of the 1966 World Cup finals. How I remember Bobby – always on guard at his post (*below right*). The nation have remembered him with the statue at the new Wembley (*below left*). It should have been built while he was alive.

Two of my goalkeeping heroes: Gordon Banks (*above*) saving at the feet of Denis Law, with Bobby Moore in close attendance, during the England–Scotland international at Wembley in 1967, famously won 3–2 by the Scots; and Pat Jennings (*below*) stopping a run by his Northern Ireland team-mate and close pal George Best during Tottenham's match against Manchester United at White Hart Lane in 1966.

popular worldwide wherever a ball is kicked. I travelled to many countries with him where children knew just two words of English – 'Bob-by Charl-ton'.

He has had a wonderful footballing life. I just wish he'd look as if he was enjoying it.

17

Gordon Banks

Born: Sheffield, 30 December 1937

Career span: 1955–78

Clubs: Chesterfield 1955–59 (23 league games); Leicester City 1959–66 (293 league games); Stoke City 1966–72 (194 league games); Cleveland Stokers 1967 (12 games); St Patrick's Athletic 1977 (1 game); Fort Lauderdale Strikers 1977–78 (39 games)

England: 73 caps

Club honours: 2 FA Cup runners-up, 1 League Cup (all with Leicester); 1 League Cup (Stoke)

World Cup 1966

Footballer of the Year 1972

THE toughest job I had in compiling my file of most unforgettable footballers was choosing between Gordon Banks and Peter Shilton as the greatest of all England goalkeepers. The restrictions put on me by my demanding editor meant there was not room for both of them.

There was always a little of the master and apprentice about Banksie and Shilts. Peter grew up in the shadow of Gordon at Leicester, learning his trade by watching Banks in action in the first team.

He learned his lessons so well that when Gordon returned from the glory of helping England win the World Cup in 1966, the Leicester directors decided they could afford to let him move on to Stoke, because in the young Shilton they had a ready-made replacement.

Shilts developed into a magnificent goalkeeper. The arguments will always continue about whether he became even better than Banks. I finally came down on Gordon's side because of a save that was made and one that was missed.

The one that *was* made, of course, was when Banks denied Pelé with the famous 'Save of the Century' during the 1970 World Cup game against Brazil. Every time I see it replayed on television I am convinced Pelé is going to score! Gordon just had no right to get across his goal to fingertip the header over the bar.

I had gone to Mexico the unorthodox way, competing in the World Cup Rally. My co-driver Tony Fall and I finished sixth in a Ford Escort. By the time I left Mexico – bound for a holiday in the Caribbean – Banks was the talk of the World Cup because of that save. This is how he described it when we got together for a recent reunion:

I have seen the save so many times on video that I can talk about it in detail now, but to be honest at the time I was too busy following my instincts to know exactly what was going on. I can remember the move starting with a pass from Carlos Alberto that was like nothing I'd ever seen before. He struck the ball with the outside of his right foot from just beyond his penalty area and it

*swerved right round our left-back Terry Cooper and into the path
of the sprinting Jairzinho. I knew they could perform banana free-
kicks, but this was a banana pass! Poor old Terry had been left
for dead.*

*Tostao drifted to the near post and I went with him as I sensed
that Jairzinho would try to hit him with a diagonal pass. What
I didn't see was Pelé running beyond his marker Alan Mullery
at the far post. Jairzinho lofted a dipping centre high in the direction of Pelé and I suddenly had to scamper back across my goal.*

*Pelé got above the ball and powered it low and hard towards
the corner of the net. It was the perfect header. I was now into a
dive to my right and as the ball hit the ground just in front of
the goal-line I flicked it with my outstretched right hand as it
came up. I had managed to divert it up and over the bar. Alan
Mullery told me later that Pelé had been shouting 'Goal' as I
reached the ball.*

*Mooro slapped me on the arse and muttered, 'F****** marvel-
lous, Banksie.' And then we got on with defending the corner. It
was only afterwards that I realised it was something pretty special
when Pelé told the press, 'It was the greatest save I have ever
seen.'*

And the save that got away? This involved Peter Shilton in the
1974 World Cup qualifier against Poland at Wembley. Norman
Hunter, the most feared tackler in English football, mistimed a
challenge out on the right touchline and the ball was transferred
to unmarked Polish striker Domarski. His low shot went under
the diving Shilton and into the net for a goal that ended England's
World Cup life and also virtually finished the reign of England
manager Alf Ramsey.

I am convinced that Banksie would have stopped that shot from
Domarski. For him, it would have been a bread-and-butter save.

So on that evidence I have selected Gordon as the number-one

England goalkeeper, just a fingernail ahead of Shilts, who went on to make a record 125 appearances for England.

Gordon would have got many more than his 73 caps but for the car smash that robbed him of the sight of his right eye in the summer of 1972, just a few weeks after he had been voted Footballer of the Year. Even with only one eye he managed to get himself voted the 'Most Valuable Goalkeeper' in the United States soccer circus after he had failed to get back into league football because of his handicap.

His record with England was phenomenal. He let in just 57 goals in his 73 appearances, a miserly average of just 0.78 goals per game. And he kept a remarkable 35 clean sheets, and was not on the losing side for a sequence of 23 matches between 1964 and 1967, which embraced the 1966 World Cup, when he went unbeaten right up to the Eusebio penalty in the semi-final.

I wonder how differently everything would have turned out if he had not missed the 1970 World Cup quarter-final against West Germany? He was lying in bed back at the England hotel shivering and feverish while his last-minute replacement Peter Bonetti – playing his first competitive game in two months – was making a mess of two saves that let the Germans in for a 3–2 victory after trailing 2–0.

To this day Gordon remains convinced that somebody nobbled one of his drinks. Nobody else in the squad was ill, and he had been studious in selecting what to eat and drink in a country notorious for Montezuma's Revenge.

Whenever Gordon and I get back together and reminisce on all our good times together, we have a giggle over a goal I scored against him when he was playing for Leicester against Tottenham at White Hart Lane. This is how Gordon remembers the goal:

It was the craziest goal ever allowed. Spurs had been awarded a penalty on a wet and churned-up pitch. I needed to wipe my hands before facing the penalty and went into the back of the net to find some grass that was not muddy. Greavsie, the sod, side-footed the ball into the other corner of the net while I was bending down, and the twit of a referee went and gave a goal. What made it worse was instead of telling the ref he was wrong, even my own team-mates were falling about laughing. I chased the referee to the centre-circle and all I got for my trouble was a booking for 'ungentle-manly conduct'.

Ah, happy days! What I do know for sure is that when Gordon was between the posts in international matches, the England defence was as safe as the Banks of England.

18
Jim Baxter

Born: Hill O'Beath, Scotland, 29 September 1939
Died: Glasgow, 14 April 2001, aged 61
Career span: 1957–69
Clubs: Raith Rovers 1957–60 (58 games, 2 goals); Rangers 1960–65 and 1968–69 (254 games, 24 goals); Sunderland 1965–67 (87 league games, 10 goals); Nottingham Forest 1967–68 (48 league games, 3 goals)
Scotland: 34 caps, 3 goals

Club honours (all with Rangers): 3 Scottish championships, 3 Scottish
Cups, 4 Scottish League Cups

J UST the mere thought of Jim Baxter brings a smile to my face.
He was such a cheeky, lovable sod on and off the pitch that I
always grin at the memory of him, whether it was taking the piss
out of the English at Wembley or joking about a life that he never
took very seriously.

I had my well-publicised problems with the booze, but – like
our mutual mate George Best – Jim never saw his drink dependency as a problem, more a bonus. When he told me at the end of
his glittering career that he was going to open a pub, I said, 'What
are you going to call it . . . "Paradise Jim"?' It was like putting a
sex addict in charge of a brothel.

In all probability, Jim tossed up between running a pub and a
betting shop. He was also addicted to gambling. I once asked him
what difference it would have made to him earning £80,000 a
week rather than the £80 wage he collected in the 1960s. 'Och,
Jim,' he replied, 'I would have been able to gamble £50,000 a week
instead of £50!'

'Slim Jim' waltzes into my 'best of the best' list, not only because
of what he achieved with Rangers but for the breathtaking skill
that made him, arguably, the finest Scottish midfield schemer of
any time. He used to call his left foot 'The Glove', and he could
almost make it talk.

Anybody who witnessed his stunning performances in the Home
Championship matches of 1963 and 1967 will agree they were
watching a genius of a footballer at work. I played in both games,
and might have applauded him if not for the fact that Alf Ramsey
would have strangled me. He hated losing to the Jocks. I remember
being with Alf when we arrived at Glasgow Airport for an international, and we were met by the larger-than-life Scottish reporter
Jim Rodger, who held out a hand in greeting and said, 'Welcome

to Scotland, Alf.' It was before his knighthood. Alf glared at him and replied, 'You must be f****** joking.'

Both Baxter-dominated games were at Wembley, the first while the Scots were still sulking in the shadow of that 9–3 defeat by the Auld Enemy, and the second following England's 1966 World Cup triumph, which left most Scots totally underwhelmed. In the 1963 match Scotland were reduced to ten men after five minutes when skipper and left-back Eric Caldow was stretchered off with a broken leg, which made Baxter try that much harder. He cleverly and completely ran the game from his midfield command post, scoring both Scotland's goals in a 2–1 victory and swaggering off at the end with the ball famously stuck up his jersey. He had owned the match so it was only right that the ball should also belong to him.

Jim was in seventh heaven that day, and showed that he was a team player as well as an outstanding individualist. He ran his legs off to make up for Scotland being a man down in those pre-substitute days. 'We'd had that 9–3 result stuffed down our throats so many times,' he said later, 'that I was determined to try to get some sort of revenge. Beating the English with ten men on their own turf was some consolation.'

Four years later he teased and tormented the new World Cup holders, taking the mickey with the full range of his tricks, including continually playing 'keepie-uppie' as he challenged our lads to try to get the ball off him. He steered the Scots to a 3–2 victory that had their supporters claiming they were the true world champions – ignoring the fact that England were reduced to nine fit men!

This was my comeback match, and I was reduced to half pace by a knock. We already had Jack Charlton hobbling at centre-forward with a broken toe, and Ray Wilson limping with an ankle injury. 'Och, ye're all excuses, Greavsie,' Jim said when I pointed out these minor points. 'Yer should have given us the Jules Rimet trophy there and then because on that day we were the greatest team in the world.'

I could never fall out with lovely Jim, because most of the insults he aimed at the English were tongue-in-cheek. Mind you, he did like to show who was the boss and few could match him for ball control. If he had been less of a piss-artist and better behaved away from the game, he would have doubled his 34 caps. 'But I wouldnae have enjoyed mysel' as much,' Jim would say. He won ten of his caps while playing in England with Sunderland before moving on to Nottingham Forest, by which time he was like an overblown caricature of himself. In fact, by the end of his career 'Slim Jim' had become 'Fatboy Jim'. It was not a pretty sight.

Born in the Fife mining village of Hill O'Beath, Jim combined his early playing career at Raith Rovers with working down the pits. It was when he moved to Rangers in 1960 that the football world sat up and took notice of his mesmerising ball control and passing skills.

In the first of two spells at Ibrox he won three championship, three Scottish Cup and four League Cup winner's medals. He was never quite the same formidable force after breaking a leg in a European Cup-tie against Rapid Vienna in December 1964.

Sadly, when Jim moved into the English game he became more noted for his playboy activity off the pitch rather than his perform-ances on it. There were only occasional flashes of the magic that had made him the Great Entertainer of the Scottish football stage.

Even today, forty years on, he is remembered with awe in Nottingham – not for his football, but for his drinking exploits. He fell into the company of my old England colleague Joe Baker and cricketing legend Sir Garfield Sobers, who was playing for Notts at the time. They could both drink until the cows came home. Baxter and Sobers were so often legless together that they came known as Drunk and Sobers.

Famously after one night on the town, Forest coach Tommy Cavanagh – on his way for early-morning training – found Jim dishevelled and bleeding in the gutter. He had been beaten up by nightclub bouncers, and was in such a state, boozed and bruised, that Tommy made him train on his own for the rest of the week so that his team-mates could not see him.

Rangers took him back after what were virtually three lost years in England, but the unique talent had disappeared and he hung up his 'talking boots' in 1970 after bringing his league appearances total for Rangers to 254 games and 24 goals. What the record books do not show is how many goals he made with passes that were delivered with perfect precision. Jim, at his best, played his football with a smile on his face, and with an arrogance that could be irritating to the opposition but irresistible for the lucky spectators.

Deciding to run a pub at the end of his career was not his wisest decision. In fact, it was the worst possible environment for a man who could never say no to a pint or three.

Long after he had retired I met up with Jim for a photo session at a hotel near Stansted Airport. I had made a joke about the modern Scottish football team lacking a player of Baxter's class – 'the only decent Baxter in Scotland now is a soup,' I said. Neil Custis, *Sun* football writer, brought us together to discuss the state of the game.

'You still on the wagon, James?' Baxter asked as we walked into the hotel bar.

'Never touch the stuff any more,' I said.

'I've cut right back, too,' Jim said. 'It's the sensible thing to do.'

I went to the bar and said, 'What are you going to drink?'

Without hesitating and not joking, he said, 'Och, just a triple vodka and a pint of red bull will do fer now.'

Neil Custis and I doubled over. If this was Jim cutting back, what would he have ordered if he had still been drinking seriously?

His heavy drinking lifestyle led to two liver transplants in the 1990s, and he finally succumbed to cancer on Saturday, 14 April 2001. It had been April Saturdays when he had made April fools of England in the summertime of his unforgettable career.

Jim Baxter. Most footballers today would not be fit to lace his boots, or his drinks. Think of him and smile.

19

Denis Law

Born: Aberdeen, 24 February 1940

Career span: 1956–1974

Clubs: Huddersfield Town 1946–60 (81 league games, 16 goals); Manchester City 1960–61 and 1973–74 (68 league games, 35 goals); Torino (27 games, 10 goals); Manchester United 1962–73 (309 games, 171 goals)

Scotland: 55 caps, 30 goals

Club honours (all with Manchester United): 2 league championships, 1 FA Cup

European Footballer of the Year 1964

Voted Scotland's 'Golden Player' of the last 50 years 2003

IT's fitting that Jim Baxter should be followed by another of my all-time favourite Jocks, Denis 'The King' Law. He was as influential as 'Slim Jim' in the defeats of England in 1963 and 1967, but – as I am always quick to remind him – he also played in the 9–3 rout in 1961.

Denis and I feel a bit like footballing brothers. We were born just four days apart, and our paths continually crossed, including during our miserable times in Italy after we had both been sucked in and seduced by the lure of the lira.

We knew that Denis meant business in the 1967 match against

England at Wembley. For the first time that any of us could remember, the Lawman came out on to the pitch wearing thick shinpads. He was ready to run through a brick wall (well, the tackles of his Manchester United clubmate Nobby Stiles) to win that one.

A fiercely proud Scot (aren't they all!), Denis refused to witness England playing West Germany in the 1966 World Cup final. On the day of the match at Wembley he booked himself a solo round of golf. ('The course was empty,' he said. 'It was lovely.') But his day was ruined as he came off the final green when somebody shouted England had won the World Cup. He reacted to the news by throwing his golf bag to the floor in disgust.

'It meant that Bobby Charlton and Nobby Stiles had bragging rights for years,' he said. 'That's why winning at Wembley in 1967 was so important to us. It ended a run of nineteen unbeaten matches by England, and from then on we could wind up our England clubmates by saying that we were the *real* world champions.'

'Denis the Menace' was a true icon of the swinging sixties, the showman and the swordsman in the celebrated Best–Charlton–Law trio that dismantled defences in such stunning style. George Best was the genius, Bobby Charlton the commander, and Law the executioner.

He would score with a rapier thrust, turning a half-chance into a goal in the blinking of an eye. Then the showman would emerge, his right arm punched into the air and held there in a salute that inspired a procession of imitators. Allan Clarke and Rodney Marsh were just two who admitted copying their idol in the way they autographed goals.

Denis was the first and true King of Old Trafford, long before the emergence of Eric Cantona. He had come a long way from his Aberdeen roots, where his father was a trawlerman who could get work only in the good weather. Winters were so bad that Denis and his six brothers and sisters had hardly anything to eat. He did not have a new pair of shoes until he was 14, wearing cast-offs until then, and before he could start a professional football career with Huddersfield he had to have a badly squinted eye surgically corrected.

Bill Shankly, his manager at Huddersfield before moving to Liverpool, said, 'We didn't know who the hell he was looking at when he used to talk to us. Once he got the eye corrected, the defenders didn't know which way he was going!'

I have never seen a player before or since with quicker reflexes than Denis and he was always looking for opportunities to do the unexpected in the penalty area, be it a bicycle kick or a stunning header after appearing to hang motionless in mid-air.

Denis made his league debut with Huddersfield at the age of 16 in 1956, and two years later he became Scotland's youngest ever player at the age of 18 years 236 days. He marked his debut with a goal in a 3–0 victory against Wales at Ninian Park on 18 October 1958. That was the start of an international career that brought him a record 30 goals in 55 appearances. The first manager to pick him for Scotland was Matt Busby, who never made any secret of his belief that Denis was one of the finest players ever to come south of the border.

Manchester City snapped up Denis and then cashed in on him just a year later when – like me – he got dazzled by talk of all the money that could be earned in Italy at a time when there was a maximum £20-a-week wage in Britain. City bought him for £55,000 and doubled their money when selling him on to Torino just twelve months later. Huddersfield were sick.

Also like me, Denis struggled to settle in Italy where players – particularly forwards – were treated like prisoners, with little freedom for movement on or off the pitch.

He tried to get rid of his homesick blues by enjoying himself off the pitch in the company of his Torino team-mate Joe Baker, the Englishman from Hibernian who had a thicker Scottish accent than Aberdonian Denis. Their exploration of the Turin nightlife very nearly cost them their lives. Joe was at the wheel of a flash new Alfa Romeo with Denis beside him when the car tipped over going the wrong way around a roundabout. Both were lucky to escape with their lives.

It got to the point where Denis had to threaten to walk out of the game to get a move back to the Football League. He went home to Aberdeen and told Torino where to stuff their lire. They had been trying to sell him on to neighbours Juventus for a huge profit, but eventually they had to give in to his demands and allowed him to join Manchester United in 1962 for a record £115,000. This was after Tottenham had rescued me from AC Milan for £99,999.

Long ago, Denis told me that he felt he was a marked man as far as referees were concerned. Encouraged by manager Matt Busby, he reported a referee to the Football Association for continually taking the piss out of him during a First Division match early in his career at Old Trafford. 'He'd say things to me like, "Oh aren't you the clever one," and, "What sort of a shot was that? Call yourself a professional?" It really got to me and when I told Matt about it he insisted that we report the ref to the FA. The upshot was that he got severely censored and walked out on the game in protest. From then on the other referees were gunning for me.'

His temper was as quick as his reflexes, and he was often in trouble with referees for retaliating. He was once involved in a full-blooded fist-fight with Arsenal centre-half Ian Ure at Old Trafford. Both got their marching orders, and long suspensions. What made it even more of a compelling spectacle is that they were good pals who roomed together when on Scottish international duty. Friend or foe, Denis refused to concede a penalty-area inch to any opponent. A Red Devil, if ever there was one.

Over the next ten years, Denis ignited the United attack with his fire and flair. He was an FA Cup winner in 1963, European Footballer of the Year in 1964, and a league championship winner in 1965 and 1967. He remains the only Scot to have been elected European Footballer of the Year.

Sadly, because of a knee injury, he missed the ultimate prize of a European Cup winner's medal in 1968.

He scored 171 league goals for United in 309 matches, and took his FA Cup haul to what was then a record 40 goals. That total did not include the six he scored for Manchester City against Luton in a 1961 tie that was abandoned because of rain.

His Manchester United career ended in bitterness in 1973 when Tommy Docherty let him go on a free transfer. 'The first I knew about it was when I saw the news being announced on television,' a disgusted Denis said. 'I thought I would end my career at Old Trafford.'

Shrugging off his recurring knee problem, Denis returned to Manchester City and in the last game of the following season almost reluctantly back-heeled the goal that helped push Manchester United down into the Second Division. 'People wrongly say that my goal relegated United,' Denis said. 'But other results that day meant United were going down regardless of how many goals we scored against them.'

He had the satisfaction of making his World Cup finals debut in the last season of a magnificent career in which he inspired hundreds of youngsters to try to play the Lawman way. They could copy his style but few could get close to imitating his unique ability.

A good family man with five sons, Denis – like me – is now a sixty-something granddad, and after beating cancer is a regular meeter and greeter at Manchester United and an amusing after-dinner speaker with scores of stories up those famous sleeves of his.

It has been quite a voyage of adventure for the trawlerman's son from Aberdeen. I am so glad that we sailed for much of the journey on the same route. For me, he was and will always remain the King of Old Trafford.

20

Pelé

Born: Tres Coracoes, Brazil, 23 October 1940

Career span: 1955–77

Clubs: Santos 1955–74 (605 league games, 589 goals); New York Cosmos 1975–77 (64 games, 37 goals)

Brazil: 92 caps, 77 goals

Club honours: 13 equivalent of Brazilian league titles

World Cup 1958, 1962 (did not play in the final), 1970

Voted Athlete of the Twentieth Century by the Olympic Association 1999

Named Footballer of the Century by Fifa 2000

L ET me tell you about the twenty minutes I once spent in the company of one Edson Arantes do Nascimento, better known to you perhaps as Pelé. When I say, 'spent in his company', it would be fairer to say, 'spent chasing his arse'.

It was back in 1964 during a four-team tournament in Rio de Janeiro that had been arranged to celebrate the fiftieth anniversary of the Brazilian FA. The other teams taking part were Argentina and Portugal. We, England that is, got the short straw and were drawn to play reigning world champions Brazil in the opening match in front of 150,000 screaming fans at the magnificent Maracana Stadium.

Our manager, Alf Ramsey, came up with this cunning plan designed to paralyse Pelé in what was his peak period as the greatest player on the planet. 'We will stop the ball getting to him,' he said simply in the pre-match tactics talk.

Then, turning to his 'hard-tackling' inside-forwards, he added, 'Jim [little old me] and George ['Matchstick Man' Eastham], I want you to drop back whenever necessary and help Gordon [Milne] and Bobby [Moore] to cut out the passes meant for him.'

'Anything you say, Alf,' I agreed. It seemed a good idea on paper, but would it work on the pitch? Stop the ball getting to Pelé. Even the Master couldn't play without the ball. Nice one, Alf.

The plan worked to perfection for the first forty minutes but then, just before half-time, a frustrated Pelé at last got possession and threaded the ball through to a young newcomer called Rinaldo, who whipped the ball first time past our goalkeeper Tony Waiters. Brazil 1, England 0.

Despite this late set-back, we felt satisfied with our first-half performance and Alf demanded more of the same in the second half. 'You're every bit as good as they are,' he said, with that steely-eyed confidence we were to get to know so well on the way to the 1966 World Cup finals. 'Just keep working, and remember – *don't let Pelé have the ball.*'

This was the equivalent of saying 'don't let Louis Armstrong sing' . . . 'don't let Neil Armstrong walk on the moon' . . . 'don't let Lance Armstrong ride his bike'. But it *was* a good plan.

It got even better early in the second half when I pounced on a loose ball in the Brazilian penalty area and stuffed it into the back of their net. Suddenly in the Maracana you could have heard a pin or a pun drop, and it was England who were laughing.

Alf on the touchline bench grinned like the cat that had got the cream, and waved his fists to call for more of the same.

The game was now more than an hour old. Brazil 1, England 1.

Budgie Byrne and I put shots inches wide, and goalkeeper Gilmar had to become an acrobat to tip a George Eastham shot on to the bar. Pelé was nowhere to be seen. Alf's cunning plan was working like a dream . . . and it was England who were dreaming of a victory.

Then, like a black panther coming out of a sleep, Pelé roared into the game as if he had been deliberately sitting it out while he weighed up what we had in our ammunition.

First, with me chasing his arse and failing to stop the ball reaching him, he went this way, that way and then – after making a pretence at shooting – passed the ball again to Rinaldo, whose whiplash left-foot shot gave Tony Waiters no chance. Brazil 2, England 1.

'Who the f*** is this Rinaldo?' George Cohen gasped, doing his best to mark and contain a player none of us had ever heard of.

Moments later I had a shot scrambled off the Brazilian goal-line. The ball was cleared to Pelé, who set off on a magic-carpet ride through the England defence. He ran fully 40 yards with the ball at his feet, going past tackles as nonchalantly as if he was knocking aside daisies. He looked up and picked his spot before beating Tony Waiters all ends up with a fiercely hit right-foot shot. Poor old Tony, a Blackpool beach lifeguard in his spare time, was in danger of drowning. Brazil 3, England 1.

We had forgotten Plan A. *Don't let Pelé have the ball.*

Now the Maracana was a madhouse. Ever heard 150,000 Brazilians screeching their heads off? It's like standing on the runway at Heathrow. Bobby Moore, who was in danger of getting a sunburned tongue from chasing Pelé, shouted something to me, but all I could see were his lips moving. He later revealed he was saying, 'Come back and help us mark f****** Pelé.'

Within two minutes of this third goal, Tony Waiters was picking the ball out of his net again. Pelé, of course, was the instigator. George Cohen was protesting to the referee about two Brazilian players being in offside positions when Pelé pushed a pass into the path of Julinho. The flag should have gone up as he slotted the ball wide of Waiters, but perhaps the linesman didn't fancy upsetting the frenzied fans baying behind him. In his shoes I wouldn't have been brave enough to raise the offside flag. Brazil 4, England 1.

In fifteen minutes of sheer brilliance, Pelé had turned the game on its head. And he still hadn't finished. I was again chasing that arse of his (what muscular buttocks, almost animal-like) when Bobby Moore ran across his path and conceded a free-kick a yard outside the box. Pelé dummied as if to take the free-kick, and then Dias ran in alongside him and chipped the ball wide of a despairing dive by Waiters, who would have much preferred at that moment to be diving off Blackpool beach. Brazil 5, England 1.

We just could not believe what had happened to us as the referee blew the final whistle. No, that's silly. We *did* know what had happened to us. Pelé had happened to us. We had let him have the bloody ball.

I can honestly say that the football he produced in those final twenty minutes was the greatest I had ever witnessed from an individual in my life. I knew I had seen something special that, one day, I could tell my grandchildren about. That day is now, and the memory of it still sings in my head. While it hurt at the time, the pain has long gone and the beauty of it is what remains. I know that on that afternoon in the Maracana Stadium in Brazil I had been in the presence of sheer genius.

For that twenty minutes of magic alone I would have Pelé top of my all-time list of great footballers. But he did manage a thing or two besides, like scoring 1,216 goals in 1,254 matches from his debut at the age of 15 until his first retirement on 2 October 1974, 21 days short of his 34th birthday.

His peak year for goals was 1958 when he scored the little matter of 139 times, including two classic goals in the World Cup final, when we first became aware of the developing legend that was Pelé. He went on to collect 12 goals in four World Cup final tournaments, and he remains the only player to have been a member of three World Cup-winning teams (1958, 1962 and 1970), although he missed the final stages of the 1962 tournament because of a pulled muscle. European clubs queued to try to buy him but the Brazilian government, fearing street riots, declared him a National Treasure so that he could not be taken abroad.

Born on the poverty line in Tres Coracoes in the same year as me, 1940, he came under the influence of former Brazilian World Cup player Waldemar de Brito while playing for his local team Noroeste. De Brito, realising he had unearthed a diamond, whisked him off to Santos in São Paulo, where he made a scoring first-team debut at the age of 15.

A year later he was in the Brazilian international team, and the following year he became, at 17, the then youngest ever World Cup debutant. The rest, as they say, is history.

Pelé was no angel, by the way, despite his carefully cultivated public persona. There was quite a bit of devil in him. Let me tell a story to illustrate just how competitive he could be.

After the match in which he took us apart in Rio, we flew up to São Paulo to watch the second match of the 'mini World Cup' between Brazil and Argentina, and I can say hand-on-heart that I have never witnessed scenes like it. Because there were no seats left in the stand, the entire England party – including players, journalists and officials – were assigned to touchline benches that were just two yards from the pitch and eight or so yards from the fenced-in capacity crowd. It was far too close for comfort.

As soon as we sat down the spectators spotted us and set up a deafening chant of *'Cinco-Una!'* – Portuguese for five-one – and a derisive reminder of our defeat in Rio (when we foolishly let Pelé have the ball). Born joker Budgie Byrne could not resist the bait and stood up on the bench and started conducting the fans like the man in the white suit before the old Wembley Cup finals.

The Brazilians loved it and started chanting in time to Budgie's waving arms.

Budgie's choir switched their attention to cheering the Brazilian team when they came out on the pitch, and they lit up the night sky by firing three-stage firework rockets high above the stadium. Then we had fireworks of a different kind on the pitch.

Right from the first whistle, Argentinian hatchet-man defender Messiano made it clear that his one intention was to stop Pelé from playing. He was not only going to stop him having the ball, but was also determined to give him a good kicking. It was a duel that underlined the naked hatred between Brazil and Argentina.

Messiano kicked Pelé at every opportunity, tripped him, spat at him, wrestled him to the floor and pulled his shirt any time he seemed likely to get past him. Finally, after about thirty minutes of this almost criminal assault, the devil came out in Pelé as he completely lost his temper. Right in front of us on the touchline bench, he took a running jump at Messiano and butted him full in the face. It made Zinedine Zidane's head-butt in the 2006 World Cup final seem like a harmless kiss.

The Argentinian was carried off with his broken nose splattered across his face, and – incredibly – the Swiss referee allowed Pelé to play on. He knew that if he had ordered him off there would have been crowd riots.

The calculated, cynical fouling by the Argentinians had knocked all the rhythm and style out of the Brazilians, and the stadium became as quiet as a morgue when two minutes from the end the player substituting for the flattened Messiano scored his second goal of the match to make it 3–0 to Argentina.

Budgie Byrne unwisely chose this moment to do an insane thing. He stood on the bench again to face the fans and, holding up three fingers, invited them to join in a chant of 'Three-Zero'. It was the worst joke of Budgie's life. Suddenly bricks and fireworks rained down from the terraces as the fans turned their disappointment on us. They would have much preferred to reach the detested Argentinians but we were nearer targets.

The usually impassive Alf Ramsey took one look at the avalanche of rubble, rubbish and rockets coming our way and gave his shortest ever tactical talk. 'Run for it lads . . .' he said.

Luckily, the final whistle had been blown and we made a mad dash for the safety of the centre-circle. Villain Budgie Byrne then turned hero as his quick wits finally got us off the pitch in one piece. As the fans began to scream blue murder, and despite the intimidating presence of armed police, Budgie shouted the wise instruction, 'Grab yourself a Brazilian player.'

He seized goalkeeper Gilmar lovingly by the arm and walked him off the pitch, knowing full well that no fans would try to harm one of their idols. We all followed Budgie's lead and went off arm-in-arm with bewildered Brazilian players.

You may think we were over-reacting, but uppermost in the minds of everybody in the stadium was the fact that just ten days earlier 301 people had been killed in a riot at the national stadium in Peru where Argentina had been the opponents.

I think the way Argentina had played against Brazil that night – brutally and with deliberate violence aforethought – stayed imprinted on Alf Ramsey's mind and was one of the reasons he made his infamous 'animals' outburst against them after the 1966 World Cup quarter-final.

Pelé, of course, was mercilessly kicked out of the 1966 World Cup, but he got his old appetite back in time to steer the greatest of all the Brazilian teams to the 1970 World Cup triumph. He played on for four more years before announcing that his fantastic career was over.

In 1975 former *Daily Express* football writer Clive Toye, then general manager of New York Cosmos, persuaded Pelé to make a comeback in the North American Soccer League. He made a final final farewell appearance against his old club Santos in New Jersey before a sell-out 60,000 crowd on 1 October 1977. It was Pelé's 1,363rd match and he naturally marked it with a goal to bring his career total to 1,281.

Anybody who knows me will understand that these statistics are coming from my writing partner, Norman 'Boring' Giller. I prefer to think in terms of flesh and blood rather than facts and figures, and what I can say with complete authority is that Pelé was the greatest footballer ever to grace a football pitch.

I know, because I once chased his arse.

21

Bobby Moore

Born: Barking, Essex, 12 April 1941

Died: London, 24 February 1993, aged 51

Career span: 1957–78

Clubs: West Ham 1957–74 (544 league games, 22 goals); Fulham 1974–77 (124 league games, 1 goal); San Antonio Thunder 1977 (24 games, 1 goal); Seattle Sounders 1978 (7 games)

England: 108 caps, 2 goals

Club honours: 1 FA Cup, 1 European Cup-Winners' Cup (both with West Ham), 1 FA Cup runner-up (Fulham)

World Cup 1966 (captain)

Footballer of the Year 1964

BBC Sports Personality of the Year 1966

PREPARE to shed tears of sadness and frustration as I talk about the player who was my best mate in football, Robert Frederick Chelsea Moore. We had a friendship that transcended the game, and his early passing hurts to this day.

Every time I think of him, the memories of our experiences and adventures together – off as well as on the pitch – fill me with warm nostalgia. This is then overtaken by feelings of hot anger for the way he was treated after he had hung up his boots.

They have erected statues to him at Wembley and at West Ham, named a stand after him, television documentaries have lauded him, and people who barely knew him have compiled books and websites galore about the master.

To top it all, the Football Association – the f****** FA – in 2003 named him their 'Golden Player' of the last fifty years.

Where the f*** were all these fawning people when Bobby was alive? Why couldn't the FA have let him know how precious he was to them before cancer claimed him? They turned their backs on him after he had captained his country 90 times in 108 appearances, and played a key role in winning the World Cup for them in 1966. He climbed the thirty-nine steps at the old Wembley for three successive years to collect major trophies, and later had to climb down and almost beg for jobs in the game he had served so well.

Surely it was obvious that the blazered brigade at their then headquarters in Lancaster Gate could have employed him in an ambassadorial role. He was known and admired throughout the world of football, and would have been welcome anywhere as representative of all that was best about our country. Instead of that, when he applied for the England manager's job, he didn't even get the courtesy of a reply.

One of the greatest defenders the world has ever seen was forced to scratch a living on the periphery of the game after a few business projects had gone belly-up. He went to Denmark, Hong Kong and those soccer hotspots of Oxford and Southend to earn his bread and butter. He then became 'sports editor' of a daily paper that peddled soft porn before winding up as a pundit-commentator on London radio station Capital Gold, giving his opinions on football in between the pop songs.

What a way to treat one of England's finest sportsmen – ignored when alive, acclaimed and applauded in death. It was like reducing Admiral Lord Nelson to the job of looking after the rowing boats at the local park, and then erecting a statue to him. The hypocrisy makes me sick.

I gave a lot of thought to how best I could represent my mate in this book, and decided to dig out an interview that my writing partner Norman Giller and I had with him when he was struggling to overcome the cancer that eventually killed him. Norman knew him as well as I did, and they shared a love of boxing, travelling miles together to catch any fight involving their hero Cassius Clay/Muhammad Ali.

We talked about the good and bad times we had together on and off the pitch. So, if you're sitting comfortably, I shall begin . . .

JG: *What a jammy git you were, Mooro, to last ninety matches as England captain. I did my best to cost you the job.*

BM: Alf was often on the point of giving me the chop after incidents involving you, James. He went ballistic in New York in 1964 after I'd talked you into breaking a curfew to sneak away from the team hotel to see Ella Fitzgerald singing at Madison Square Garden.

JG: *Dear old Alf. When we told him we'd been to see Ella he thought it was an elephant at the zoo. All he knew about was football and westerns.*

BM: Yeah, he loved his westerns. Remember when we were in East Germany and Alf found out there was a western showing with subtitles? He rounded us up and we all went off to the cinema. The film was dubbed in German, and as the subtitles started crawling along the bottom of the screen they were in Polish!

JG: *We pissed ourselves. Alf loved us to do things together, to go round as a team as if tied by a rope.*

BM: You were too much of an individualist for him, Jim. Don't forget that we were together on the best day of my life and the worst of yours.

JG: *Knew you'd bring that up. We were room-sharing in the Hendon hotel during the 1966 World Cup. It was weird when we woke up on the morning of the final because you knew you were going to captain the side and I guessed I wouldn't be playing. Alf had not said a dicky bird to me, but I sensed I'd been given the elbow.*

BM: What could Alf do, Jim? You'd been injured for the quarter- and semi-final and the team had been magnificent in both games. If there had been substitutes then you would have got on, and Geoff probably wouldn't have got his hat-trick.

JG: *That's all blood under the bridge, Mooro. I always knew we would win the World Cup but, to be honest, I never envisaged that I would be a spectator. I wonder if people realise how close you came to not playing in the finals?*

BM: Oh, you mean the West Ham contract business. I was virtually blackmailed into signing a new contract with the club just before the first match against Uruguay. Ron Greenwood came to the hotel with all the papers, and it was made clear to me that as I was out of contract with West Ham I would not, under Fifa rules, be eligible to play for England. So I put my name to the contract and came off the West Ham transfer list. I wasn't being greedy. I just knew I was getting paid half of what many of the players at other clubs were earning.

JG: *You were there for Alf Ramsey's greatest triumphs, but also for the bad times. There were the cock-ups he made with the substitutions in Mexico in 1970.*

BM: Yes, it was the one weakness with Alf, apart from his lack of communication skills with the media. He hated the substitute rule because it had never been part of his thinking in all his time in the game. He never experienced it at club level, and just didn't feel comfortable with the rule. His decision to pull off Bobby Charlton, who was motoring nicely in the 1970 quarter-final against West Germany, was a shocker. Franz Beckenbauer was standing close to me as Bobby got the hook, and his eyes lit up. He had suddenly been given unexpected hope that Germany could turn the game.

JG: *And you were involved in Kevin Keegan's embarrassing exposure at Wembley.*

BM: That was in the 1974 World Cup qualifier against Poland. I'd been dropped after I'd had a bit of a nightmare in the game in Poland. I sat alongside Alf, and had never seen him so lacking in ideas as England struggled to get the ball into the net. I kept on at him in the second half to get a substitute on to mix things up a bit. But the longer the game went on he just seemed to freeze. Sitting to my right were our subs, including Ray Clemence, Kevin Keegan and Kevin Hector. Suddenly, with just five minutes to go and with me nagging him, Alf finally decided he should send on a sub. 'Kevin, get stripped,' Alf ordered. This was the moment when the drama on the bench turned to farce. Ray Clemence helped Kevin Keegan off with his tracksuit bottoms, but he was so eager that he tugged his shorts down to his knees. While he was suffering this over-exposure he became even further embarrassed when Alf made it clear he meant Kevin Hector not Keegan. I helped Hector off with his tracksuit bottoms, but by the time he got on there were just one hundred seconds left – the shortest England debut on record. England went out of the World Cup, and it eventually cost Alf his job.

JG: *The most shocked I'd ever seen you, Bob, was when I dropped in* *from nowhere to see you in Mexico City when you were under lock and key in the British ambassador's villa.*

BM: That was when I'd been sent back from Colombia after being arrested on that charge of stealing a bracelet from a jeweller's shop on the eve of the 1970 World Cup.

JG: *I'd arrived in Mexico at the end of the World Cup rally to find out that you'd been nicked. Our mutual mate Norman did some detective work and found out where you were being held until allowed to rejoin the England squad. I climbed over the wall of the villa to avoid all the press and photographers at the front, and the ambassador's wife caught me wandering around the garden. She gave me a bollocking and then demanded that I go to the front door. When I rang the door she let me in!*

BM: She almost fainted, Jimbo, when your first words to me were, 'Show us the bracelet then, Mooro.' I was so pleased to see you after the nightmare I'd been through. We cleared the ambassador out of all his drink that night.

JG: *It was disgraceful the way Alf and the rest of the Football Association freebie-chasers left you out to dry in Colombia. You could have got thousands out of the jewellery shop for destroying your reputation with a false charge.*

BM: I thought of going down that road, Jim, but it would have cost a fortune in legal fees, and knowing what crafty people they were I ran the risk of them inventing some witness who would have pointed the finger at me. Bobby Charlton was in the jewellery shop with me at the time of me supposedly stealing the bracelet. Can you imagine him having any part of something that dodgy!

JG: *Or* anything *dodgy. You could trust him with your last bottle of water in the desert. Remember our dance, Mooro?*

BM: You, you silly sod, suddenly grabbed hold of me in the penalty area in the middle of a First Division match between West Ham and Tottenham. You twirled me around as if it was a Cockney knees-up. It was hilarious. Can't imagine that happening in today's game. It's all so bloody serious. As we danced you said, 'See you later at the Black Lion,' one of our watering holes.

JG: *Happy days. Of course, we wound up together at West Ham.*

BM: Yes, and you got me in trouble again.

JG: *Here we go. I'm going to get blamed for the 'Blackpool Incident' now.*

BM: Well it was you, Jim, who called the cab to take us to Brian London's nightclub when you heard one of the hotel porters say there was no chance of the Cup-tie being played the next day because of all the snow on the pitch.

JG: *That porter seemed to know what he was talking about, and let's be honest, Mooro, eskimos couldn't have played football in those conditions. And by the way, I didn't call the cab. It just happened to arrive with a fare that was being dropped off at the hotel.*

BM: I felt sorry for Clyde Best, who we dragged along with us at the last minute.

JG: *Yes, Clyde came along for the ride and Brian Dear for the drink. We were not pissed when we got back to the Imperial, but we had been seen having a few pints in the nightclub by a supporter. He reported us to the club after we had lost to Blackpool on a skating-rink pitch that should have been ruled unfit for play.*

BM: It all blew up a week later. Everybody had kept quiet about it because, unbeknown to me, Eamonn Andrews was planning to hit me with the *This Is Your Life* book, and they waited until after the show before the newspapers started headlining what had happened at Blackpool.

JG: *I thought Ron Greenwood let you down big time. I didn't care about myself because I was planning to get out of the game at the end of the season. But he just threw you to the wolves. We were both suspended and even Alf Ramsey dropped you for a match. If you'd played, you would have beaten Billy Wright's record of captaining England ninety times, instead of equalling it. The biggest mistake* *we made, Mooro, was losing that Cup-tie at Blackpool. If we had won, or got a replay, nothing would have come of it. Greenwood could have punished us privately, but he decided to let the press have a field day. He used us as scapegoats.*

BM: D'you think he was getting his own back for what happened on the plane?

JG: *Oh, you mean when your business pal Freddie Harrison spiked his drinks.*

BM: We were in the upstairs bar of a Jumbo jet on the way to New York for an exhibition match against Pelé's Santos. You and I were knocking back pints when Ron joined us and asked for a Coke. Freddie decided to lace the Coke with Bacardi, a pretty juvenile thing to do but we giggled behind Ron's back.

JG: *During the next hour or so Ron must have had five or six Cokes, all of them doctored by the mischievous Freddie. Ron finally realised what was going on and, to his credit, he laughed it off. The alcohol made his tongue much looser than he would have liked and he confessed he was thinking of resigning.*

BM: Yes, that was embarrassing. And when he went back to his seat he went into a heavy, drink-sedated sleep. Peter Eustace, who was not exactly Ron's greatest fan since being dropped from the team, had the rest of us in fits of laughter as he leaned over the snoring Greenwood, miming as if telling him exactly what he thought of him. Ron would have had a fit if he'd woken up.

JG: *He never mentioned the resigning business again, but the Blackpool farce certainly gave him the chance to get his own back.*

BM: Let's be fair, Jim, for all his faults Ron was a gentleman who gave a lot to the game. He was as good a tactician as I ever met in the game, and he taught me a lot when I was a kid with the England Under-23s and then when he took over from Ted Fenton at Upton Park.

JG: *Yeah, Ron was out of the Walter Winterbottom school. A scholar and a gentleman. He couldn't understand how you and I could be* *less than serious about the game when we were off the pitch. With a gun to your head, who would have been your first choice for a World team from all the players you played with or against?*

BM: That's easy, Jim. Pelé by a mile. He had everything – perfect balance, could shoot with either foot, had tremendous vision, was as brave as they come and had the agility of a gymnast.

JG: *And if I was picking a World team defence, Mooro, I'll say this to your face because it's what I say behind your back . . . you would be my first choice.*

BM: Stop it, Jim. You're making me blush.

That was where we finished our interview, making a date for later when we could pick it up again and talk purely football rather than about our adventures off the pitch. Norman and I had arranged to meet him at the Capital Gold studio, but got a call from their switchboard, sending Bobby's apologies and asking us to postpone our meeting until a later date.

The interview never took place. Within a month lovely old Mooro had succumbed to his cancer.

One of England's greatest ever footballers – 'Sir' Bobby Moore – had gone, and suddenly everybody cared.

But where were they all when he needed them?

22

Eusebio

Born: Mozambique, 25 January 1942

Career span: 1957–78

Clubs: Lourenco Marques 1957–60; Benfica 1961–75 (301 league games, 317 goals); brief appearances with Rhode Island Oceaneers, Boston Minutemen, Monterrey, Beira-Mar, Toronto Metros, Las Vegas Quicksilver, Uniao Tomar 1975–78 (74 games in total, 26 goals)

Portugal: 64 caps, 41 goals

Club honours: 10 Portuguese league championships, 5 Portuguese Cups, 1 European Cup-Winners' Cup, 3 European Cup runners-up

European Footballer of the Year 1965

World Cup Golden Boot winner 1966

EW people outside Africa and Portugal had heard of Eusebio when I first played against him. It was in Tottenham's European Cup semi-final saga against Benfica back in 1961–62. I remember saying to anybody who would listen, 'Portugal have found another Pelé.'

He wore the same No. 10 shirt, had a similar physique, and – without argument – a harder shot than the great man. He had the power, particularly in his right foot, to launch the ball like an Exocet missile. They shared the same nicknames – 'The Black Pearl' and 'The Black Panther' – until Pelé became known simply as 'The King'.

Eusebio was the outstanding player when Benfica beat us 4–3 on aggregate in a two-legged semi-final that neutral onlookers called 'the most exciting two games in the history of the European Cup'.

Tottenham had no fewer than three goals disallowed for offside, and I will swear until the day I kick the bucket that my third one at White Hart Lane was perfectly legal. But this chapter is about the unique Eusebio, not me, so I shall stop whingeing (but it *still* wasn't offside).

Eusebio da Silva Ferreira – his full name – was Benfica's secret weapon. He had joined them just a few months earlier from Lourenco Marques in Mozambique, then under Portuguese rule. The Brazilians were given first refusal on signing the 19-year-old inside-forward, but passed because they thought they had plenty of players at home who were better than he was. Next in line to sign him were Sporting Club of Lisbon because they used Lourenco as a nursery club.

The story goes that Bela Guttman, Benfica's verbose Hungarian-born manager, was sitting in his barber's chair in Lisbon when he overheard some gossip about Sporting Lisbon being interested in an exceptional prodigy with Lourenco.

Guttman got the next flight out to Mozambique and came back with Eusebio safely locked in to a contract. Sporting Lisbon cried 'foul' but the young African was bound for Benfica despite all the legal fisticuffs.

At the end of his first season with Benfica, Eusebio scored two memorable goals in the 5–3 European Cup final victory over Real Madrid (a match in which Tottenham should rightfully have been playing but I'm not complaining). The following year he scored another European Cup final goal, this time Benfica finishing runners-up to AC Milan at Wembley.

Over the next thirteen years he became a footballing legend, despite the handicap of a recurring knee injury that finally forced him into what were virtually walk-on parts with a cluster of clubs in Mexico, the United States and Canada.

Who will ever forget his impact on the 1966 World Cup, when his nine goals earned him the Fifa Golden Boot? I remember watching his quarter-final performance against North Korea at Goodison Park on television with the rest of the England lads. The tiny-tot Koreans had raced into an unbelievable 3–0 lead and then Eusebio took over. He scored four goals and won the match for Portugal virtually single-handed . . . or, I guess, right-footed would be a more appropriate way of putting it.

As we watched a recording of the match at the England hotel headquarters in Hendon, one player was taking particular note – a short-sighted, toothless tiger called Norbert 'Nobby' Stiles. Alf Ramsey gave him the job of marking Eusebio in the semi-final at Wembley, and there was no better player on the planet for following orders than Our Nobby. The little feller told Alf, 'I'll stick closer to him than sh*t to a blanket.'

True to his word, Nobby hardly allowed the Portuguese Man o' War a kick, and Eusebio's only real impact on the match was when he scored from the penalty spot, the first goal England had conceded throughout the finals. One of the most touching images of the 1966 finals was the sight of Eusebio using his shirt to wipe away tears that flowed after the 2–1 defeat by England.

When lists are drawn up of the world's greatest players, Eusebio often misses out in favour of Pelé, Maradona, Best, Cruyff, Di Stefano, Puskas, Muller, Ronaldo and Zidane. Why? Because of that man Stiles.

In two of his biggest tests Eusebio failed to produce anything like his peak form because he could not shake off the pesky Stiles, who used to get almost inside his shirt with him. The second time that Nobby got the better of him was in the 1968 European Cup final, when Manchester United beat Benfica on an emotion-charged night at Wembley.

Mind you, Eusebio very nearly won the match for Benfica in the closing moments of ordinary time when he at last managed to slip the Stiles shackles. He unleashed a signature shot – with his left foot – that had goal written all over it. Everybody in the stadium thought Benfica were about to take a 2–1 lead until goalkeeper Alex Stepney produced one of the great saves to keep the ball out of the net somehow. 'If I had been able to shoot with my right foot,' Eusebio said later, 'I would have made no mistake. But I was having problems with my knee even then, and so I shot with my left. It was a good save by Stepney, but with my right foot I would have put the ball out of his reach.'

Eusebio, arguably the greatest footballer ever to come out of Africa, had tremendous sprint speed to go with his natural power, and he topped the Portuguese League scoring list seven times. In 1965 he was voted European Footballer of the Year, and was European Golden Boot winner in 1968 and 1973 before his knee problems reduced both his pace and power.

In his retirement he has become a roving ambassador for Portugal, just the sort of job the Football Association should have given to Bobby Moore. He works as a spokesman against racism, representing the views of the world union of 57,500 professional footballers.

Yes, Portugal had a Special One long before Jose Mourinho surfaced. One of Jose's proudest possessions is a photograph of himself taken bouncing on Eusebio's lap when he was five years old. He often contacts his old hero to talk football, and puts him up on a pedestal with Pelé and Maradona.

In all competitions for Benfica, Eusebio scored 727 goals in 715 matches. That is a phenomenal output. How glad he must have been that a certain Mister Nobby Stiles was not playing in the Portuguese League.

And how lucky he was that a certain goal scored for Tottenham against Benfica in the 1962 European Cup semi-final was unjustly ruled offside. But I'm not complaining.

23
Gianni Rivera

Born: Alessandria, Italy, 18 August 1943

Career span: 1959–79

Clubs: Alessandria 1959–60 (26 league games, 6 goals); AC Milan
1960–79 (501 games, 124 goals)

Italy: 60 caps, 14 goals

Club honours: 3 Italian championships, 4 Italian Cups, 2 European
Cups, 2 European Cup-Winners' Cups

European Footballer of the Year 1969

World Cup runner-up 1970

D
URING my brief unhappy spell with AC Milan in 1961 there
was a young player in the squad who was as gifted a teenaged
footballer as I had ever clapped eyes on. While I was becoming
known as the Rebel of Italian football, he was collecting a nickname that stuck – 'The Golden Boy'.

This was Gianni Rivera, a midfield player so beautifully balanced
and silky smooth that you could imagine him playing in ballet
tights and gliding across the pitch. He could pass the ball through
the eye of a needle, and had the sort of ball control that was a gift
from the footballing gods, because there was nobody on this earth
who could have taught him his skills.

I can never recall seeing Gianni sweat. He was all inspiration, no perspiration, and – the mark of a great player – seemed to have twice as long to do things as the players around him.

Back in those miserable days in Milan, I quickly discovered that he had an old head on young shoulders as I fought against the prison-like regime of a club where they thought they owned you twenty-four hours a day.

Most of my four months with AC Milan were spent in conflict with their coach, Nereo Rocco. And Nereo was a name that fitted him down to the ground because he was always giving me the thumbs down no matter what I did. If there had been lions around, I'm sure he would have tossed me to them.

Rivera, all of 18 and three years younger than I was, used to take me to one side during training and put an arm around my shoulder. 'Yimmy,' he would say in fractured English, 'why-a you fight Rocco all the time? Why-a you do these things? Why-a not go for the easy life and do-a what he says?'

That good common sense one day took Gianni into political life – but that was after he put together one of the great footballing careers.

He and Italian football were so good for each other that he became wealthy enough to buy out the AC Milan club president and install his own man, while himself holding the position of club vice president.

Even as a schoolboy Rivera stood out head and shoulders above all other potential professionals. He made his *Serie A* debut for Alessandria at the age of 15 against Inter Milan, who were *talking* about buying him while AC Milan were *acting*. They snapped him up when he was 16, giving him the responsibility of taking over from the Uruguayan master Juan Alberto Schiaffino. It was the equivalent of filling the boots of Tom Finney. And they were never too big for the Golden Boy.

Rivera quickly became the chief architect of the AC Milan attack, and his precise passes took them to the league championship in

1962, by which time I was collecting an FA Cup winner's medal with Tottenham. It was Rivera more than anybody who turned Milan into the European kings of the mid-sixties. The Golden Boy had become the man with the golden boots. Even back then he was earning the equivalent of £1,000 a week. This, remember, was when in England £100-a-week footballers were few and far between.

He had the most famous face and feet in Italy. Huge commercial deals brought his good looks to advertising campaigns. On the pitch he was the role model for every Italian schoolboy, with his stylish appearance and seemingly effortless way of playing the game.

Our paths have often crossed since we were club-mates, and whenever we meet we hug each other like long-lost brothers. I really appreciated his friendship and support during my four lost months in Milan and always kept an eye on his progress.

He made his debut for Italy at 18 and became their major motivator in four World Cup finals. There was almost civil war in the Italian camp at the 1970 tournament in Mexico. Coach Ferruccio Valcareggi got it into his head that Rivera could not – as he put it – 'co-exist' with another exceptional player, Sandro Mazzola. I suppose it was something like the Lampard/Gerrard situation in the modern game – two outstanding players handicapping rather than bringing the best out of each other.

'I will play them in relays, Mazzola for the first half, and Rivera for the second half,' Valcareggi told an astonished Italian press, who ripped him apart for his indecision. The atmosphere was so bad in the squad that the players refused to give interviews.

I smiled to myself because this was the sort of in-fighting I had witnessed in my brief stay with Milan.

Between them, Mazzola and Rivera guided Italy to the final, with skilled support from exceptional players of the calibre of Luigi Riva and Roberto Boninsegna. The madness of not playing Mazzola and Rivera together cost them any chance of winning the trophy.

It is history now that the brilliant Pelé-propelled Brazilian team took Italy apart and won the final 4–1, with Rivera – 1969 European Footballer of the Year – insultingly being brought on for just the last eight minutes, by which time the game had been won and lost.

In fairness, Mazzola had a cracking game and there was no way he could be called off at half-time as had been planned. But why oh why Valcareggi could not have played both his artists will remain a mystery. They were only on the pitch together throughout the World Cup for those last eight minutes of the final, because it was Boninsegna who was ultimately sacrificed so that Rivera could get into the game.

Rivera played on for Milan for another nine years, and made his fourth appearance in World Cup finals in 1974. He did it all without seeming to have a hair out of place. Gianni always looked immaculate, even in the heat of battle.

He ended his long association with AC Milan in 1986 when Silvio Berlusconi bought the club. Rivera, by this time a centre-left politician with a huge public following, was elected to Parliament, and rose to the position of under-secretary for defence in Romano Prodi's government.

Rivera retained his interest in football as a television commentator and pundit, and caused uproar during the 1982 finals when he dismissed Italy's chances as being next to hopeless. Don't you just hate these know-all ex-pros who make a career in television when their playing days are over?

When the Paolo Rossi-inspired Italians won the World Cup Rivera said publicly, 'I will wear the habit of a penitent and follow the procession of Saint Bartholomew in repentance at my home village.'

That wasn't quite the advice he gave me in the springtime of our footballing lives together, and the only repentance I felt was for agreeing to join AC Milan in the first place. The bonus was that I played with one of the finest young footballers of my generation, Gianni Rivera – the Golden Boy.

24

Pat Jennings

Born: Newry, County Down, 12 June 1945

Career span: 1961–1986

Clubs: Newry Town 1961–63; Watford 1963–64 (48 league games); Tottenham 1964–77 (472 league games); Arsenal 1977–84 (237 league games)

Northern Ireland: 119 caps

Club honours: 1 FA Cup, 1 League Cup, 1 Uefa Cup (all with Tottenham); 1 FA Cup (Arsenal)

Footballer of the Year 1973

PFA Player of the Year 1976

THE Man with the Bucket Hands, Pat Jennings was the best of all British goalkeepers that I played with or against. Yes, I would put him just a fingertip ahead of Gordon Banks and Peter Shilton.

Yet when he first arrived at Tottenham from Watford in 1964 you would not have given tuppence for his chances of making the grade at the highest level. He came into a team that was being rebuilt after the sudden collapse of the 'Super Spurs' – Danny Blanchflower forced into retirement by a knee injury, and dear John White killed by a freak flash of lightning while playing golf.

Big Pat was a bag of nerves when pitched into the Spurs first team, and I used to see those spade-like hands of his visibly shaking in the dressing room. I remember Pat telling me that he was concentrating so hard that he would suffer from headaches. Manager Bill Nicholson had to leave him out a couple of times until he conquered his nerves, and he then developed into just about the finest British goalkeeper of all time – with challenges, I have to say, from old-timers Frank Swift, Harry Hibbs and another outstanding Irish goalie, Elisha Scott.

All the signs were that Pat would be an exceptional Gaelic footballer when he was at school, and he was quite casual about playing in goal in his spare time for Newry Town, while building his considerable physique by chopping down trees.

Manager Bill McGarry persuaded him to come across the Irish Sea and start a Football League career with Watford, and within a year he had done enough to convince Tottenham that he was the ideal successor to 'Super Spurs' goalkeeper Bill Brown.

He gradually became an idol at White Hart Lane, and popular throughout the club. Modest and quite shy, he was as lovely and likeable a man as you could wish to meet, with a deep, soft-spoken voice that was rarely raised even when suggesting defensive colleagues should pull their finger out.

As well as building impressive credentials at club level, he started an international career that made him a world star. I once scored a first-half hat-trick against him at Windsor Park, but I won't mention it here.

Making his debut with Pat in the same match against Wales in 1964 was a young winger called George Best. They became good pals, although leading contrasting lifestyles. Pat settled down to a long and happy marriage with Hilton Irish Showband singer Eleanor Toner, while 'settled down' and 'George Best' never sat comfortably in the same sentence.

A little bit of trivia for you – Pat was brought up in the same Chapel Street in Newry where ten years before him Peter

McParland had grown up. Peter collected an FA Cup winner's medal with Aston Villa in 1957, and a decade later Pat got the first of his two winner's medals in the 1967 final against Chelsea. Not a bad record for one street.

Pat played more than 1,000 competitive games in all, and was voted Footballer of the Year in 1973. The highlights of that season were two penalty saves for Tottenham against Liverpool at Anfield on the morning of the Grand National – one from Tommy Smith, and then one from Kevin Keegan. All the stuff of legend.

Three seasons later he was voted the PFA Player of the Year, and he is one of the few sportsmen who has been awarded both an MBE and an OBE. It all came as a surprise to Pat, whose next boast will be his first.

The thing people always noticed about Pat on a first meeting was the size of his hands. I used to marvel at the way he could catch the ball one handed, a legacy of his days in Gaelic football.

My abiding memory of him is of Jennings the goalscorer! Tottenham were playing Manchester United in the Charity Shield at Old Trafford in the summer of 1967. Alan Gilzean and I were upfield facing the United goal when suddenly we saw the ball going first bounce over the head of goalkeeper Alex Stepney and into the net.

We looked back to see big Pat doing a jig on the edge of the penalty area. He had drop-kicked the wind-assisted goal a distance of 120 yards. With the new season about to start, I said to Gilzean, 'You realise, Gilly, that this makes Pat our top scorer.'

The only time I ever saw this affable gentle giant lose his temper was against Don Revie's Leeds Kickers at Elland Road in 1968. Mick Jones came roaring in like a mad bull and caught him with an unnecessary flying boot in the thigh. The suddenly enraged Jennings took careful aim and kicked Jones up the arse. What should have been a free-kick for Spurs became a penalty for Leeds, which Allan Clarke converted for the only goal of a bad-tempered match.

Our skipper Dave Mackay, I recall, was so incensed that he grabbed the ball and kicked it with all his might out of the ground.

I thought the Tottenham directors were bonkers to allow Pat to move to deadly rivals and neighbours Arsenal in August 1977, when he was 32. It was like Paul McCartney going from The Beatles to The Stones. Spurs obviously thought he had little left to give, and they had Barry Daines as a replacement. I also know that Pat was pissed-off with the Spurs board at the time because they would not give him a loan to help him buy the house of his dreams. They just had no idea how to repay him for his great service to the club.

Pat answered Tottenham's lack of faith in him by playing on for another eight years at Arsenal, and he became as big a hero at Highbury as he had been at White Hart Lane.

He played a major part in getting the Gunners to three successive FA Cup finals, emerging as a winner in the middle one, 1979. 'I know a lot of Tottenham supporters were upset with me going to Arsenal,' Pat said. 'But it suited my domestic life, because there was no need for the big upheaval of having to move to a new area. I was just happy to still be playing at the top level and I gave Arsenal the same one hundred per cent commitment I had always given to Spurs. Of course, the fact that my old Northern Ireland captain Terry Neill was in charge at Highbury helped make it a smooth transition.'

Pat semi-retired in 1986 to concentrate on golf, which he loved, but he kept his eye in by returning to Tottenham in a coaching capacity while retaining his player registration. At the back of his mind was playing his last game in the 1986 World Cup finals, and he tuned up by going in goal for the reserves.

His dream finale came true when Northern Ireland qualified for the World Cup finals in Spain. All eyes were on him when he made his last competitive appearance with what was then a record 119th international match against Brazil. To add to the fairytale finish, it was his 41st birthday. Brazil won 3–0, but Pat was carried off at the end as an all-time hero of Irish football. And he will always be an all-time hero of mine (even if I did score a first-half hat-trick against him, which I have agreed not to mention. Sorry Pat).

25

Franz Beckenbauer

Born: Munich, 11 September 1945

Career span: 1964–83

Clubs: Bayern Munich 1964–77 (427 games, 60 goals); New York Cosmos 1977–80 and 1983 (132 games, 21 goals); Hamburg 1980–82 (28 games)

West Germany: 103 caps, 14 goals

Club honours: 5 *Bundesliga* titles, 4 German Cups, 3 European Cups, 1 European Cup-Winners' Cup

World Cup 1974, runner-up 1966; managed World Cup winners Germany 1990 European Championship 1972

European Footballer of the Year 1972 and 1976

I T would not surprise me in the least while I am preparing this chapter if Franz Beckenbauer arrives at my side and writes it himself. Let's face it, he has done everything else in football and is not happy unless he has his fingers (it used to be his feet) in every pie.

'Been there, done that' should be tattooed on his chest. He won just about everything there was to win as a player, and then, after managing the World Cup winners in 1990, climbed ever higher until he was the big white chief overseeing the 2006 World Cup.

Since hanging up his golden boots, he has led his life the way he used to play the game as a pioneer of the 'sweeper' system. He is here, there and everywhere, negotiating and cajoling, sweet-talking and spin-doctoring, wheeling and dealing. I don't think he will be happy until he is President of Fifa. *Der Kaiser* wants to be *El Presidente*!

Beckenbauer has a brain the size of Mars, and it seems to me he uses it to better himself at every turn. Nothing wrong with that, but sometimes you can think a man has too much power, too much sway and too much say.

There is little doubt in my mind that England should have staged the 2006 World Cup, but our negotiating team – led by the football knights Sir Bobby Charlton and Sir Geoff Hurst – were outmanoeuvred by crafty Franz, just as he outthought them on the playing field at Leon in the 1970 World Cup finals.

The only time he got it wrong against England was in the 1966 final, when his abundant skill was sacrificed while he sat on Bobby Charlton in a man-to-man marking role that took those two creative players out of the match. Of course, Franz was quick to point out that those were the tactics of manager Helmut Schoen. 'If I'd had my way,' he said, 'I would have played an attacking role.'

Beckenbauer strolled into my selection. As much as I have disliked his arrogance, I cannot dispute that he was an absolute master of the footballing arts. My mate Bobby Moore was a great admirer, and unashamedly copied his sweeping technique when Franz started attacking from the back in the late 1960s.

As upright as a member of *Der Kaiser*'s guards, Beckenbauer was elegant and confident on the ball to the point of being conceited. He was tactically astute and an outstanding captain, a superstar in every sense of the word.

He has come a long, long way since the schoolboy days when he supported Bayern Munich's deadly rivals, 1860 Munich. Playing in a friendly match for his local youth club side against a team from 1860 Munich in the 1957–58 season, he got thumped in the face by an 1860 opponent. He was so upset that he vowed he would never play for them and instead signed with Bayern Munich to start an association that has lasted, with a few brief breaks, nearly half a century.

German football folklore has it that Beckenbauer became known as Kaiser Franz following an incident in the 1969 German Cup final. He dispossessed Schalke's star player Reinhard Libuda with what many considered a foul tackle. He then strolled the length of the pitch with the ball at his feet while the Schalke fans booed him every inch of the way. He defiantly stood deep in the Schalke half of the field and for a full thirty seconds juggled the ball until even the fans booing him had grudgingly to applaud his skill. Libuda was known as *König von Westfalen* (king of Westphalia) and the watching reporters had to reach for something superior for Beckenbauer, and came up with *Der Kaiser*.

Beckenbauer won 103 caps for West Germany before the Berlin wall came down, and captained his country fifty times. He was voted European Footballer of the Year twice, and was the brains behind the rise of Bayern Munich as a major power in Europe, steering them to three successive European Cup triumphs.

He was also a brave bugger. Evidence of his courage came in Mexico in 1970 when he played on with a dislocated shoulder in the dramatic 4–3 semi-final defeat by Italy.

In his third and last World Cup finals, played in his Fatherland in 1974, Beckenbauer peaked at exactly the right time, and he led West Germany to a memorable 2–1 victory over Johan Cruyff's

Holland in the final in his hometown of Munich. It completed an amazing full house for Franz. He and the left-foot wizard Wolfgang Overath became the only players to collect World Cup gold, silver and bronze medals (they finished third in 1970).

The 1974 final was the one in which Wolverhampton referee Jack Taylor awarded Holland a first-minute penalty after they had put together a stunning sequence of fifteen passes without a single German touching the ball. Beckenbauer later revealed, 'As Neeskens scored from the penalty spot I said to my team-mates, "Don't worry. This referee will give us a penalty before long."' Sure enough, master butcher Taylor cut a joint for the Germans, awarding them a penalty from which Paul Breitner equalised. Gerd 'Der Bomber' Muller scored the winning goal with a magnificent shot on the turn in the 43rd minute, and it was Kaiser Franz who collected the World Cup.

Always aware of his value, Beckenbauer picked up a fortune to play with Pelé for New York Cosmos at the back end of his career. He still had the legs and the appetite to return to Germany and help Hamburg win the *Bundesliga* in 1982. He knew just how to market himself, and made bags of money with commercial ventures that took in lucrative advertising contracts with adidas and a leading mobile phone company.

He touched a pinnacle in 1990 when he became the first and only man to both captain and then coach a World Cup-winning side. While all this was going on, Beckenbauer found the time to marry three times and to father five children.

In every interview these days he talks like a statesman rather than a football man. Asked recently what sort of hold football has on the world, he replied, 'Football has an incredible power that goes well beyond sport. Especially in Africa, in countries where people wage war against each other because some of them come from the north and others from the south. A tribe here, a tribal chieftain there – but football brings them all to the same table, football makes them peaceful. It can instil order and a sense of community. Football is for all of the people all of the time.'

Now doesn't that sound like *El Presidente* speaking! I suppose it beats 'sick as a parrot' and 'over the moon, Brian'.

You can't knock the man's record. He is a bloody genius. I just wish he had been a little less supercilious about it all. Envious, moi?

26

Gerd Muller

Born: Nördlingen, Germany, 3 November 1945

Career span: 1964–81

Clubs: Bayern Munich 1964–79 (453 league games, 398 goals); Fort Lauderdale Strikers 1979–81 (80 games, 40 goals)

West Germany: 62 caps, 68 goals

Club honours: 4 *Bundesliga* titles, 4 German Cups, 3 European Cups, 1 European Cup-Winners' Cup

World Cup 1974

Scored a then record 14 World Cup finals goals

Golden Boot winner 1970 World Cup

European Championship 1972

European Footballer of the Year 1970

WHAT is it with goalscorers? So many of us seem to turn to the bottle after the shooting and the shouting are over. Is it that our thirst for goals has to be replaced by a substitute? The question is prompted by the fact that Gerd Muller, who was arguably the greatest of all marksmen, is yet another who had serious alcohol problems when his career was finished.

He is in good company. George Best, Garrincha, Ferenc Puskas, Jim Baxter, Paul Gascoigne, I suppose I had better include myself, and Diego Maradona – although cocaine was a bigger problem for him – were among those who had an alcohol dependency after hanging up their boots.

We all went from boots to booze. Muller was another who thought opening a bar was a good idea when he retired, and – like Jim Baxter before him – did his best to drink his premises dry.

Stocky and seeming to be almost as wide as he was tall, Muller had to watch his weight throughout all his years plundering goals. Once all restrictions were lifted, he dived into the life of an alcoholic until rescued by his old friends in football.

Bayern Munich, the club where he spent fifteen mostly glorious years, brought him back into their family, helped him get straightened out and, as I write, he is happily helping coach the next generation of Bayern football stars.

Remember Muller at his peak, banging in goals galore in the 1970 and 1974 World Cups? Black haired, brooding, built like a brick shite house and dynamite in the penalty area. Today he is white haired, with a beard and looking, what shall I say, very un-athletic.

This is the man who back in the early 1960s was told by Bayern Munich that he was too fat and slow to make the grade. They changed their mind when he started to rattle in goals for his local youth team in his Bavarian birthplace of Nördlingen. He earned the nickname 'Der Bomber' as he blitzed defences with more explosive results than any other striker in European and World Cup history.

Including qualifying matches, Muller scored 19 goals in the 1970 series with a then record ten in the finals.

His contribution to West Germany's World Cup triumph in 1974 was four goals, including the all-important winner against Holland in the final on his favourite hunting ground in Munich.

He was just as prolific in club football with Bayern, scoring more than 600 goals in all competitions. His 36 goals in European Cup football made nonsense of the early predictions that he would be too weighed down with muscle and fat to make an impact at the top level.

At just 5ft 6in tall, Muller was squat almost to the point of squashed in build. His short, tree-trunk legs gave him a low centre of gravity, and as well as his finishing accuracy with either foot, his secret was stunning acceleration. Like so many goalscorers, he was carthorse slow over 100 metres, yet like a flash of lightning in the space of a hall room carpet.

For a short man, he was a nuisance in the air and was brave enough to challenge the tall, strong central defenders in aerial combat. His ability to shoot on the turn made him as dangerous in the penalty area as a wild-west gunman in a bar duel.

His speciality was to swivel and shoot all in one rapid move-ment. His golden goal that beat Holland in 1974 was a typical example of this technique, which caught out dozens of defenders.

Very few players matched his scoring ratio at international level. His 68 goals in just 62 matches is mind-blowing stuff.

Asked about his gift for goals, Muller said, 'I have this instinct for knowing when a defence is going to relax, or when a defender is going to make a mistake. Something inside me says, "Gerd, go this way; Gerd, go that way." I don't know what it is.'

Like the rest of us, Gerd followed his instincts and did not have a clue how he achieved it. If any of us knew, we would bottle it and make a fortune selling the secret formula.

Gerd the Girth was at the forefront of all the great German successes of the late 1960s and into the 1970s. He helped Bayern

Munich to an unprecedented run of success in the *Bundesliga* as they dominated at domestic and then European level.

Along with team-mates of the calibre of goalkeeper Sepp 'Big Gloves' Maier, smooth-as-silk full-back Paul Breitner, scheming scorer Uli Hoeness and Kaiser Franz Beckenbauer, Muller was part of the Bayern 'dream team' that also formed the foundation of the national side.

It was, of course, Muller who broke English hearts in the quarter-finals of the 1970 World Cup in Mexico by cleverly poaching the extra-time goal that completed West Germany's extraordinary revival and their 3–2 victory in a match that looked lost when they were 2–0 down.

He was on fire in Mexico, scoring what was then a record ten goals in six matches, including a hat-trick against Bulgaria and two goals in the classic semi-final against Italy.

Two years later he was the main marksman as West Germany lifted the European Championship, collecting the scalp of England at Wembley along the way. And guess what, their 3–1 win included a shot-on-the-turn goal by *Der Bomber*.

Then it was on to the 1974 World Cup victory, when he made up for having had a quiet tournament – *only* four goals – by netting the winner in the final.

Who could have guessed that this would be the last international goal Muller would score, and indeed the last international game he would play. He was just 28 and at the peak of his powers. It all ended in tears because of a huge bust-up at the after-match victory banquet.

The spirit in the German camp had been fragile throughout the tournament, following a bitter dispute over win bonuses, finally sorted out – of course – by Kaiser Franz Beckenbauer.

When the players arrived at the hotel for the celebrations, they found loads of German officials but no wives or girlfriends. They had been banned from attending. Just like the English FA, the

German association was full of old farts who thought they were more important than the players.

Uli Hoeness led a mass walk-out in protest, and Muller not only joined in but announced instantly that he would never play for Germany again. He made his statement in a downtown bar, where most of the players had headed after the banquet fiasco. Wolfgang Overath, Jurgen Grabowski and Paul Breitner were equally angry, and they too declared that their international careers were over. The World Cup-winning side had broken up overnight.

This all came in the middle of a run of three successive European Cup final victories by Bayern Munich from 1974 to 1976. It was domination on a Real Madrid scale.

Then came the downhill run as Muller started to feel the effects of his dynamic action. His back started to give him problems and he wound down his career playing with the United States circus, teaming up with George Best at Fort Lauderdale. I'm surprised there was elbow room for them both.

He returned to the Fatherland and got lost in a sea of alcohol until helped back to the shores of sobriety by his old Bayern Munich chums Beckenbauer and Hoeness, who is now the club's general manager.

During his playing career *Der Bomber* built a mountain of goals that will guarantee him a place in football history. You could say that he had an unquenchable thirst for goals.

27

George Best

Born: Belfast, 22 May 1946

Died: West London, 25 November 2005, aged 59

Career span: 1963–84

Clubs: Manchester United 1963–1973 (361 league games, 137 goals); Stockport County 1975 (3 league games, 2 goals); Cork Celtic 1975–76 (3 games, 0 goals); LA Aztecs 1976–78 (61 games, 29 goals); Fulham 1976–77 (42 games, 8 goals); Fort Lauderdale Strikers 1979–80 (33 games, 7 goals); Hibernian 1979–80 (22 games, 3 goals); San Jose Earthquakes 1979–81 (86 games, 34 goals); Bournemouth 1983 (5 league games, 0 goals); Brisbane Lions 1983 (4 games, 0 goals); 1984 Tobermore United (1 game)

Northern Ireland: 37 caps, 9 goals

Club honours (all with Manchester United): 2 league championships, 1 European Cup

Footballer of the Year 1968

European Footballer of the Year 1968

SIMPLY the Best seems too glib and clichéd a description for George Best, but I am comfortable using it because it just happens to be totally accurate. George *was* simply the best British footballer of my lifetime, probably of anybody's lifetime.

OK, I admit to bias because George and I were close pals with much more in common than just our footballing careers. They have a lovely saying in Belfast – which you are likely to hear soon after touching down at George Best Airport: 'Maradona good; Pelé better; George best.'

That's better than anything I can coin. I'm choked just thinking about the loveable, cheeky sod. He used to take the piss out of me for giving up being pissed. I never ever felt it my business to try to talk him out of his 'have-booze-will-travel' existence. In many interviews he would tell journalists with that mischievous grin of his, 'Jimmy has chosen his way, I've chosen mine . . . and I know who's getting the most enjoyment out of it!'

How could I argue with that Irish logic? George lived his life like there was no tomorrow, laughing, joking, shagging, staggering and brawling through his middle-age. Eventually, there was no more tomorrow. But I honestly think – no, I *know* – George would not have had it any other way.

George did everything by the bucketload. He played football better than almost anybody on the planet, he loved many of the women he bedded (which was on the Casanova scale), he drank more than was good for him but loved every drop, and he spent every penny as if money was coming out of a tap. It was George, of course, who famously said, 'I've spent my money on booze, women and fast cars, the rest I squandered.'

Everybody, the world and its brother, had an opinion on George. And d'you know something, he didn't give a monkey's about any of them. He lived his life the way he wanted to, and – surprisingly, for somebody pictured so many times with a tasty blonde on his arm – he was happiest as a loner.

He once told me that his most contented times were spent sitting alone at continental-type cafés just watching the world go by. For all his exposure across front pages and on the box, he remained a shy man at heart.

George cared about other people that other people didn't care about. I will let you read that sentence twice to see that it makes sense.

I remember before one of our road shows up in Leeds we were sitting having a meal in a pizza restaurant when, shuffling in, came the vaguely familiar figure of somebody we suddenly realised had been a pioneering player when George was first making his name in the game.

It was Albert Johanneson, the black South African winger, who had been a runner-up in the 1965 FA Cup final with Leeds. He had gone on the skids after his retirement and had become yet another loser to booze.

I left George and Albert talking over old times to get prepared for the evening's show. Bestie, not for the first time, failed to turn up, and later admitted that he and Albert had gone out on the piss.

'Well,' said George, 'I at least had the satisfaction of giving Albert one more decent night out. Nobody gives a f*** about him. He deserved my full attention for just one night.'

That was the caring side of Bestie, who was an easy touch for hard-luck stories. But even 'Generous George' became a little disillusioned when people would get him to sign all sorts of things 'for sick friends and relatives' only to find them appearing on eBay a few days later.

When George was desperate for money after his liver transplant, his conscientious agent, Phil Hughes, persuaded him to have the trophies, medals and mementoes he had won and the shirts he had worn auctioned. Phil could not believe how little was left when he went to George's house. Most of those prized possessions had been given away, stolen or lost.

One thing that always amuses me is when people talk about George having had a short career. He actually played on for eleven years after his ten eventful seasons at Old Trafford. Sadly, many of the games were for teams not really worthy of his regal presence. It was like finding a Goya in a garage sale.

As a winger, George was like Stanley Matthews on steroids. He had mesmerising ball control, the speed of an Olympic sprinter over 20 yards and a deadly eye in front of goal. And he was recklessly brave. Any defender threatening him physical harm – and there were a lot of them in his peak years – were treated to the full monty. He would tease and torment them, risking serious injury as they kicked out trying to stop him. George rarely came off a pitch without having got the better of his marker.

They kept telling us that Pelé and Maradona were better players, but if George had performed in those highly skilled Brazilian and Argentinian teams, surrounded by gifted footballers, he would have been acclaimed worldwide as, well, simply the Best.

He used to be searingly honest on our road shows when it came to the question and answer sessions with the audience. I used to wince sometimes, hoping there were no legal eagles in listening distance. Here is a vetted version of some of George's answers in a tape-recorded version of the Best & Greavsie show. All the questions were pitched by members of the audience:

Q: *If you were starting out all over again as a player, George, would you lay off the booze?*

GEORGE: You must be pissed to ask that question! I would have done everything the same. I'm not one of the people who look back and regret things. I did what I wanted to do at the time and thoroughly enjoyed myself.

Q: *How big an influence did Matt Busby have on you?*

GEORGE: He was like a second father to me, and I had great respect for him. People said he was too easy on me, but he gave me several bollockings that almost brought me to tears. He was not the soft fella that was portrayed in the press. Sir Matt could be ruthless when necessary, but he had soul. I loved the man.

Q: *Why did you and Bobby Charlton hate each other?*

GEORGE: That's bollocks. We misunderstood each other, rather

141

than hated each other. Bobby and I came from different worlds. He did not approve of my lifestyle, and I was not over-impressed by his. What I do know is that I have got a lot of fun out of life. I'm not sure Bobby can say that. Have you ever seen him laughing? Let me say in front of all you witnesses that I rated him highly as a player, and it was a joy to have Charlton and Denis Law on my side. Three European Footballers of the Year together. It didn't come better than that. Even Real Madrid had only two of those!

Q: *With a gun to your head, George, who was the greatest player of your generation?*

GEORGE: In Europe, Johan Cruyff. He was magical when at his peak. On the world stage I have to go along with the general view – Pelé just ahead of Maradona, but Alfredo Di Stefano and Ferenc Puskas were something special when playing together for Real.

Q: *Did you ever go on the pitch drunk?*

GEORGE: I played with hangovers a few times, but I was a good enough professional to make sure I was fit to play in my Manchester United days. Mind you, there were a few games in the United States where I might have struggled to pass the breathalyser test.

Q: *Is it right you bedded seven Miss Worlds?*

GEORGE: Total rubbish. It was only four. I didn't turn up for the other three.

Q: *Were you caught in bed with a blonde on the afternoon of an FA Cup semi-final?*

GEORGE: That's another lie. She was a brunette. Seriously, I was amusing myself with a lady in my hotel room on the afternoon of the 1970 FA Cup semi-final against Leeds. We were just talking and flirting when Wilf McGuinness, then the Manchester United boss, came knocking on the door like a maniac. I didn't see what harm I was doing. It was surely better to be relaxing, talking to a nice lady, than worrying about that evening's game.

Q: *Did anybody ever threaten to break your leg while you were playing against them?*

GEORGE: Only a few dozen times. They didn't realise it but they just made me play better because I wanted to prove they did not belong on the same pitch as me. I know that sounds arrogant, but without that sort of confidence don't bother to try to play at the top.

Q: *Are you jealous of the thousands of pounds today's players are earning each week?*

GEORGE: No, it's their time and my advice is enjoy it while it lasts. I was a big earner throughout my career and have no complaints. Mind you, if Greavsie and I were playing now, I've no doubt we'd both be on more than £100,000 a week. Think of the booze that would buy!

Q: *What was your lowest moment, George?*

GEORGE: Getting sent to prison. I know I deserved it, but what good did it do anybody? I could have done something for the community, something like training under-privileged kids. But they wanted to make an example of me. As I was sent down, I turned to my solicitor and said, 'I suppose that's the knighthood f****d.' I even got hammered for that by the press when it became public what I'd said. Surely a sense of humour is the only thing that keeps people sane at times like that.

Q: *How do you rate David Beckham?*

GEORGE: Well, he can only kick the ball with his right foot, can't head the ball, can't tackle and doesn't score nearly enough goals. Apart from that, he's not bad.

Q: *Who were the hardest players you played against?*

GEORGE: There were a squad of hit men in the days when Jimmy and I were playing. Every team had an assassin. Don't forget, they could tackle from behind then. We were not given any protection by the referees. I was kicked by the best of them, Norman 'Bites Yer Legs' Hunter, Ron 'Chopper' Harris, Tommy 'Iron' Smith, Dave Mackay, Billy Bremner, and we had a good marker in little Nobby Stiles, who would have tackled his granny if Matt Busby had asked him to. But the hardest of them all was Peter 'Cold Eyes' Storey at Arsenal. He seemed a real psycho to me. He used to prowl around the pitch almost grunting as he waited to chop anybody trying to get past him.

Q: *If you could turn the clock back, George, what major change would you make?*

GEORGE: I would play on for Manchester United for another five years and break every record in the books. I think if Matt Busby or Alex Ferguson had been in charge, I would never have stopped playing at the top so early. But let's say Tommy Docherty was not my sort of manager. I always thought he was more interested in his own image rather than the club's.

Q: *Why did you go missing so much?*

GEORGE: Well wouldn't you have gone missing if waiting for you in the bedroom were Miss United Kingdom, Miss United States, Miss World?

Q: *What's the truth about that story of you and a Miss World in a Manchester casino?*

GEORGE: It's been a bit embroidered, but this is the true version. I was playing roulette in a Manchester casino, got lucky and won twenty thousand pounds. The girl who brought me luck that night was the Swedish Miss World, Mary Stavin. She was hanging on my arm as I cashed in my chips. She put a few wads in her handbag, and I stuffed the rest in my jacket and trouser pockets. Then we got a chauffeured limousine back to the Manchester hotel where we were staying.

As the little Irish night porter let us in, I tipped him twenty quid to bring a bottle of chilled Dom Perignon up to our room.

Mary, in a see-through negligee, was just coming out of

the bathroom and the twenty grand was spread over the bed when the porter arrived with the bubbly.

As he put the tray on the bedside table, the porter asked a little nervously, 'I wonder, Mr Best, if you'd mind a fellow Ulsterman putting a personal question to you?'

'Fire away,' I said, peeling off another tenner from the stack of money and handing it to the old boy.

'Well, I was wondering,' said the porter, 'where did it all go wrong?'

Q: *Weren't you ashamed of yourself when you turned up drunk on Terry Wogan's live television show?*

GEORGE: It's the people around Terry who should feel ashamed. They later denied it, but I'm sure they deliberately plied me with booze in the hospitality room before the show started, knowing full well that I was getting drunk. They wanted me pissed when I walked on set. I have no doubt about that. Well, they got their wish and I was not proud of my performance that night. I don't think Terry was part of it. He was shocked when I walked on stage as pissed as a fart. It was his production team. I think they were struggling in the ratings at the time.

Q: *I read a Michael Parkinson article in which he wrote that you were thinking of committing suicide when you were a young man. Is that true?*

GEORGE: If Parky wrote it, it must be true. I have a lot of time for him. I did tell him years ago that I had the feeling that one day I would top myself. I was a complicated mess then and had many different moods. Now I love life, and want to grow old disgracefully.

When George passed on in November 2005, a light went out on the football stage. I played against him, I drank with him, I laughed with him, I liked him a hell of a lot . . . I never ever pitied him. George chose his path and did it his way right to the last.

Yes, he *was* simply the best.

28

Johan Cruyff

Born: Amsterdam 25 April 1947

Career span: 1964–84

Clubs: Ajax 1964–73 and 1981–83 (265 league games, 204 goals); Barcelona 1973–78 (143 league games, 48 goals); LA Aztecs 1979–80 (27 league games, 14 goals); Washington Diplomats 1980–81 (32 league games, 12 goals); 1981 Levante (10 games, 2 goals); 1983–84 Feyenoord (33 games, 11 goals)

Holland: 48 games, 33 goals

Club honours: 8 Dutch league championships, 5 Dutch Cups, 1 Spanish championship, 1 Spanish Cup, 3 European Cups

European Footballer of the Year 1971, 1973 and 1974

World Cup runner-up 1974

IT is arguable that Johan Cruyff was a finer footballer than almost any of the other outstanding players featured on my list of the élite of the élite. What is *definite* is that he smoked more cigarettes than most of the rest of them put together.

When he used to join us in the ITV studios to lend his punditry to major football tournaments, he was rarely without a cigarette in his hand. And it was the same during his playing career. He would smoke in the dressing room before and after matches, smoke during meals and smoke during breaks in training. He smoked like a bloody steam engine.

I used to enjoy a puff, but I was an apprentice compared to the chain-smoking Cruyff. It is amazing what he achieved on the football field considering what the medics tell us is a huge hazard for athletes.

The pioneer of 'Total' football, Cruyff was *the* 'Total' footballer. He could play here, there and everywhere and have an important influence on the game no matter where he was on the pitch.

Out of superstition – and later for marketing reasons – he always wore the No. 14 shirt (which had first been given to him when he came on as a substitute for Ajax in 1970 and from then on he didn't want to let it go). He could have worn any of the outfield shirts and been comfortable with the ball at his feet.

I thought the most depressing sight of the 1978 World Cup was seeing Cruyff sitting in the ITV studio talking about games in which he should have been playing.

Had he been in Argentina for the finals, I am convinced Holland would have won the World Cup at a canter rather than finishing runners-up to the hosts. He was a stubborn git, and ignored all pleas to join Holland's challenge, because of a long-running dispute with the Dutch FA.

Four years earlier, with Cruyff pulling the strings, Holland were comfortably the best team there but were psyched out of it in the Munich final by their arch rivals West Germany. Bitter in-fighting in the Holland camp between rival factions of players showed in the lack of team spirit as they waved the white flag of surrender in a sterile second half.

It was during this World Cup tournament that a new trick was born. It became known as the 'Cruyff Turn'. He would give his marker the impression he was going to cross the ball, but then suddenly drag it behind his planted left foot with the inside of his right foot and turn through 180 degrees before accelerating away on the outside of a completely bewildered defender.

This wonderful bit of skill was action-replayed a hundred times during the 1974 tournament, and not only became Cruyff's signature move but inspired thousands of youngsters worldwide to copy it. More than thirty years on you see the 'Cruyff Turn' cropping up as part of the modern player's box of tricks.

In England we first became aware of the emergence of Cruyff as a player to watch in the winter of 1966, when he was a precocious teenage talent with Ajax. Bill Shankly was building the foundation of the Red Revolution at Anfield, and our eyes popped when we saw a European Cup result in our newspapers: Ajax 5, Liverpool 1. The game was played in a swirling mist at Amsterdam's Olympic Stadium.

'Och, they got lucky,' Shanks said. 'They could see better in the fog than we could, and they had a young kid called "Cruff" who just got lucky every time he got the ball.'

Shanks managed to make 'Cruyff' sound like the bark of a dog, and over the next decade and more Johan proved he had bite to go with his thoroughbred skills.

The way Cruyff started his career is the stuff of fairytales. His mother was a cleaner at the Ajax club, and kept nagging the coaching staff, saying that her son was better than any of the players on the staff. Johan, just 12 years old, was invited to join the Ajax youth academy and within four years he really *was* the best player on their books. Former Spurs player Vic Buckingham, who was in charge at Ajax at the time, spotted his potential and when Vic returned to England to manage Fulham, he reported, 'There's a kid I left behind in Amsterdam who is going to be a better player than Pelé.'

Never free of his tinderbox temperament, Johan had worrying disciplinary problems early in his career, and was continually at war with referees. After being sent off in his second appearance in the famous orange shirt of Holland, the Dutch FA banned him from playing for the national team for a year. That was the start of a long-running feud with the Dutch authorities. But once he started to mature he developed into possibly the greatest footballer ever to come from Europe.

He was European Footballer of the Year three times in the 1970s while helping Ajax to dominate the European Cup, and then he became known as *El Salvador* (The Saviour) in Spain, where he inspired Barcelona to break Real Madrid's monopoly of *La Liga*. Playing in tandem with him at Barcelona was his old Ajax team-mate Johan Neeskens, who would also have been on my list but for my editor's restriction on foreign players.

Cruyff was always his own man, often swimming against the tide of authority. When adidas won sponsorship of the Dutch shirts, he doctored his logo so that the three stripes became two. Cruyff was a Puma client.

A deep-thinking tactician and theorist, he was always trying the unusual and the unexpected. In a 1982 game for Ajax against Helmond Sport he took a penalty that caused huge controversy, but it was within the rules at the time. From the spot, he squared the ball into the path of team-mate Jesper Olsen, took the return pass and stroked the ball into the net. The Helmond goalkeeper did not know whether he was coming or going. That move has since been outlawed.

In Barcelona they still talk about what they call the 'impossible' goal that he scored against Atletico Madrid. A high ball into the penalty area seemed certain to be collected by the goalkeeper. Suddenly Cruyff took off and scissored the ball into the net when seeming to be five feet off the ground.

He says of his approach to football, 'The hardest thing is to convince players that football is a simple game, and should be played simply. I always followed my instinct on the pitch, and did not practise any tricks. I did what came naturally. I say time and time again, "*Don't* complicate a simple game."'

It is rare for a great player to become a great manager. Super-brain Cruyff did the double. I once watched one of his training sessions, and was fascinated at how innovative he was with his coaching. He had ten players on a pitch roughly half the size of a penalty area, and demanded that they play one touch, or at most two touch. Six of the players attacked, against four defending. Cruyff explained, 'With an area this small, players become accustomed to quick thinking, quick movement, and they appreciate the importance of instant control. Passes have to be pin-pointed. Faced with a match situation, they will benefit from having worked in such confined space.'

I smiled to myself, thinking back to when I first came into the game and training consisted of six laps of the pitch! Cruyff was a player and a coach supreme.

Married to his childhood sweetheart Danny since 1968, they have three grown children, including Jordi, who was a good-class player with Barcelona and Manchester United.

Johan maintained his rebellious spirit right up to the end of his playing career, electing to play for bitter rivals Feyenoord after a contract row with Ajax. It was the equivalent of Thierry Henry turning out for Tottenham. As if to give two fingers to the Ajax club, with which he will always be associated, he helped Feyenoord win the League and Cup double for the first time in their history.

A rebel without a pause, Cruyff has never been frightened to take a political stand. He chose to play for Barcelona ahead of Real Madrid because he did not approve of 'that Fascist' General Franco's links with Real. In dispute with the Dutch FA before the 1978 World Cup finals, he finally decided not to take part as a protest against the military junta that had taken over in Argentina.

Cruyff took his superior tactical knowledge into coaching and management. He guided a young Ajax team to the European Cup-Winners' Cup in 1987 before returning to Barcelona where he added to his legend by steering them to eleven trophies in eight years, including four Spanish titles and the European Cup in 1992.

All that smoking finally caught up with him, and he had a quadruple by-pass operation following a severe heart attack. After that he swapped the cigarettes for lollipops and became a leading anti-smoking campaigner. I wasn't going to be the one to tell him that the lollipops to which he had become addicted would rot his teeth.

That trail of cigarette smoke he left behind could not fog the fact that Johan Cruyff was one of the all-time greats – ahead of even Pelé and Maradona, some would argue, because of his all-round ability.

29

Kevin Keegan

Born: Armthorpe, Yorkshire, 14 February 1951

Career span: 1967–1984

Clubs: Scunthorpe United 1967–71 (124 league games, 18 goals); Liverpool 1971–77 (230 league games, 68 goals); Hamburg 1977–80 (90 league games, 32 goals); Southampton 1980–82 (68 league games, 37 goals); Newcastle United 1982–84 (78 league games, 48 goals)

England: 63 caps, 21 goals (31 games as captain)

Club honours: 3 league championships, 1 Second Division championship, 1 German championship, 1 FA Cup, 2 Uefa Cups, 1 European Cup
Footballer of the Year 1976
PFA Player of the Year 1982
European Footballer of the Year 1978 and 1979

KEVIN KEEGAN took a little talent a long, long way, and he makes it into my all-star selection for his energy, enthusiasm and ability to compete on equal terms with the best players in the world – even though he was not blessed with their natural skills.

He obviously did something right because he remains the only British footballer to win back-to-back European Footballer of the Year awards. They were won during his eventful three years with Hamburg, where he was idolised as 'Mighty Mouse'.

We had 'The Wizard of Dribble' Matthews, 'The King' Pelé, 'The Black Panther' Eusebio, 'The Golden Boy' Rivera, '*Der Kaiser*' Beckenbauer, '*Der Bomber*' Muller . . . and suddenly it was the era of Mighty Mouse!

It sums up, for me, how the game had gone from admiring and applauding the exceptional individualists to praising and approving of the functional footballers.

Keegan's great strength was that he could make the team play, galvanising everybody around him with his high-octane energy and his sheer determination. He used almost to shame his team-mates into trying to match his effort. You can't knock it, but – sorry, Kev – it wasn't pretty to watch.

He started right the way at the back of the queue, failing to impress his local club Doncaster Rovers during a trial run. And so it was that one of the most glittering careers in British football began at Scunthorpe's Old Showground, not exactly the hotbed of the game.

In 1971, the same year that I decided to get off the football roundabout, Keegan got his big break when Bill Shankly took him to Liverpool for a fee of £35,000. Shanks liked players who could run all day and were prepared to soak their shirts with sweat for the team. With Keegan, he hit the bullseye.

Within two years of arriving at Anfield Keegan had helped Liverpool capture their first league title for seven years, forming what became a famous and feared striking partnership with John Toshack. That Little and Large double act detonated First Division defences.

By the time he departed for Hamburg in 1977 for a then record fee of £500,000, he had added two more championships, two Uefa Cups, an FA Cup, the Footballer of the Year trophy and – the top prize – the European Cup to his collection.

He achieved all of this during my 'lost' years, when I was having a personal battle with the bottle. In my sober moments I used to watch Kevin on the box and wonder how he had achieved so much with so little talent. I thought perhaps I was still pissed.

With Hamburg he had three more hugely successful years, helping them win the *Bundesliga* in 1979 and reach the European Cup final the next season, when they were beaten by Cloughie's Nottingham Forest.

Always a shrewd one for the commercial opportunity, Keegan shocked the football world by returning to English football with unfashionable Southampton rather than accepting an offer to join European giants Juventus.

By then I had managed to kick the bottle and was starting a career as a football pundit on the box, so I was getting a close-up view of the Keegan phenomenon. And I at last began to see that he had a gift that some managers would consider gold dust. He was born industrious – not inventive or creative, but *industrious*.

He used to cover more grass in one match than I used to in a season. His work rate was astonishing, and I could appreciate why Bill Shankly regarded him so highly.

His success story continued at Southampton where he scored 37 goals in 68 league games and added the PFA Player of the Year award to his heaving trophy cabinet before a swansong couple of seasons with Newcastle.

My old team-mate Bobby Robson had by then become England manager, and ended Keegan's 63-cap international career at a stroke. Bobby was from my generation of footballers who looked for skill first, stamina second, and he axed Mighty Mouse without giving him a whiff of a game during his regime. I don't think Kevin ever forgave Bobby for that, particularly as he found out from the press that he was no longer wanted for an England team he had always represented with pride and passion, including 31 games as captain.

At the end of his playing career Kevin switched to management with mixed results. He selected teams to play in a way that was completely the opposite of how he had performed. The trademark of a Keegan team was that it always put the emphasis on flair and adventure, forgetting the little matter of disciplined defence.

Keegan got through his footballing days without scandal or the sort of boozy episodes that scarred a few of us, but he was involved in a strange incident just before his managerial debut with Newcastle.

He had taken a few months out of the game to recharge his batteries on the golf courses of Spain, and drove the 1600 miles back from the Costa del Sol alone. He was so knackered when he arrived in England that he pulled into a layby close to the M25 at Reigate in Surrey and fell asleep in his Range Rover, only to be violently awoken. Three men were attacking him. They beat him up, bashed him with a baseball bat and robbed him. Three drug addicts were later arrested and charged with assault. Welcome back to England, Kev!

As somebody who had always been pretty harsh with my

criticism of Keegan the player, I had to admit to admiring the team he created at Newcastle. He steered them to promotion and then built a side of outstanding individual players, including Peter Beardsley, Andy Cole, David Ginola, Alan Shearer, Philippe Albert and Faustino Asprilla.

They made a great early charge for the championship, but frittered away a 12-point lead to hand the title to Manchester United. The pressure got to Kevin, as he famously showed in a live post-match interview on Sky. Responding to Alex Ferguson's wind-up suggestion that teams tried harder against Manchester United than they did against Newcastle, he responded with a nonsensical outburst that gave comedians and impersonators across the land wonderful material. This was it verbatim, snarling into the camera, wearing lopsided headphones that made him look like Enid Blyton's Big Ears:

'When you do that with footballers like he said about Leeds . . . I've kept really quiet, but I'll tell you something: he [Fergie] went down in my estimation when he said that – we have not resorted to that. But I'll tell ya – you can tell him now if you're watching it – we're still fighting for this title, and he's got to go to Middlesbrough and get something, and . . . and I tell you honestly, I will love it if we beat them – *love it!*'

Keegan walked out on Newcastle soon afterwards, and I thought he had turned his back on the game. But he took three more jobs that he failed to complete, managing Fulham and Manchester City either side of a strange stint as England boss.

A disastrous Euro 2000 challenge was followed by defeat by Germany in the last match at the old Wembley. Keegan shocked everybody at the after-match press conference when he announced his resignation, stating with the brutal honesty that was his trademark, 'I did this job to the best of my ability but the truth is that Kevin Keegan is a little bit short for this job. It was one thousand per cent my decision to go. Tactically, I was not quite up to it.'

So what is Kevin's legacy as he trawls new ground with an

ambitious, Glasgow-based Soccer Circus for kids dreaming of being the next Kevin Keegan?

Well, there's his seventies perm . . . a Top 40 record hit *Head Over Heels* . . . thousands of twenty-something Germans walking around with the first name Kevin . . . and, let's be fair, proof that you can achieve your dream if you are prepared to work hard for it. Nobody worked harder to get on to my list of heroes and entertainers than Kevin Joseph Keegan.

30

Kenny Dalglish

Born: Glasgow, 4 March 1951

Career span: 1969–1990

Clubs: Celtic 1969–77 (324 games, 167 goals); Liverpool 1977–1990 (511 games, 172 goals)

Scotland: 102 caps, 30 goals

Club honours: 4 Scottish league championships, 4 Scottish Cups, 1 Scottish League Cup, 6 league championships, 1 FA Cup, 4 League Cups, 3 European Cups

Footballer of the Year 1979 and 1983

PFA Player of the Year 1983

WE now come to a player blessed with all the talent that Kevin Keegan lacked, the man who replaced him as the footballing god of Anfield, Kenny Dalglish. And as I write, Keegan is based in Kenny's hometown of Glasgow, selling the football dream to Scottish kids. Yes, it really *is* a funny old game!

Few players in history have won more honours, and none have managed to be so successful on both sides of the border. He remains (and will, I bet, always remain) the only player to score more than one hundred league goals in both the Scottish and English leagues.

Yet, in his middle-age, Kenny's memories are haunted by three footballing tragedies that throw a dark shadow over all the great things that he achieved on and off the pitch.

Freakishly, this dream of a footballer suffered the nightmare of witnessing three of the worst crowd catastrophes ever: he was at Ibrox during the 1971 'Old Firm' match when stairway 13 at the decaying stadium collapsed, killing 66 fans; in 1985 he was a member of the Liverpool team playing against Juventus in the European Cup final when a wall came down as fans rioted, and 39 Italian supporters died; after the horror of Heysel came the heartbreak of Hillsborough, 96 Liverpool fans dying in a crowd crush on the day the Dalglish-managed Reds met Nottingham Forest in the 1989 FA Cup semi-final.

No man should have to be burdened with such grief and tragedy, and the impact of it on Dalglish – particularly the Hillsborough disaster – had us worrying about his health. I have no idea how I would have handled all that grief and stress, but he had the strength of character to come through the storm with his head held high and somehow to find the appetite to tackle new challenges as manager at Blackburn, Newcastle and, briefly, back at his old Celtic hunting ground.

Dalglish has always been a fiercely private man, allowing few people to get close to him. Football reporters accustomed to having their notebooks filled with quotes galore from Bill Shankly suddenly had to get used to a curt, 'Nae comment.'

When Liverpool manager Bob Paisley bought him from Celtic

as replacement for Keegan in the summer of 1977, he handled the press with a suspicion that could have been interpreted as contempt. Journalists who were there have told me that he would answer questions in mumbled monosyllables, and when he did decide to utter sentences, few English ears could understand his heavy Glaswegian accent.

Scottish sportswriter Ian Archer had forewarned us of his abrupt manner. Ian was once walking through the centre of Glasgow, minding his own business, when out of nowhere he found himself confronted by the young, blond, red-cheeked Dalglish.

'Wisnae,' said Dalglish to a startled Archer.

'Wisnae what?' Archer responded (understanding that Kenny was saying 'wasn't').

'Wisnae offside,' replied Dalglish before disappearing into the crowd.

Archer was baffled, and it was only after several minutes of excavating his brain that he remembered that a month earlier he had written in a match report that a Dalglish goal for Celtic had looked suspiciously offside.

'This was,' said Ian, 'the most piercing, informative and longest interview Dalglish ever gave me.'

Kenny's golden years were those he spent at Anfield, yet Bill Shankly always considered him 'the one that got away'.

He had a trial at Liverpool as a 15-year-old schoolboy in August 1966, playing for the 'B' team in a 1–0 victory against Southport reserves in the Lancashire League. Shanks had his mind focused on the upcoming season and took no notice when his training staff sent Dalglish home without signing him.

When Shanks saw Dalglish playing for Celtic a few seasons later he nearly blew a gasket as he realised Liverpool could have had him for nothing. It was eleven years after that trial that Kenny finally arrived as a Liverpool player, for a fee of £440,000, by which time Shankly had put himself out to grass.

Born in Dalmarnock in the East End of Glasgow on 4 March 1951, Kenneth Mathieson Dalglish was brought up in the docklands area of Govan, a goalkick from Ibrox, home ground of his favourite team, Rangers.

Like the great Hughie Gallacher before him, he started out as a goalkeeper, playing between the posts for his Milton Bank primary school team – a classic case of goalkeeper turned poacher. By the time he was capped as a Scottish schoolboy international he had moved forward to right-half, scoring twice on his debut in a 4–3 victory over Northern Ireland schoolboys.

His ambition was to play for Rangers, but they completely ignored him. After failing to impress Liverpool, he then showed his wares at West Ham later in that summer of 1966. Again, no interest.

So it was back to Glasgow for young Kenny, and the Protestant son of an engineer signed as a part-time professional for Jock Stein and the very Catholic Celtic. Assistant manager Sean Fallon clinched the deal, leaving his wife outside in the car while he popped into the Dalglish home. 'Just be a few minutes,' he said to his wife. Three hours later he returned with the Dalglish signature safely on a contract. His wife pointed out the little matter of it being their anniversary. He was supposed to be taking her out.

Between playing for Celtic's nursery side, Cumbernauld United, Dalglish worked as an apprentice joiner, which could explain why he later showed he knew all the angles on a football field.

A year later, Celtic were the newly crowned kings of Europe and Kenny became a full-time professional. He played in the Parkhead reserve team that became known as the Quality Street Gang. Just imagine walking casually into a ground to watch a reserve match and finding players of the calibre of Dalglish, Lou Macari, Danny McGrain and Davie Hay performing in front of you.

Jock Stein was never one for shooting off his mouth, so we all sat up and took notice when he said, 'I've got a couple of forwards who are going to become the talk of the game, Kenny Dalglish and Lou Macari. They're a bit special.'

Tommy Docherty sent 20-year-old Dalglish on for his international debut in a 1–0 European Championship victory over Belgium at Aberdeen.

'He will develop into one of the all-time greats, take my word for it,' the Doc said later as he celebrated the news that the win at Pittodrie had clinched his appointment as full-time manager of Scotland.

'I've got the job at just the right time,' he went on. 'It's years since we've been so rich in young talent. As well as Dalglish, I can call on players like Alan Hansen at Partick, Danny McGrain and Lou Macari at Celtic, and Martin Buchan at Aberdeen. The future's bright.'

What would Scotland give for players of that calibre coming through today?

Dalglish went on to win a record 102 caps and scored 30 goals. Denis Law scored the same number in 55 matches for Scotland. In truth, Kenny was rarely as impressive for his country as his club. I rate him one of the greatest British club players I have seen in my fifty-plus years in and around the game, but there are many I would put ahead of him on the international stage. Perhaps he needed the familiarity of club team-mates around him, but whatever the reason was, he often struggled to find his club form for Scotland.

Anfield was plunged into mourning when Kevin Keegan decided to take the Deutschmark and transfer his talent to Hamburg in 1977. Little did the Liverpool fans realise that his replacement in the No. 7 shirt, the modest, unassuming Dalglish, would prove himself the greatest player in the club's history. He continually comes out top in the polls despite support for Keegan, my old side-kick Ian St John, Billy Liddell, Roger Hunt, Ian Rush, Graeme Souness and, more recently, Steven Gerrard.

Dalglish plundered his goals with the cold professionalism of an assassin gunning down a victim. He had a great awareness of what was happening on the periphery around him, and I have seen few forwards to match him as a shielder of a ball. He would frustrate defenders into committing themselves to a tackle, side-step them and then either dart for goal or bring a team-mate into play with a perfectly weighted pass. Kenny reminded me in some ways of my former Tottenham partner Alan Gilzean, another wonderfully skilled Scot who could somehow find space to make things happen no matter how crowded the penalty area.

One thing's for sure, I know I would have loved to play along-side Dalglish, because he made life so much easier for the players around him by his positioning and precise passing.

Kenny was an unselfish team player who was quite happy to share the goal glory with colleagues. His partnership with Ian Rush was even more destructive than the Keegan-Toshack double act in the previous Liverpool purple patch. They seemed to have a telepathic understanding, and Kenny made dozens of goals for his Welsh partner. 'I knew that if Kenny was in possession and I ran into space, the ball would arrive just where and when I wanted it,' said Rush. 'There was nobody to touch him for making an accurate pass in a packed penalty area.'

Dalglish was appointed player-manager in the wake of the Heysel Stadium tragedy, and put the smile back on Liverpool faces by capturing the league championship and FA Cup double in his first season.

Kenny repeated the championship success in 1988 and 1990, making his final league appearance in May 1989. Bob Paisley reached down into his long memory and said, 'Of all the players I have played with, coached and managed in more than forty years at Anfield, I have no hesitation in saying that Kenny is the most talented.'

Following the Hillsborough disaster, Dalglish was magnificent in the way he carried the city's grief on his shoulders. He worked tirelessly to try to ease the pain of survivors and the distressed relatives of those Liverpool fans who lost their lives so senselessly on the terraces of a tired football ground. Dalglish was dignity personified. He attended as many funerals as possible, read lessons, helped out with counselling and dug deep down into his very soul to try to bring solace to the bereaved.

Kenny never made an issue of the stress and strain he was under, but it must have taken its toll. He got his mind back on football and lifted the FA Cup after a 3–2 extra-time victory over Everton at Wembley. Liverpool were beaten to the league championship – and another double – in the last seconds of the 1988–89 season, when Michael Thomas scored an injury-time goal that clinched the title for George Graham's Arsenal.

The Dalglish-dictated Reds regained the championship the following season, and were going for another hat-trick – following the treble of the early-1980s – when Dalglish astonished everybody by announcing that he was quitting. He was walking out with the club top of the table and locked in a fifth-round FA Cup saga with Everton, that had ended 4–4 the day before Kenny decided to leave.

As we all guessed, Dalglish's health was suffering under the enormous pressure he had been under. He said that he was 'a person pushed to the limit' and admitted that on match-days he felt as if his head was exploding.

He took eight months out of the game before making a shock reappearance as manager of Blackburn Rovers. Bankrolled by chairman Jack Walker, he led Rovers to promotion from the old Second Division in his first season, and captured the Premier League championship three years later. Kenny was only the fourth manager to win the championship with two different clubs – Tom

Watson (Sunderland and Liverpool), Herbert Chapman (Huddersfield and Arsenal) and Brian Clough (Derby and Nottingham Forest) were the others.

Dalglish then decided that the pressure at Ewood Park was too great, and took the less demanding role of director of football. In 1997 he followed Kevin Keegan as manager at Newcastle, an unhappy association that lasted only until the summer of the following year. After that, he returned to his roots at Celtic where he became director of football with John Barnes in tow as manager. It was a less than successful comeback and ended with the sack, his disappointment cushioned by a pay-off of more than £600,000. He started the New Millennium on the outside looking in at a game to which he had given so much, but then started a world-wide talent hunt as the Director of Football Operations for the Proactive company. He still has much to give to a game he played better than almost anybody else.

Dalglish went through his playing career expressing himself the best way he knew how, with his feet. And the message was loud and clear – Kenny Dalglish was here. Few Scots have had such a deep and lasting influence on the English game. What a pity he did not want to tell us more about it. Nae comment!

31

Graeme Souness

Born: Edinburgh, 6 May 1953

Career span: 1970–1991

Clubs: Tottenham 1970–73 (1 game, no goals); Montreal Olympique (10 games, 2 goals); Middlesbrough 1973–77 (176 league games, 22 goals); Liverpool 1977–84 (247 league games, 38 goals); Sampdoria 1984–86 (56 games, 8 goals), Rangers 1986–91 (49 games, 3 goals)

Scotland: 54 caps, 4 goals

Club honours: 5 league championships, 4 League Cups, 3 European Cups, 1 Second Division championship, 1 Italian Cup, 1 Scottish Premier title, 2 Scottish League Cups

WHEN they were making the film *Braveheart*, I reckon the producers missed – right on Scotland"s doorstep – an ideal person to play a leading warrior. I refer, of course, to Graeme Souness, who could have stepped into any of the gory-glory roles without requiring an acting lesson. He would simply need to have played it the way he played his football. His tackling would have been enough to frighten the English invaders to death.

Of all the players featured in this book, I promise you that Souness is the one you would have least wanted to face in a confrontation for a 50-50 ball. He had such a will to win that he gave the impression he would have kicked his own granny to come out on top.

Graeme, born in the tough Broomhouse district of Edinburgh on 6 May 1953, went to the same Carrickvale school that Dave Mackay had attended a generation earlier. They must have been hewn out of the same lump of granite, because Souness had all the Mackay motivating mannerisms and liked to boss the pitch in the same intimidating way that his schoolboy idol did.

His encyclopedic knowledge of all that Mackay achieved swayed him to join Tottenham at the age of 15 when any of the Scottish clubs would willingly have opened their doors to him.

I learned earlier than most that Souness was not only a star in the making, but also a headstrong boy who knew his own mind. He was the talk of the club after a powerhouse performance that helped Spurs win the coveted FA Youth Cup in 1969. Then, as I was on the verge of leaving Tottenham for West Ham, Graeme was on the point of walking out on Spurs before he had kicked a ball in first-team football.

He went home to Edinburgh, claiming he was homesick. The whisper among the players was that his real sickness was because he had yet to make the breakthrough into the league team. He was impossibly impatient.

What was at first a small domestic story was suddenly blown up out of all proportion. It reached the ludicrous stage when questions were being asked in the House of Commons, as the story crossed from the back to the front pages. Graeme had spent two years at Spurs as an apprentice who considered himself more of a sorcerer.

When he walked out and returned to Edinburgh, Tottenham reacted by suspending him without pay for two weeks. Graeme's local MP took up the case, and questioned in the House what right a football club had to deal with 'a minor' like this when his only 'crime' was to suffer from homesickness. 'Is homesickness something that should be punishable?' demanded the MP, managing to make Souness sound as hard done by as Oliver Twist. The story became the property of columnists with poison pens, and Bill Nicholson, fatherly manager of Tottenham, was unfairly pilloried. Souness was suddenly the best-known teenaged player in the land.

The suspicion at Spurs was that their hot young property had been 'got at' and was being tempted away from Tottenham.

'I have never known such an ambitious and impatient young man,' an exasperated Bill Nick told me. 'He has a wonderful future in the game, but he wants to run before he can walk. He can't understand why I'm not already considering him for the first team. He wants to jump ahead of established professionals, such as Alan Mullery and Steve Perryman. His chance will come, but he must show patience. If he's ever picked for Scotland, I wonder if they will find a cap big enough for his head.'

A suitably repentant Souness returned to Tottenham, but he wore out the carpet to Bill Nick's office to the point where the veteran Spurs boss decided, reluctantly, he had no option but to let him go. He had made one brief first-team appearance in a Uefa Cup-tie (substituting for Martin Peters in a match in Iceland) before being sold to Middlesbrough in December 1972 for £27,000, which was a hefty fee in those days for a virtually unknown and untried player. During the previous summer he had got valu-able first-team experience with Montreal Olympique in the North American Soccer League.

Within five months of signing the young Scot, Middlesbrough manager Stan Anderson was replaced by Jack Charlton. Big Jack took an immediate shine to Souness.

'I could see straightaway that the lad had enormous potential, an opinion shared by Graeme!' said Jack, who was making his managerial debut. 'I felt that he was being played out of position as a left-sided midfielder or left-back, so I moved him to a central midfield position, and gave him more responsibility.'

Jack gave a hint that Souness was still hot to handle when he added, 'It took a lot of nagging before he would do what I wanted him to do. He liked to dwell on the ball and tended to be over-elaborate. I had to give him a few rockets before he got the point and started to make the sort of quick, positive passes that were right for the team. He had an arrogant streak in him, but that's no bad thing if you're going to try to dominate the midfield the way that he does.'

It was the Souness power and drive in midfield that played a prominent part in pushing Middlesbrough to the Second Division championship in 1973–74, by an extraordinary record margin of 15 points.

His cap fitted perfectly when manager Willie Ormond picked him for his international debut against East Germany in 1974, and he went on to play 54 matches for Scotland and became an outstanding captain and leader. It was exactly what the supremely self-confident Souness expected of himself.

Kenny Dalglish, one of his regular Scotland team-mates, was impressed by the Souness competitive spirit on which you could warm your hands. He recommended him to Bob Paisley when he moved to Anfield, and within six months Graeme was performing a supporting role in midfield to Dalglish. Perhaps Kenny preferred the thought of playing with rather than against him! The fee of £352,000 was, at the time, a record deal between two English clubs. Liverpool money has rarely been better spent.

Souness had at last found the stage that he felt his talent deserved. He was an instant hit with the Anfield fans – and an instant hit on opponents, who could not believe how fiercely he tackled in Liverpool's cause. At the end of his first season Liverpool retained the European Cup, Dalglish's delicate chip beating Bruges at Wembley, with Souness and Alan Hansen helping to give the team a strong Scottish heartbeat.

With his Pancho Villa moustache and pugilistic nose, Souness looked every inch a gladiator, and he used to put the fear of God into any fancy-Dan opponent who was not prepared to risk life and limb to win the ball. Once he got it, Graeme knew exactly how to use it in the best interests of the side. He would find team-mates with perfectly placed passes, and also knew how to find the net with shots delivered, like his tackles, with vicious intent. He could have been a mirror image of his boyhood idol, and my old Tottenham pal and skipper, Dave Mackay.

In seven success-soaked seasons at Liverpool, more than half of them as captain, Souness won everything there was to win. The highlight came in 1984 when he led the Reds to the unique treble of league championship, Football League Cup and the European Cup.

Souness, whose motto could have been 'Go to work on an ego', now needed new challenges, and he spent two seasons with Sampdoria, steering them to the Italian Cup for the first time in their history. Then came a call to return home that he could not resist. He was wanted as player-manager at Rangers. It was a role that suited this born leader down to the Ibrox ground.

Souness, more than any other person, changed the face of Scottish football for all time. He recognised that if Rangers wanted to be a global rather than just a domestic force, he would need to import players from outside Scotland. He brought in English international stars of the calibre of Mark Hateley, Chris Woods, Terry Butcher, Trevor Francis, Ray Wilkins, Mark Walters, Trevor Steven and Nigel Spackman. For more than a century English clubs had been plundering the cream of the Scottish players. Now the football boot was on the other foot.

He was treading all over tradition, and turned the faces of many Rangers fans green when he paid Nantes £1.5 million to bring in former Celtic striker Mo Johnston. Mo became the first prominent Catholic player to wear the blue shirt of Rangers in their 116-year history. It was an incredibly defiant – some said daft – thing to do, and it proved beyond doubt that Rangers were now in an 'anything goes' period. As new chairman David Murray, who was bankrolling the exceptional enterprise, said, 'Graeme has turned the big ship around single-handed.'

Souness came out all guns blazing from the moment he set foot inside Ibrox, and he was so wound up that he managed to get himself sent off in his first game for Rangers. He was leading by example, his actions saying to his players, 'This is the sort of competitive spirit I want.'

The result of the revolution was astonishing. In his first season in charge, the swashbuckling Souness lifted the Scottish championship and the League Cup, beating Celtic 2–1 in the final. Two more championships followed, this time in successive seasons (1988–89 and 1989–90), and two more League Cup finals, with victories over Aberdeen in 1988–89 and Celtic in 1990–91.

Rangers were on the threshold of another championship in 1991 when Souness stunned the Ibrox faithful by agreeing to return to Anfield as successor in the manager's chair to his old team-mate Kenny Dalglish.

This should have been all sweetness for Souness, but it turned into the sourest experience of his career. He just could not get the players to function for him as he had at Rangers, and the Liverpool fans, who had once worshipped the ground he tackled on, turned on him in an ugly way following a gross misjudgement on his part.

Souness underwent a major heart operation, and the first most people knew of it was when his exclusive story was splashed across the front page of the *Sun*. At that time even mention of the *Sun* was poison on the lips of many Anfield supporters because of the way the paper had covered the Hillsborough tragedy, and they would not forgive Souness for what they saw as an act of treachery.

He had 'only' the 1992 FA Cup to show for his three years in charge at Liverpool when he had a less than amicable parting with the club in January 1994.

Licking his wounds, Souness went on a whirlwind tour of the football map. He had a year in Turkey as manager of Galatasaray, and brief spells with Torino, Southampton and Benfica before planting his feet firmly at Blackburn Rovers.

He steered Blackburn back to the Premiership in his first season, and was soon on his travels again, this time taking over from Bobby Robson as Newcastle manager. That was a Tyne Bridge too far for Graeme. He was hounded out by the fans, who had never really forgiven the club for the way they dumped 'Uncle Bobby' Robson.

Graeme has since been patrolling on the periphery of the game, working as a TV pundit and once coming close to taking over at Wolves with the support of a powerful consortium. He still has the appetite to be involved at the hub of a club, and is spitting blood over stories linking him with the on-going 'bung' culture that seems to run like a poison in the veins of the Beautiful Game. The rat race of football has become a writ race, and he threatens anybody who mentions his name and 'bung' in the same sentence with legal fisticuffs.

As a manager, he used to prowl the touchline like a hungry lion, giving referees the angry eye, and evoking memories of when he was bossing the pitch for Liverpool, Sampdoria, Rangers and Scotland. There has rarely been a more dominant midfield player in the history of the game. Yes, he would have been perfect for that *Braveheart* role.

32

Michel Platini

Born: Joeuf, France, 21 June 1955

Career span: 1972–1987

Clubs: Nancy 1972–79 (175 games, 98 goals); St Etienne 1979–82 (107 games, 58 goals); Juventus 1982–87 (147 games, 68 goals)

France: 72 caps, 41 goals (49 games as captain)

Club honours: 1 French championship, 1 French Second Division title, 1 French Cup, 2 Italian league championships, 1 Italian Cup, 1 European Cup-Winners' Cup, 1 European Cup

European Championship 1984

French Footballer of the Year 1976, 1977

European Footballer of the Year 1983, 1984 and 1985

World Player of the Year 1984

IF Beckenbauer is *Der Kaiser*, then Michel Platini is *le Roi* of European football. Like the German master, Platini has made an impressive impact off as well as on the pitch and he is the current big white chief of European football.

As with Beckenbauer, Platini has schemed both as a player and as a football politician. He now knows how to place a palm for a vote-winning handshake as expertly as he used to place a pass on the pitch when he was the supreme playmaker of the 1980s.

I was in a privileged position during his peak years of having the best TV studio seats at the major international tournaments, and I got the perfect view of the maestro in action.

In their famous *Carré Magique* (Magic Square) France had four of the most gifted creative players in the world – Alain Giresse, Luis Fernández, Jean Tigana and, of course, *le Roi* Platini. They might easily have had a World Cup as well as their 1984 European Championship triumph but for falling foul of the Germans.

I chose that phrase carefully. In the 1982 World Cup semi-final in Seville, German goalkeeper Harald Schumacher nearly got away with murder. He flattened Patrick Battiston with one of the worst fouls I ever witnessed on the football field. He launched himself at Battiston – who was clear through – and his hips smashed into the Frenchman's face, knocking him cold and breaking his jaw.

Goodness knows what game the referee was watching, but after the seriously injured Battiston had been stretchered off he awarded the Germans a goalkick. There is no doubt whatsoever in my mind that Schumacher should have gone off with Battiston and into a long suspension.

The game finished in a 3–3 draw, and Germany won the first-ever World Cup final penalty shoot-out. Four years later Platini-propelled France reached the semi-final again, and once more it was Germany who put them out.

This meant that Platini, one of the most accomplished foot-ballers of all time, left the game without the World Cup winner's medal that his skill deserved.

He had always been the architect, the free-kick specialist and the main marksman for all of his teams at club and country level. He was like the composer, arranger, conductor and lead violinist of an orchestra.

Platini did everything with style and panache, and was a gentle executioner. He could have played the game in carpet slippers.

The little Napoleon had come a long way from the days when his schoolmates called him 'Fatty'. Coached by his Italian immigrant father, Aldo – a top-quality footballer – he steered his local club Nancy to the French premier division, moved on to St Etienne and moulded them into champions of France.

With his Italian heritage, Platini had always dreamed of playing in *Serie A*, and jumped at the chance when Juventus came calling for him. There were petty jealousies when he first arrived, and just as he was considering returning to France the other Juve players realised what a master they had in their squad. Once he was accepted, he quickly developed into one of the world's outstanding midfield generals.

He was the main motivator behind Juve's two *Serie A* championships, one European Cup, one Cup-Winners' Cup, one European Super Cup and one Intercontinental Cup title in a four-year span of non-stop success.

Platini was doing things in threes. He was *Serie A* top scorer three times and was voted European Footballer of the Year three times in succession from 1983.

Anybody not around in the mid-1980s who wants to find out just how special Platini was should dig out footage of his performances in the 1984 European Championship in his homeland. He dominated the tournament from start to finish. His nine goals in five games came from all points on the football compass – free-kicks, diving headers, after dazzling combination play, long-range shooting. He just could not miss. Even a mis-hit free-kick against Spain in the final found the net.

France had never won anything on the international football front before this triumph, and they knew they owed everything to the poised and polished Platini. He was just magnificent.

In 1985 he was severely shaken by the harrrowing events at the Heysel Stadium when thirty-nine Juve fans were killed before the Liverpool–Juventus European Cup final. A lot of the sparkle went out of his game and he lost his appetite completely after France had fallen at the semi-final stage of the World Cup in 1986, when he was handicapped by recurring tendinitis.

Like me, he decided to retire at the relatively young age of 31. Without him, Juventus had to wait eight years before their next *Serie A* championship. Without him, France failed to qualify for the World Cup finals again until they were the host nation in 1998.

But Platini was far from finished with football. After a brief flirtation with the business world, he became French team manager and included a run of nineteen successive matches without defeat. He was voted World Manager of the Year in 1991 before a slump led to his resignation.

Michel is quite the philosopher. Listen to him on the Beautiful Game: 'Football is a fantastic and intelligent game, which teaches us how to live together, how to share when you are better than others. Football is an extraordinary education for life.'

And listen to the football politician Platini: 'When I follow the finals of the European Cups, I look at all the aspects surrounding protocol, to get some ideas. I am interested in personalities, sponsors and the stands. But as soon as the whistle goes, my concentration is all on what is happening on the pitch. We must never lose sight of the fact that it is the game at grassroots level that is the lifeblood of football. The World Cups and the European Cups are the icing on the cake.'

He switched from coaching to administration and was a key man on the organising committee for the 1998 World Cup finals in France, and did such an impressive job that he began to develop a powerbase on both the Uefa and Fifa executive committees.

In 2007 he defeated the previously immoveable Lennart Johansson in a vote for the role of Uefa President.

How soon, I wonder, before we see a head to head duel for the Fifa presidency between Platini and Franz Beckenbauer?

Le Roi versus *Der Kaiser*. Wonder if it will go to penalties?

33

Paolo Rossi

Born: Santa Lucia, Italy, 23 September 1956

Career span: 1975–87

Clubs: Como 1975–76 (6 games); Vicenza 1976–79 (94 games, 60 goals); Perugia 1979–80 (22 games, 13 goals, then a two-year suspension); Juventus 1982–85 (87 games, 25 goals); AC Milan 1985–86 (28 games, 2 goals); Verona 1986–87 (20 games, 4 goals)

Italy: 48 caps, 20 goals

Club honours: 2 Italian championships, 1 Italian Cup, 1 European Cup, 1 European Cup-Winners' Cup

World Cup winner 1982

World Cup Golden Boot winner 1982 (6 goals)

European Footballer of the Year 1982

THE Paolo Rossi story could have come out of an episode of *The Sopranos*. The boy wonder of Italy in the 1978 World Cup was caught up in a bribery scandal in 1980 that shook Italian football to its foundations. AC Milan were kicked down to the Second Division and their president banned for life. Heartbroken Rossi was told he could not play for three years.

This would have meant Rossi missing the 1982 World Cup in Spain, but the ban was cut to two years on appeal. He returned to action just ten weeks before the finals by which time he had transferred to Juventus, who had part-owned him early in his career.

Italian team boss Enzo Bearzot decided to gamble – and gamble was the operative word – on including Rossi in his squad for Spain. He went into the finals with just three *Serie A* games under his belt in the previous two years.

I was on the ITV panel of experts (I use the word in its loosest form), and everybody fell about laughing when I picked Italy as my tip for the World Cup. After all, they were in the same second-round group as Diego Maradona's Argentina and also Brazil. With Eder, Falcao, Junior, Socrates and Zico playing at their peak, those Brazilians were looking almost in the class of the Pelé-led team of the 1970 tournament.

Italy produced a two-faced performance in Spain – and the first face was not a pretty sight. Rossi looked like a rusty ghost of the player who had lit up the 1978 World Cup with his stunning skill, and Italy stumbled through the preliminary stages without winning a single game. They made it through to the second round by drawing all three of their matches, and playing sterile stuff that stank of the old defence-dominated Italian football.

The ITV panel, including such know-alls as Brian Clough, Jack Charlton, Mike Channon, Denis Law, Ian St John and George Best, had a good laugh at my expense. 'Italy to win?' said Cloughie, in his usual no-punches-pulled style. 'I thought Jimmy had come off the booze!'

The saddest sight of all was having George Best sitting in the studio with us watching his former Irish international team-mates progressing to the second phase. They would have done even better had they had the sense to select George, who was looking trim and fit following two seasons on the North American soccer circuit.

Like the rest of the pundits, George laughed out loud at my insistence that Italy would lift the trophy. 'I'm the one who's supposed to be on the piss, Greavsie,' he said with that cherubic grin of his.

I understood the Italian psyche better than any of the other panellists, and knew they would adopt a different attitude once they had survived the first phase of the tournament.

To Italy, the preliminary matches were like a phony war. They were saving the real stuff for the vital second round. Now we saw the finer face of Italian football as they out-thought and out-fought Maradona's Argentina, stealing a 2–1 victory during which Rossi began to show signs of shaking off the rust and the dust collected during his two years' enforced absence from the game.

But I was in a very small minority who considered they could beat the brilliant Brazilians. Rossi had not scored in the four games to date, and Brazil had been so exceptional that I was heavily outgunned in the studio as I tried to make out a case for Italy winning.

We then witnessed one of the greatest games and one of the greatest individual performances in World Cup history. Rossi, suddenly alive and alert, put Italy into the lead after just five minutes with a delicately headed goal. Socrates equalised seven minutes later, breaking away from the violently close attentions of the ill-named Gentile to score with an angled shot as the action swung rhythmically from end to end with the timing of a pendulum. The standard of football by both teams was out of this world.

It was the reinstated and revived Rossi who put Italy back in the lead in the 25th minute, pouncing on a mistake by the Brazilian defence to drill in his second goal with exquisite timing that made nonsense of his long lay-off. I was watching in the ITV studio on a monitor, and don't mind admitting that I punched the air as he proved my instincts right. I just knew that a thoroughbred player like him could not have suddenly become a bad player.

Twenty-two minutes into the second half Brazil pulled level for a second time with one of the outstanding goals of the tournament. Falcao dribbled on a bewildering path across the penalty area, saw a gap that nobody else had spotted and beat goalkeeping master Dino Zoff with a sizzling left-foot shot.

That seemed to be it for brave Italy. Brazil needed only a draw to clinch a place in the semi-finals. Surely they would now shut up shop.

But Brazil being Brazil, they continued to attack, which meant there were still chances for Italy. A game that deserved to be the final was settled by a moment of magic from Rossi as he completed one of the most famous World Cup hat-tricks.

Skipper Zoff made a desperate save in the 75th minute, the ball was quickly swept into the Brazilian half and a corner was conceded. Tardelli drove the ball into the penalty area when the corner was only half cleared, and before anybody else could move a muscle Rossi turned a half chance into a goal with electric reactions that were nothing short of miraculous considering his two years out of the game.

Back in the ITV studio everybody suddenly came round to my way of thinking – Italy *could* win the World Cup.

There was now no stopping Rossi. He pulverised Poland with both goals in Italy's 2–0 semi-final victory, and his headed goal in the 56th minute of the final put Italy on the way to a convincing 3–1 victory over favourites West Germany.

Rossi, the assassin with the choirboy looks, had emerged as the star of the tournament and the Golden Boot winner with six goals. For the second time in his career he had proved everybody wrong. When he first started, three major knee operations led to Juventus losing faith in him, convinced that he would not be fit enough to stand up to the stresses and strains of *Serie A* football.

He was farmed out to Como, and later played on loan for Perugia, which was where he became embroiled in the bribery scandal.

I could not understand why he would risk his career by taking money to throw a match, and he always pleaded his innocence, claiming that he had been stitched up by a prosecution witness.

Long after Rossi retired to concentrate on a property-development company and local politics, the witness whose evidence had got him banned confessed that he had invented the story under pressure from unnamed mystery men.

Yes, it could all have come out of an episode of *The Sopranos*. Paolo Rossi had everybody singing his praises, particularly this happy man in the ITV studio.

It was one of football's great comeback stories, and Rossi's name will always be written large in World Cup history. You can bet on it.

34

Diego Maradona

Born: Villa Fiorito, Argentina, 30 October 1960

Career span: 1976–97

Clubs: Argentinos Juniors 1976–81 (167 games, 115 goals); Boca Juniors 1981–82 and 1995–97 (69 games, 35 goals); Barcelona 1982–84 (36 games, 22 goals); Napoli 1984–91 (188 games, 81 goals); Sevilla 1992–93 (25 games, 4 goals); Newell's Old Boys 1993 (3 games, 0 goals)

Argentina: 91 caps, 34 goals

Club honours: 1 Argentinian league championship, 1 Spanish Cup, 2 Italian league championships, 1 Italian Cup, 1 Uefa Cup

World Cup 1986

Golden Ball for Player of the Tournament at World Cup 1986

Argentinian Footballer of the Year twice

South American Footballer of the Year 5 times

Fifa 'Best Footballer of the Century' (people's choice)
Fifa Goal of the Century (v. England 1986 World Cup, the one scored with his foot)

THE often-disgraced but always fascinating Diego Maradona tried to be best at whatever he turned his hand to (particularly his left hand) – whether it was scoring goals, creating goals, drinking, taking drugs or just plain cheating. He was one of the great untouchables.

And a lot of English football fans would not have wanted to touch him with a bargepole after his behaviour in Argentina's 1986 World Cup quarter-final against England.

During this tournament Maradona confirmed that he was the greatest player on the planet. Unfortunately for followers of the most popular sport on earth, he was also confirmed as the greatest cheat.

To make it worse, the only footballer who could look Pelé in the eye was unrepentant, and boasted that his immoral moment was a divine intervention – 'the hand of God' he called it.

I remember watching it with Ian St John as we were preparing our *Saint and Greavsie* slant on the match. The action replays confirmed that he had definitely punched it into the net. The Saint, being a Jock, found it highly amusing. My first reaction was that Maradona had got away with murder, but under cross-examination from the Saint I had to confess I had claimed goals that should have been disallowed. There was one in particular for Tottenham against QPR when the referee and linesmen were the only people in the ground who did not see that I had handled the ball as I scored. Our reaction when the referee gave a goal was to laugh like drains and say, 'Thanks very much.'

The difference with Maradona's sleight of hand is that he did it on the world's biggest football stage.

Let me remind you that Bobby Robson's England would have reached the semi-final if they could have overcome Argentina.

Watched by a crowd of 114,580 spectators in Mexico City's Azteca Stadium, the match was heavy with tension because of the over-spill of feeling from the Falklands War. Squads of military police brandishing white batons patrolled the ground, but apart from a few isolated skirmishes the rival England and Argentine fans gave all their attention to the game, which was electric with action and atmosphere.

All eyes were on Diego Maradona, who was in the form of his life and forcing good judges to reassess whether Pelé really was the greatest footballer of all time. He might have been the shortest man on the field at just over 5ft 4in, but the chunky, wide-shouldered Argentine captain paraded across the pitch with the assured air of a giant among pygmies.

England's defenders noticeably quivered every time he took possession, which was often because he was continually demanding the ball the moment it reached the feet of any team-mate.

When he had the ball on his left foot, he would glide past tackles with the ease of a Rolls-Royce overtaking a Reliant Robin; and when he did not have the ball he was still a menace because of the speed with which he ran into areas of space to make himself available for a pass.

England defender Terry Fenwick, who gave the impression of being out of the retaliate-first school of football, decided that a physical assault might be the best way to keep Maradona quiet. Wrong! All he got for his clumsy effort was a booking and a cold stare from the Master. That cool look could have been interpreted as meaning Fenwick would eventually pay for his attempted ambush. Maradona would pick his moment to provide action to go with that look.

England might have fared better in a goalless first forty-five minutes had they been more adventurous, but they were so conscious of Maradona's match-winning ability that they cautiously kept players back in defence. They would have been better employed supporting raids against an Argentine back line that looked vulnerable under attack.

The second half belonged almost entirely to Maradona, and the two goals that he scored became the major talking point of the entire tournament and remain fresh in the memory to this day. The first will always be remembered for its controversy – many would say cheating – and the second for its quite astounding quality.

Six minutes had gone of the second half when Maradona swept the ball to the feet of Valdano and raced into the penalty area for the return. As he made his break, some England defenders were appealing for offside but the linesman's flag stayed down and Valdano's centre was deflected across the face of the England goal by Steve Hodge. Goalkeeper Peter Shilton came off his line prepared to punch clear.

There seemed no way the stocky Maradona, dwarfed by the powerfully built England goalkeeper, could get the better of Shilton in the air. He would have needed stilts to outjump Shilts. Spectators looked on in amazement as the ball cannoned into the net off Maradona with the airborne Shilton stretching out to thrash empty air.

Saint and I were astonished (along with millions of fans watching the television action replay) when we got confirmation of what we thought we had just seen. There was the instant evidence. No doubt about it, Maradona had pushed the ball into the net with his left hand.

Outraged, Shilton led a posse of protesting players trying to persuade referee Ali Bennaceur that the goal had been illegal. But from the angle that the Tunisian referee saw it, Maradona appeared to have scored with his head. He pointed to the centre circle and the little man from Buenos Aires went on a dance of celebration that should have been a skulk of shame.

Four minutes later, with the aggrieved England players trying to regain their composure, the Jeykll and Hyde character that was

Footballing royalty: the king of Dutch soccer Johan Cruyff duels with *Der Kaiser* Franz Beckenbauer during the 1974 World Cup final (*above*); *Der Bomber* Gerd Muller finishes off England with the winning goal in the 1974 World Cup quarter-final (*below*).

Kevin Keegan (*above*) took his perm for a term in Hamburg, and was replaced in the No. 7 Liverpool shirt by Kenny Dalglish (*right*), who became an even bigger hero than Mighty Mouse at Anfield.

Graeme Souness (*below*) bosses the midfield for Liverpool against Manchester United, with Old Trafford skipper Bryan Robson preparing to make a challenge.

Paolo Rossi (*above*) and Gianfranco Zola (*below*), both representing Italy in my all-star selection.

Michel Platini, an emperor on the pitch as a flair player and now the ruler of Europe as a football politician.

Maradona scores his infamous 'Hand of God' goal against England in the 1986 World Cup quarter-final (*above left*); Dennis Bergkamp and Ian Rush duel for the ball at Highbury in 1996 (*right*).

Those were the days my friends, when David Beckham and Eric Cantona were team-mates at Manchester United and the footballing gods of Old Trafford.

The way we were. Alan Shearer and Paul Gascoigne celebrate Gazza's goal against Scotland at Wembley during the Euro '96 tournament. Both Geordies make it into my élite of the élite list.

Roy Keane always liked to be in charge, as referee Mike Riley is finding out during a 2004 Premiership match against Liverpool at Old Trafford. Brian Clough described the young Keane as having 'an even bigger head than mine!'

David Beckham has a right foot to die for. Pity about the left. He is as one footed as Long John Silver.

Ronaldinho has the Real Madrid defensive wall jumping with a free-kick during a *La Liga* match at Barcelona's Nou Camp stadium in 2006. The Real players are (*from left to right*) Ronaldo, Guti, David Beckham, Zinedine Zidane and Roberto Carlos. Four of the players in this picture make it into my list.

Two of the modern masters, Ronaldo and Thierry Henry, tussle for the ball during a Real Madrid–Arsenal Champions League match at Highbury in 2006. Ronaldo is showing signs of the added pounds that were a weight on his mind.

The past, present and future faces of Manchester United – veteran wing wizard Ryan Giggs joins in goal celebrations with the new kids on the block, Cristiano Ronaldo and Wayne Rooney. All three make it into my *Heroes and Entertainers* selection.

England team-mates Steven Gerrard and Michael Owen (*below*) are fairly pleased with each other after a goal. They both started out at Anfield and became kings of the Kop. In Gerrard I saw a 'new' Duncan Edwards, and in Owen I saw a 'new' me!

Maradona unveiled the genius in his game. He produced the sort of magic that had prompted Napoli to buy him from Barcelona for a then world record £6.9 million in 1984.

To say he ran rings around England would be too simple a description of a goal that stands comparison with the very best scored anywhere and at any time. Indeed, it was voted Fifa Goal of the Century in 1999.

Running with the ball at his feet from close to the halfway line, Maradona drew England defenders to him like a spider luring its prey. Kenny Sansom, Terry Butcher and then Terry Fenwick – he who unwisely tried a physical assault in the first half – all came into the Maradona web and were left in a tangle behind him as he accelerated past their attempted tackles.

Again, it was Maradona versus Shilton, this time on the ground. Maradona did not have to cheat his way past the England goalkeeper. He sold him an outrageous dummy that left Shilton scrambling for a shot that was never made, and then nonchalantly prodded the ball into the empty net for a goal of breathtaking beauty. It was a moment of magnificence that sweetened the sour taste left by Maradona's first goal. Well, almost.

England, to their credit, battled back and substitute John Barnes laid on a goal for the razor-sharp Lineker in the 81st minute. But it was Argentina who went through to the semi-finals.

As they walked exhausted off the bakehouse of a pitch after their 2–1 defeat, the England players – led by Shilton – found the energy to continue their complaints to the referee about the first Maradona goal. But most of the capacity crowd were talking only about his second goal as they filed out of the ground at the end of an eventful quarter-final that would always be remembered as 'Maradona's Match'.

The little man had a mix between a smile and a smirk on his face as he said later:

Yes, the ball did go into the England net off my hand. It was the hand of God. It was not deliberate and so I do not in any way feel guilty claiming it as a goal. Would an England player have gone to the referee and said, 'Don't award the goal. The ball hit my hand?' Of course not. Anyway, why all the controversy? Surely my second goal ended all arguments.

Argentina duly won the thirteenth World Cup final at the Azteca Stadium on 29 June 1986 when they beat West Germany 3–2, and it was Maradona who collected the trophy as captain.

The 'Hand of God' was not there to rescue him as his private life became an horrendous mess. From the early 1990s he was battling cocaine addiction, and he was banned for fifteen months after failing a drug test in Italy, where he had almost single-handedly (no doubt, left) turned Napoli into a major force in *Serie A*.

It was astonishing what he achieved with Napoli. In that defence-dominated league he never had less than two markers following him everywhere he went. I have seen nobody better than Maradona at evading tackles with body swerves and sudden acceleration, and he would often hurdle over flying boots aimed at taking his legs from under him. The man was a footballing genius, as good as any I have seen with a ball at his feet.

Too many people have judged him by his off-the-field activities, rather than giving him the credit he deserves as a player who could have come from another planet.

Maradona's personal life was always bringing him the wrong sort of headlines, though. He became involved in a controversy over an illegitimate son, was criticised for having Mafia connections, had treatment for alcohol abuse, put on so much weight that this once super athlete waddled rather than ran, and was kicked out of the 1994 World Cup after failing another drug test.

Fifa conducted a poll on the internet in 2000 to find the people's choice as the Footballer of the Century. They stupidly forgot to take into account that most website surfers are under 30 and would not have seen Pelé in action. Maradona ran away with the vote, but Fifa then decided that a 'football family of experts' would decide, and suddenly Pelé was announced in first place.

With a classic piece of compromise, Fifa decided to make two awards, one to Maradona for the website vote and one to Pelé. Maradona accepted his prize and arrogantly walked out before Pelé received his trophy. It was pathetic.

Whenever I've met Maradona I have found him a charming, friendly little (fat) bloke. The last time I saw him he was wearing a 'Stop Bush' T-shirt and calling the President 'a garbage man', so he can't be all bad, and I have to admit that some of Maradona's goals – particularly that second one against England – have never been bettered by Pelé or anybody else.

So who gets the crown as The Greatest? I'll be honest, I cannot choose between them.

Many of Pelé's goals were created for him by others, but he was a master at putting the finishing touch. Maradona fashioned the majority of his goals himself with the sort of breathtaking, dribbling runs we witnessed against England in Mexico in 1986. He has lost out heavily to Pelé in the PR stakes, but I think it is unfair to judge either of them by their personalities or lifestyles.

Assessing them purely as footballers, I would put them on equal terms – with a bloke called George Best running them both close!

35

Ian Rush

Born: St Asaph, Wales, 20 October 1961

Career span: 1979–2000

Clubs: Chester City 1979–80 (34 league games, 14 goals); Liverpool 1980–87 and 1988–96 (469 league games, 229 goals); Juventus 1987–88 (29 league games, 7 goals); Leeds United 1996–97 (36 games, 3 goals); Newcastle United 1997–98 (10 league games, 0 goals); Sheffield United, loan 1998 (4 league games, 0 goals); Wrexham 1998–99 (18 league games, no goals); Sydney Olympic 1999–2000 (2 games, 1 goal)

Wales: 73 caps, 28 goals

Club honours: 5 league championships, 3 FA Cups, 5 League Cups, 1 European Cup

European Golden Boot 1984

Footballer of the Year 1984

PFA Player of the Year 1984

ONE of the hardest jobs I had in making my selections was deciding which striker should represent Liverpool from a choice of my old England rival Roger Hunt, his and my sidekick Ian St John and the Hammer of Wales Ian Rush.

St John was as much a maker as taker of goals, and so I reluctantly put him in third place. Sorry, Saint.

People put it about that Roger Hunt and I did not like each other because we were competitors for the same England shirt, while in truth we never had a cross word throughout our careers and there was a lot of mutual respect.

What I like about both Hunt and Rush is that they were out-and-out, no-nonsense strikers. Neither of them was a fancy-Dan. They both just got on with the job of putting the ball in the net with a minimum of fuss or frills. The way they celebrate goals today, the players are like consenting adults. Hunt and Rushie never mixed arrogance with their artistry.

I know that if my screen partner Ian St John were making this selection, he would have no hesitation in plumping for Roger Hunt. They were dynamic together, and too much of a double handful for most defences.

But against that, I had to take into account the double act of Kenny Dalglish and Ian Rush. They were equally productive partners, and probably more potent than Roger and the Saint (sounds as if Roger Moore belongs in here somewhere!).

In the end, and after much soul searching, I came down on the side of Rush, even though he failed to beat Hunt's all-time Liverpool club record of 245 league goals. Rush finished up with 229 in his two spells at Anfield, but all were scored at the top level of the First Division, while Roger's collection started in the Second Division before the Shankly-inspired Red Revolution.

Another major factor was Rush's honours haul. He collected five league championship medals to Hunt's two, and a record five League Cup winner's medals. He also picked up three FA Cup winner's medals to Roger's one, scoring a record five FA Cup final goals. Hunt, of course, had the little matter of the World Cup medal for bragging rights, not that he ever boasted. They shared the common trait of being modest, unassuming men despite having plenty to shout about.

Rush also had a European Cup medal to show off at the end

of the 1984 season in which he was in unstoppable form. He plundered 49 goals as Liverpool completed what was the 'Impossible Treble' of league championship, League Cup and European Cup (Manchester United went one better in 1999 with the League, FA Cup and European Cup).

In that memorable 1984 season Rush pulled off the individual hat-trick of winning the Football Writers' Footballer of the Year award, the Professional Footballers' Association Player of the Year trophy and the Golden Boot as Europe's top marksman.

But it all might have been a different story if wise old Bob Paisley had not given him some sound advice after he had joined Liverpool from Fourth Division Chester City at the age of 18.

Rush got impatient playing in Liverpool reserves. He was talking about finding a club where he could get first-team football when 'Uncle Bob' sat him down and explained, 'We're playing you in the reserves so that you get used to the Liverpool style of play. I promise it will pay dividends when you get into the first team. You're developing just the way we want, and if you show just a little more selfishness when you get the ball in the penalty area, I think you'll soon be the perfect Liverpool player.'

That's the way they did it at Anfield, bringing players off a conveyor belt, doing it the Liverpool way. The following season Rush scored 30 goals in 49 appearances, and proved that he was already the finished article.

He once went a remarkable run of 145 successive games with Liverpool when he was never on the losing side in a match in which he scored. He didn't just decorate matches. He *decided* them. His total league and Cup haul was a club record 346 goals.

His career went pear-shaped when he fell for that old feeling that the grass was greener on the Italian side of the football fence. He joined Juventus for £3 million in the summer of 1986. Like me when I mistakenly went to Milan, Ian soon found out that Italy was a sterile place to be after the excitement and adventure of the Football League.

It was a nightmare for Rush as Juventus suffered through their worst season for twenty years. He had been hailed as the 'new John Charles' on his arrival in Turin, a link strengthened by the fact that both were sons of Wales. But I know of no player who could live up to that billing. The Italian press nicknamed him 'The Eagle' when he kicked off with Juventus, and the cartoonists had great fun giving him the eagle image. But they soon realised that this was one eagle that had not landed. A man of simple tastes, he said that he was missing his pints in the pub at home with his pals.

The goals dried up – just seven in 29 *Serie A* games – and his brain also seemed to freeze. Asked what was wrong with Italy he famously replied, 'It's like being in a foreign country.'

He got back to Anfield as quickly as possible, and had to battle for his place against a formidable challenge from John Aldridge (who scored an impressive 329 goals in his travels with Newport, Oxford, Liverpool and Tranmere).

Ian added another 89 goals to his league collection before a less than successful final flurry to his career with Leeds, Newcastle, Sheffield United, Wrexham and – a long way to go for two games – Sydney Olympic.

Idolised in his native Wales, Rush scored a national record 28 goals in his 73 international appearances without ever reaching the final of a major tournament. The highlight for him was scoring the winning goal against world champions Germany in a Euro '92 qualifier.

In 2006 Rush came third in a Liverpool poll to find the hundred top players 'Who Shook the Kop'. The two ahead of him were Kenny Dalglish and Steven Gerrard.

Yes, he definitely earned his place in my select list. But I will always have a soft spot for Roger Hunt, my old *friendly* rival.

36

Eric Cantona

Born: Paris, 24 May 1966 (raised in Marseille)

Career span: 1983–1997

Clubs: Auxerre 1983–85 and 1986–88 (103 games, 46 goals); Martigues, loan 1985–86 (15 games, 4 goals); Marseille 1988–89 and 1990–91 (40 games, 13 goals); Bordeaux, loan 1989 (11 games, 6 goals); Montpellier, loan 1989–90 (33 games, 10 goals); Nimes 1990–91 (16 games, 2 goals); Leeds United 1992 (28 games, 9 goals); Manchester United 1992–97 (185 games, 82 goals)

France: 45 caps, 20 goals

Club honours: 1 French championship, 1 French Cup, 1 league championship, 4 Premiership titles, 2 FA Cups

PFA Player of the Year 1994

Footballer of the Year 1996

HOW fitting that Eric Cantona now makes his living on the stage and screen, because he was one of football's born entertainers, a brooding, moody genius who brought a mixture of magic, mystery and just a little mayhem to the Old Trafford theatre of dreams. He was like a pantomime villain, loved and hated in equal measure.

It was like watching a whole series of *Tales of the Unexpected* when Eric was performing for Manchester United, and long before

Alex Ferguson stole him from Leeds he was a constant companion of controversy and the central figure in French footballing farce.

Cantona and Manchester United were made for each other. Eric was looking for a stage big enough for his production skills and megawatt personality. United were looking for a player to spark their challenge for the newly introduced Premiership title.

And how they delivered – talk about *entente cordial*! United not only won the inaugural Premiership title but three more championships. Eric schemed and scored to inspire astonishing success that included two league and FA Cup doubles. At the end of the second FA Cup final in 1996 – after scoring the winning goal against Liverpool – he became the first foreign captain to collect the treasured trophy.

He did it all with such regal style – trademark turned-up collar, arrogant stance and straight-ahead stare after scoring – that he was even crowned King of Old Trafford, a title that up until then had belonged exclusively to the idolised Denis Law.

But there was a dark side to the French musketeer, and the violent rebel inside him emerged when he infamously kung-fu kicked a jeering spectator after being sent off at Crystal Palace.

Following that moment of madness I did some research on Eric for a proposed television documentary, trying to find out what made him tick and then explode like a time-bomb. These were among the incidents I uncovered in Eric's previous life before he became a legend at Old Trafford . . .

In 1987 he was fined for punching his own goalkeeper and giving him a black eye . . . 1988, banned for three months for a reckless tackle . . . suspended from international football for a year for calling the national coach 'a bag of shit' . . . 1989, told he would never play for Marseille again after ripping off his shirt and throwing it at the referee, and the club owner said that he belonged in a lunatic asylum . . . suspended for two matches for throwing a boot in temper at a team-mate . . . 1991, threw the ball at the referee and walked off before the red card could be shown, and then had a dressing-room fight with another player.

When he protested at the length of a suspension, a member of the French disciplinary panel told him, 'You can't be judged like any other player. Behind you is the trail of the smell of sulphur.'

Eric reacted by going up to each member of the panel and saying to their face, 'Idiot.' They immediately doubled his suspension to two months, and Cantona announced that he was giving up football. He could not suffer fools at all, let alone gladly.

He had always been a volcano waiting to erupt, and admitted that he admired the likes of Jim Morrison, Mickey Rourke and Marlon Brando for their 'independence and rebelliousness'.

Yet the demons only seemed to manifest themselves within the world of football. Away from the game he lived quietly, fiercely protecting his privacy. His then wife, Isabelle, whom he had known since his teens, became a French teacher at Leeds University. Unlike several of his team-mates there were no tabloid exposés about Cantona drinking, womanising or fighting.

He was content to live in a modest semi-detached house in Manchester, veering away from the rich trappings and status symbols of the modern footballer. Perhaps this was because he had grown up in a cave that had been converted into a home by his paternal grandfather, a Sardinian stonemason.

There was something about Eric that tugged at the heartstrings of influential people in the game. When he announced that he was retiring from football following his fall-outs with the French authorities, Michel Platini and Gérard Houllier pleaded with him to continue playing, and suggested that he should try his luck in England.

The temper tantrums continued when he arrived in England after a trial run at Sheffield Wednesday that went hopelessly wrong. Leeds gave him a platform to show his skills, but in 1992 he fell out with manager Howard Wilkinson after playing a key role in helping the Elland Road club win the league championship, claiming that Wilko was jealous of the way the fans worshipped him ('Oh-ah-Cantona' was a chant started by the Leeds supporters) . . . 1993, fined £1,000 by the Football Association for spitting at a Leeds fan in his first game back at Elland Road with Manchester United . . . sent off in Manchester United's European Cup defeat by Galatasaray in Turkey for accusing the referee of cheating, and then scuffled with Turkish police . . . 1994, banned for five games after being sent off twice in four days, including for stamping on an opponent . . . arrested and handcuffed by security guards in a dispute over accreditation before the 1994 World Cup semi-final between Brazil and Sweden in Los Angeles.

But when Eric was good at Manchester United, he was very, very good. Who can forget his stunning volley against Wimbledon in the 1994 FA Cup-tie, and then his pair of penalty kicks that sank Chelsea in the Cup final at Wembley the same season. Then there was his audacious chip against Sheffield United in the third round the following year, and a classic goal against QPR, plus two goals against Manchester City in both derbies of the 93–94 season.

You could cite a whole gallery of great moments, but the Cantona volcano erupted once too often with the kung-fu kick. It looked as if Eric's breathtaking career was over as he was handed a record eight-month ban and a prison sentence that was later reduced to community work.

Hard-bitten reporters, reared on 'over the moon, Brian' and 'sick as a parrot' quotes, looked on dumbstruck when the Frenchman told them after a judge had quashed his jail sentence, 'When seagulls follow a trawler it is because they think sardines will be thrown into the sea.' That was all he said at the news conference. The press boys were, well, sick as parrots.

Alex Ferguson, one of the few people on earth who could handle the wild Frenchman, talked him out of quitting the game and he came back for two more seasons of success before suddenly walking off stage as abruptly as he had arrived. He decided, at the age of 30, to seek new challenges and horizons in the theatre and film world. It was not so much a retirement as an abdication. His only involvement with football was as manager, coach, captain and main goalscorer for a professional beach football team. 'The future,' Eric said, 'is sand.'

Like all great thespians and entertainers, he had left us wanting more.

He entertained us as much with his tongue and thoughts as his feet. Let him have the last word. Here are a few of the sayings of King Eric:

- *'Goals are like babies – they are all beautiful.'*
- *'I had heart, and I know without heart you cannot play.'*
- *'I am searching for abstract ways of expressing reality, abstract forms that will enlighten my own mystery.'*
- *'I stopped playing football because I'd done as much as I could. I needed something that was going to excite me as much as football had excited me.'*
- *'I'm proud of what I achieved at Manchester United, but a life built on memories is not much of a life.'*
- *'If you have only one passion in life – football – and you pursue it to the exclusion of everything else, it becomes very dangerous. When you stop doing this activity it is as though you are dying. The death of that activity is a death in itself.'*
- *'The ball, it is like a woman. It (and she) likes to be caressed.'*
- *'Whatever happens, there are always things you could have done better. You score two goals and you usually feel you could have done better. You score two goals and you usually feel you could have scored a third. That's perfectionism. That's what makes you progress in life.'*
- *'An artist in my eyes, is someone who can lighten up a dark room. I have never and will never find difference between the pass from Pelé to Carlos Alberto in the final of the World Cup in 1970 and the poetry of the young Rimbaud, who stretches*

cords from steeple to steeple and garlands from window to window. There is in each of these human manifestations an expression of beauty that touches us and gives us a feeling of eternity.'

- *'My best moment? I have a lot of good moments but the one I prefer is when I kicked the hooligan.'*

Eric Cantona. *Magnifique.*

37

Gianfranco Zola

Born: Oliena, Sardinia, 5 July 1966

Career span: 1984–2005

Clubs: Nuorese 1984–87 (31 league games, 10 goals); Torres 1987–89 (88 league games, 21 goals); Napoli 1989–93 (105 league games, 32 goals); Parma 1993–96 (102 league games, 49 goals); Chelsea 1996–2003 (229 league games, 59 goals); Cagliari 2003–05 (74 league games, 22 goals)

Italy: 35 caps, 9 goals

Club honours: 1 Italian league championship, 1 Uefa Cup, 2 FA Cups, 1 League Cup, 1 European Cup-Winners' Cup

Footballer of the Year 1997

I WONDER if Gianfranco Zola realises that he was born in the same week that the 1966 World Cup kicked off at Wembley?

It was fitting then that thirty years later he should join Chelsea and help steer them to two FA Cup final victories at the old Wembley.

It was no accident that much of the magic Zola produced at Chelsea bore a startling resemblance to Maradona's bag of tricks. He had come under the influence of the Argentinian Master while playing understudy to Diego early in his career at Napoli.

Gianfranco said in an interview during his memorable stay at Stamford Bridge, 'I used to spy on Diego at every opportunity. Every time he was in training I would be in the background, watching like a hawk. I studied the way he curled balls at free-kicks, how he dribbled and how he made space for himself with his acceleration. Then I would practise all the things I had noticed. As you can imagine, I am a great admirer of Maradona. He remains the best footballer I have ever seen.'

While all the good things rubbed off on Gianfranco, he was wise enough not to take on any of Maradona's dubious baggage. Off the pitch, they are as alike as grass and granite. Zola's lifestyle could not be more different. A teetotaller, he quickly settled into his London home with wife Franca and their three children. Away from the football crowds, he loves nothing better than playing Beethoven on his grand piano.

He eventually got to take over Maradona's No. 10 shirt, and his goals and passes helped Napoli win the *Serie A* championship in 1989–90. A £1.4 million move to Parma in 1993 coincided with him taking over from Roberto Baggio as a key man in Italy's attack. He was a major influence on the Parma team that developed from a domestic force in Italy to a power in Europe.

Standing a haircut taller than Maradona at 5ft 5in, Zola was always an Anglophile and he jumped at the chance when Chelsea player-manager Ruud Gullit came calling for him in November 1996. He made such an impression in his first season in England that he was voted the Football Writers' Footballer of the Year. The move had revitalised his game just as he was losing his appetite at Parma. This is what he said about his early experiences with Chelsea:

> *My first season in English football was just unbelievable. The memories of it will live with me forever. It was very important to me that I should help Chelsea win something after Ruud [Gullit] had put so much faith in me.*
>
> *Our victory against Middlesbrough in the FA Cup was unforgettable. To be part of that wonderful occasion was fantastic. I have never known anything quite like the atmosphere of a Wembley Cup final. It sent shivers down my back.*
>
> *Two days earlier I had been honoured to be presented with the Footballer of the Year award. It was an overwhelming experience, particularly as the legendary Sir Stanley Matthews handed it to me. That was just awe-inspiring. My father was there on his first visit to England and for the entire trip he kept saying, 'I have met Stanley Matthews.' Even to this day, there are few bigger names in football. In Italy he is known as Mister Football.*
>
> *I was privileged to have a long talk with Sir Stanley, and he told me that he used to play for twenty pounds a week. Today he would be worth all the money in the Bank of England!*

Zola was the first player to win the Footballer of the Year award without playing a full season, and was the first Chelsea player to win the accolade.

He had seven wonderfully happy and satisfying seasons at Chelsea before heading into the sunset by holding his passing-out parade with Cagliari on his home island of Sardinia. Chelsea supporters went into mourning when they heard that the player known as 'Magic Box' was leaving Stamford Bridge, where he had such a rapport with the fans that he was voted 'Best Loved

Chelsea Player Ever'. Many of his 80 goals for Chelsea were conjured – back-heels, volleys, side-foots after dazzling dribbles and scissor kicks. One FA Cup goal against Norwich – a back-heel delivered while he was in mid-air – was described as 'pure fantasy'.

Roman Abramovich took over at Chelsea just after the little man had committed himself to Cagliari, and did all he could to persuade him to change his mind and stay at Stamford Bridge. But Zola is a man of his word, and refused to break his verbal promise to join his home-island club. Everywhere he went, Abramovich heard people saying how Zola was the greatest player Chelsea had ever had. He went to the lengths of trying to buy Cagliari – as you do – so that he could lay claim to Gianfranco, but his offer for the club was rejected.

Zola was a magnificent ambassador for his country and for the whole of football, and is the perfect role model for any young professional just coming into the game.

Even at 38, he still had the power to influence matters on the pitch and – in the role of skipper and schemer – he steered Cagliari back to *Serie A* before hanging up his shooting boots.

I remember the then Chelsea manager, Claudio Ranieri – once his coach at Napoli – saying that he had never known a player get a reception like Zola did at away grounds. 'They applaud him as he steps off the coach and again as he comes on to and leaves the pitch,' he said. 'It is extraordinary how he has won the hearts of everybody.'

His off-the-field charity work at Chelsea was rewarded with the OBE, a rare honour for an overseas player.

'My greatest satisfaction is the way people respect me,' he said on hearing of his OBE honour. 'Many people excel in games but when you have achieved that level of respect, it is something extra special. Money can give you many things but respect cannot be bought. What I have achieved in the way people regard me, in my mind, is remarkable. I will always have a little of London and a lot of Chelsea in my heart.'

Zola is equally well thought of in his homeland, and he and his former Chelsea and international team-mate Pierluigi Casiraghi have been trusted with the joint job of running the Italian Under-21 team.

The young players of Italy could not have a better tutor than Gianfranco, and I hope they can find out what's inside the Magic Box.

38
Paul Gascoigne

Born: Gateshead, 27 May 1967

Career span: 1985–2005

Clubs: Newcastle United 1985–88 (107 league games, 25 goals); Tottenham 1988–92 (112 league games, 33 goals); Lazio 1992–95 (47 league games, 6 goals); Rangers 1995–98 (104 league games, 39 goals); Middlesbrough 1998–2000 (48 league games, 4 goals); Everton 2000–2002 (38 league games, 1 goal); Burnley 2002 (6 league games, 0 goals); Gansu Tianma, China 2003 (4 league games, 2 goals); Boston United 2004–05 (6 league games, 1 goal)

England: 57 caps, 10 goals

Club honours: 1 FA Cup, 2 Scottish Premier championships, 1 Scottish Cup, 1 Scottish League Cup

BBC Sports Personality of the Year 1990
Scottish Footballer of the Year 1996
Scottish PFA Player of the Year 1996

W HEN it was announced in 2007 that Paul Gascoigne was going to play the lead role in a horror movie called *Final Run*, I didn't know whether to laugh or cry. I wondered if it was going to be the story of Gazza's life, which has had all the twists and turns of a Hammer horror movie.

I have closely monitored the life and times of Paul since he first appeared on the football scene at Newcastle as a tubby teenager. He was regularly featured on our *Saint and Greavsie* show, and I nicknamed him 'Fat Boy' because he was always stuffing himself with Mars bars.

His saving grace was that he had the sort of football skills that are a gift from the gods. He is one of the few English-born players whom you can mention in the same breath as old-time ball-playing masters such as Len Shackleton, Wilf Mannion and Raich Carter – all of them, coincidentally, heroes of the North East. His box of tricks even matched those of Clown Prince Shackleton.

But somewhere along the football path Paul lost his way in – it has to be said – a maze of his own making. The boy who had the nation crying with him when he shed tears during his barnstorming performances at the 1990 World Cup finals never really grew up. They proved to be tears on the face of a clown.

Gazza's roller-coaster ride took him from Tyneside to Tottenham, then to Lazio in Rome, on to Rangers in Glasgow, back to the North East with Middlesbrough, across to the North West with Everton and then Burnley, down to China, of all places, with Gansu Tianma, before winding up with Boston United.

And at just about every stopping-off place he got involved in controversial – usually drink-dictated – incidents that took him

200

from the back pages to the front. The newspapers had a ball with him throughout his headline-hitting career.

He battled the demon drink, but was continually falling off the wagon and getting bruised as well as boozed. I've been down that 'sober just for today' road, so I have some idea of what Gazza has been going through. But on top of alcoholism he has the added problems of bulimia, an obsessive-compulsive disorder, bipolar disorder, ulcer and heart complications, insomnia and a flirtation with cocaine. He was also pilloried in public when branded a wife beater. And something not listed on his medical reports is what I would rate a soft brain. As his former England boss Bobby Robson said years ago, 'The boy is as daft as a brush.'

On the plus side for Gazza is that he remains what he always was from the first time I met him – a loveable, huggable lad (I can't think of him as a middle-aged man) who, for all his faults, you just cannot help but like. He is like a puppy you had as a child, for which you never lose your fondness.

I ached for Gazza when he said in a 2006 interview, 'Some people might have this problem or that problem. I've got them all. It's something I have to deal with every day and it's hard. When I wake up in the morning, I'm thinking, "Don't drink, don't take drugs, watch what you eat, take your medication." It's terrible. I've got to be on top of everything. It's a battle I've got to the end of my life.'

He played 57 times for England and scored 10 goals. It should have been several more if Glenn Hoddle had not cut off his legs on the eve of the botched France '98 World Cup finals. I am not saying Hoddle was wrong to drop him – perhaps it was because of something he did wrong in a previous life. The mistake was selecting him in the first place if he had doubts about his lifestyle. One thing's for sure, Gazza had more talent than most other players who remained in the squad.

Phil Neville was also kicked out at the last minute, and revealed later, 'I started to cry and felt a comforting arm around my shoulder. It was Gazza giving me support.'

That's the sort of caring bloke Gascoigne is. Pity that, when told earlier that he was being axed, he lost his rag with Hoddle and trashed his hotel room!

One England goal by Gazza stands out in our memories above all the rest, and it came during the Euro '96 finals at the old Wembley.

Terry Venables had taken over the England management baton from Graham Taylor, and he put together an inventive team that restored English pride with an inspiring challenge for the championship.

England came into the tournament under a cloud of controversy after some of their drink-fuelled players had got involved in a wild night out in Hong Kong following a match meant to warm them up for Euro action at home.

Gazza, who too often went a prank too far, was at the centre of it all. He and several team-mates were photographed pouring drinks down each other's throats while half lying in a pseudo dentist's chair in a nightclub. Then, on the flight home, several players were accused of causing damage to aircraft property. It was bad enough having fans as hooligans; now the players were behaving like louts.

Only an exceptional performance in the Euro Championship could restore their pride and self-respect. And that is exactly what they produced under the influence – I almost said intoxicating influence – of coach Venables.

England were held 1–1 by Switzerland in the opening game at Wembley, a harsh penalty award against Stuart Pearce cancelling out an Alan Shearer goal and costing them a deserved victory.

Then came the 'British Final' – England against Scotland, who had held Holland to a goalless draw in their first game. It was a cracker.

Trailing 1–0 to a Shearer goal, the Scots were awarded a penalty twelve minutes from the end. David Seaman saved superbly from Gary McAllister, and within a minute the one and only Gazza had scored a gem of a second goal for England. He looped the ball over Colin Hendry's head before volleying first time past goalkeeper Andy Goram to secure a 2–0 win for England. It was a carbon copy of Pelé's goal in the 1958 World Cup final.

He celebrated by going to a chosen spot at the side of the Scottish goal, and as he lay down England team-mates poured bottled water down his throat in a send-up of the dentist's chair incident. The crowd loved it, and suddenly all was forgiven. If only Gazza's drinking had stopped there.

From then on, there were more downs than ups in his career as his wild off-the-pitch lifestyle started to rob him of vital pace on the pitch. It was like being helpless witnesses, watching a close friend fall down a mountainside. The sad thing is that Gazza never quite made it to the top of the mountain. With all the skill with which he was blessed he should now be unveiling statues of himself as the finest scheming, scoring midfielder England ever produced. Instead of that, we are left thinking what might have been.

First and foremost, Gazza was an entertainer supreme. So let's leave you laughing with some of his madder moments . . .

When a Scottish referee dropped his cards during a match, Gazza picked up a yellow card and brandished it at the referee. Instead of laughing, the humourless referee booked him for dissent.

For Italia '90 the TV producers decided it would be a good idea to introduce each player with a close-up on camera and have them miming their names, with a caption going across the bottom. Gazza clearly mimed 'F***ing W*****' and it went out worldwide.

A famous picture showing Vinnie Jones squeezing Gazza where it hurts during a First Division match was not the end of the affair. Paul sent Vinnie a red rose, and got a toilet brush in return.

Gazza booked a series of sunbed sessions for his Newcastle team-mate Tony Cunningham, a black Jamaican.

Meeting the Lazio president for the first time after they had agreed to spend £4.5 million on him, Gazza shook him warmly by the hand and said, 'Has anybody told you before, you're the spitting image of Lou Costello.'

On his first night in Rome after signing for Lazio he was followed everywhere by a minder. Gazza gave him the slip, put his shoes on the window ledge of the sixth-storey hotel room, threw open the window and then hid in a cupboard. The minder arrived in the room and thought he had jumped.

He was playing for Lazio against Genoa in the Stadio Olympico when a tackle left injury-prone Gazza in a painful heap. Fearing the worst, the entire Genoa team grouped round Paul as he lay flat out on the pitch. Suddenly a grinning Gascoigne got to his feet, shook every Genoa player's hand and then limped off for treatment.

Strolling through North London with his Tottenham team-mate Gary Lineker, Gazza persuaded a protesting Lineker to follow him on to a Routemaster bus. He then talked the driver into letting him get behind the wheel, and tipped him to go off route to drop them at their destination.

Followed by a TV documentary camera crew filming a day in his life, he led them to a Glasgow house on the pretence it was one of his regular haunts. He had never been there in his life, and when a lady opened the door and found herself staring at a camera, Gazza told her he was doing the Daz doorstep challenge.

When Mirandinha became the first Brazilian to play in the English First Division, Gazza sportingly took it upon himself to act as his English teacher and as a result the Brazilian would answer the simplest of questions with a stream of swear words.

As the England team posed for a photograph, Gazza pulled down Paul Ince's shorts and Ince's bare backside made it on to every tabloid sports page.

While staying in a New Zealand hotel, he was told there was

no bacon for breakfast. 'What,' said a stunned Gazza, 'all the sheep in this country and there's no bloody bacon?'

There will never be another Gazza, which means some of the fun has gone out of the game. For all his faults, he more than most fitted the title of the Great Entertainer.

39

Dennis Bergkamp

Born: Amsterdam, 18 May 1969

Career span: 1986–2006

Clubs: Ajax 1986–93 (185 league games, 103 goals); Inter Milan 1993–95 (52 league games, 11 goals); Arsenal 1995–2006 (315 league games, 87 goals)

Holland: 79 caps, 37 goals

Club honours: 1 Dutch championship, 2 Dutch Cups, 3 Premiership titles, 4 FA Cups, 2 Uefa Cups, 1 European Cup-Winners' Cup

Dutch Footballer of the Year 1992 and 1993

Footballer of the Year 1998

PFA Player of the Year 1998

To describe Dennis Bergkamp as 'The Flying Dutchman' is a contradiction in terms. He rose to dizzy heights on the football pitch, but flatly refused to climb aboard an aeroplane because of a morbid fear of flying. I could sympathise with him because, in my playing days, I had to get a lot of drink inside me before I would venture on board. If we were meant to fly, God would have given us wings.

His decision never to fly again – following a bomb-scare flight in 1994 – meant he missed those overseas matches he could not reach by ship, Eurostar or motorcar. The 2002 World Cup in the Far East went by without him. But he still got in enough skilled action on terra firma to earn his place on my list, a centimetre ahead of his compatriot Marco van Basten. Poor old Marco's goal-gorged career was sadly cut short by injury, while Bergkamp maintained an astonishingly high standard of performance across a stretch of twenty years.

A Dutch name has been on the coveted European Footballer of the Year award on seven occasions – Johan Cruyff (three times), Ruud Gullit (once) and van Basten (three times). Bergkamp was second and third, and twice third in the Fifa World Player of the Year vote.

But he is the one I select on a par with Cruyff as the greatest Dutch footballer of them all. I have rarely seen anybody to match him for a sublime first touch, and he always seemed to be able to 'think' his way through a defence. He never tried to make himself felt physically; football for 'Ice Man' Dennis was more of a psychological battle, and he continually left shell-shocked defenders in need of a shrink.

He achieved enough with Ajax to cement his place in football's hall of fame, stalled at Inter Milan and then became a huge influence at Arsenal, where many Gooners will tell you that he is the finest footballer ever to pull on the red-and-white shirt. I will go further and say that of the flood of foreigners who have come into the English game, the non-flying Dutchman has been among the very best.

Bergkamp was famously named after his father's hero, Denis

Law. The registrar who filled out the form didn't realise there was just one 'n' in the Lawman's first name. Maria also pops up as his middle name, a common addition for Roman Catholics.

Coached in his early days by his Dutch hero Cruyff, Dennis played as a support striker with responsibility for making as well as taking goals. For three successive seasons he was top league scorer in the Netherlands.

His form inevitably drew the interest of the then mega-rich Italian clubs, and when he moved to Internazionale in 1993 he was hailed as the 'new' van Basten, who had made a massive impact with rivals AC Milan. Bergkamp was nothing like out-and-out striker van Basten, and suffered in comparison. He was much more of an artistic player, but was unappreciated by the Italian press, many of the fans and also several of his team-mates, who it was claimed froze him out and refused to give him the ball.

Bruce Rioch rescued Dennis from his Milan misery during his brief reign as Arsenal manager, a move that was negotiated by director David Dein.

Suddenly, after the suffocation of the Italian defensive system, Bergkamp found the freedom to roam, and in his energetic new partner Ian Wright found the ideal soul mate to benefit from his intelligent running and inch-perfect passing.

The arrival of Arsene Wenger as the new overlord of Highbury was the big turning point for Bergkamp. Here was somebody who could understand his football language, and Bergkamp was the perfect translator of Wenger's fresh tactical plans on the pitch.

This was how Wenger, in typical philosophic mood, summed up Bergkamp's contribution to Arsenal as he came to the close of his career in 2006:

Dennis has intelligence and class. Class is of course, most of the time, linked to what you can do with the ball, but the intelligence makes you use the technique in an efficient way. It's like somebody who has a big vocabulary but he doesn't say intelligent words, and somebody who has a big vocabulary but he can talk intelligently, and that's what Dennis is all about. What he does, there's always a head and always a brain. And his technique allows him to do what he sees, and what he decides to do.

Let me summarise that by saying Bergkamp was the thinking man's footballer. He was always a thought and a deed ahead of defenders, and he could thread the ball through the eye of a needle.

A hat-trick he scored against Leicester City in 1997–98 is the stuff of legend. For the one and only time his goals came first, second and third in the BBC's *Match of the Day* Goal of the Month competition.

At the end of that season he scored one of the great World Cup goals in a quarter-final win against Argentina in France '98, happily just a Eurostar ride away.

There were just seconds to go with the teams deadlocked when Frank De Boer struck a 60-yard through ball in the air. Bergkamp leapt to collect it in full stride, nipped around defender Roberto Ayala after nutmegging him, and slotted home a perfectly placed shot with the outside of his right boot.

'You can't imagine a goal like that,' Dennis said at the after-match press conference. 'It just happens. You just have to follow your instincts. Once Frank had the ball I sensed it would be coming my way, and he had the same thoughts and played the ball through with a fantastic pass. He has to take a lot of credit for the goal. I just happened to get myself into the right place at the right time.'

Bergkamp was noted more for the quality rather than the quantity of his goals. Probably the best he scored in England came against Newcastle in March 2002. Robert Pires slotted a pass through to him in a crowded Newcastle penalty area. All in the blinking of an eye, Bergkamp – with the ball under his mesmerising control – spun 180 degrees around a bemused close-marking defender and then beat the oncoming goalkeeper with the coolest of finishes. Not surprisingly, it was voted Premiership Goal of the Season.

The goal was recently voted the second best in the history of the Premiership, beaten only by David Beckham's lob from the halfway line for Manchester United against Wimbledon in 1996. Good as that Becks goal was, I would personally have to put Bergkamp's classic piece of individual genius ahead of it.

I have never been one for statistics, but the following fact summed up his impact at Arsenal. He scored 121 goals in 424 appearances in all matches for Arsenal, but the eye-opener is that he 'assisted' in another 166 goals. That is proof positive that the Dutch master was as creative a player as has ever been seen in British football. He was always a delight to the eye, and here's one old pro who doffs his cap to him. Bergkamp would have been considered a great in any era.

40
Alan Shearer

Born: Gosforth, Newcastle-upon-Tyne, 13 August 1970

Career span: 1986–2006

Clubs: Southampton 1986–88 (118 league games, 23 goals); Blackburn Rovers 1992–96 (138 league games, 112 goals); Newcastle United 1996–2006 (303 league games, 148 goals)

England: 63 caps, 30 goals (34 games as captain)
Club honours: 1 Premiership title
Euro '96 Golden Boot winner (5 goals)
Highest ever Premiership scorer with 260 goals
Premiership Player of the First Decade
Footballer of the Year 1994
PFA Player of the Year 1995 and 1997
Awarded an OBE 2001

THERE are a mountain of goals as evidence that Alan Shearer deserves his place here among the footballing masters. I was restricted to how many home-grown players I could select, but the sheer number of Shearer's goals guaranteed him a place.

Cut Shearer and I am sure he would bleed Newcastle black and white, but he was a long time coming home. The Geordies turned him down at the age of 15, famously putting him in goal for part of his trial.

Southampton recognised a goalscorer when they saw one, and he repaid their faith by scoring a hat-trick at the age of 17 in his first full First Division match, against Arsenal. It was just the start of the flood of goals.

Many players who were technically more gifted than Shearer are featured in this book, but few could equal his physical presence in the penalty area. That had something of the old school about it.

I would have loved to play alongside him, because he had the power and determination to create chances for the players around him and I know I would have happily fed off his passes and knock-ons.

He was something in the mould of my old Tottenham and England partner Bobby Smith, not quite so bulky but – like Smithy – he used to let his markers know that he was around. Come to think of it, he could be one of the last physical-contact players we see at top level as referees come down more and more on any player showing a sniff of aggression.

Kenny Dalglish, who knew a thing or three about goalscorers, spent Jack Walker's money to take him to Blackburn in 1992. At £3.6 million he was a steal.

Due almost entirely to his 31-goal input, Blackburn finished runners-up to Manchester United in 1993–94 and the following season went one better by lifting the Premiership title. This time Alan weighed in with 34 goals.

He had two successful S-A-S partnerships, at club level with Chris Sutton and playing with the subtle and talented Teddy Sheringham for England.

Shearer and Sheringham were particularly outstanding in the 4–1 humiliation of Holland at Euro '96. This was the pinnacle of Alan's England career. His five goals earned him the Golden Boot as top scorer in the tournament. He scored twice against Holland, with the second one completing possibly the finest collective goal ever put together by an England team. The Dutch defence was ripped asunder by a sweeping move involving Paul Gascoigne and Sheringham before Shearer pounced, applying an unforgettable finishing touch and nearly breaking the net with a rocket of a shot. They were showing Holland how to play Total football!

Shearer's form throughout Euro '96 convinced the Newcastle manager Kevin Keegan to take him home at last. The player they could have had for the price of a McDonald's beefburger ten years earlier cost Newcastle the little matter of £15 million. And even at that sky-high price it proved a bargain.

He became a god on Tyneside, up there with the likes of idols Jackie Milburn, Malcolm Macdonald and Hughie Gallacher. Alan pounded in 148 Premiership goals on his way to overtaking the all-time 200-goal club record of the immortal Milburn.

Few worthwhile trophies came his way while he was banging in goals galore for Newcastle, but he could not take the blame.

His output was nothing short of phenomenal, and he became the Mr Untouchable of St James' Park. Ruud Gullit took him on in a power struggle and lost. He discovered that Shearer was as politically astute off the pitch as he was tactically aware on it.

Bobby Robson, who filled the hot seat as manager after Kenny Dalglish and Gullit had followed Keegan out of the revolving door at Newcastle, described him as 'a very special player with a very special rapport with the Newcastle fans. He is so special that it can be very difficult managing somebody whom everybody thinks should be an automatic choice. There is not a player on earth who should be an automatic selection, including Alan. He is a good guy, but I was disappointed by his reaction when I made him a substitute. He wants to – and expects to – play in every game.'

For a player who 'put it about a bit' on the pitch, Shearer was unusually reticent about shouting off the pitch – unlike Malcolm 'SuperMouth' Macdonald. It came as a surprise to find him following a career as a BBC television pundit, because he had never been a particularly flowing talker about the game during his footballing career. But now he has found his voice, and he always speaks sense.

A good, solid family man, he managed to stay virtually scandal free throughout his playing days. Club chairman Freddy Shepherd let slip in an unintended tabloid newspaper interview that the directors knew him as 'Mary Poppins' because of his trouble-free, dignified lifestyle.

There was just one sniff of an off-the-pitch incident that made headlines.

By all accounts, Newcastle's players went out on the piss during a break in Dublin in 1997. It developed into one of those daft nights when Belgian defender Philippe Albert was walking around with a traffic cone on his head, and other Newcastle players were reduced to a near comatose state. As they became more and more legless, Irish international Keith Gillespie started flicking bottle tops at Shearer, who warned him that if he didn't stop, he would get a good hiding.

More bottle tops hit Shearer, and in good old-fashioned style our hero invited Gillespie outside. Suddenly the other players looked out of the window to see a pair of legs going up in the air. 'We ran out,' witness David Batty recorded later, 'and saw Gillespie spark out in the gutter. There was blood everywhere. Keith had apparently taken the first swing and Al just turned and decked him.'

Mary Poppins had briefly become more like Marvin Hagler.

Shearer has always been his own man. He surprised everybody when he climbed off the England bandwagon after the Euro 2000 tournament. Skipper of the side, he was just 29 and there seemed plenty of goals he could have added to the 30 he scored in his 63 England appearances.

He decided to retire from the international scene because he felt he owed it to Newcastle to give them his total commitment. It typified his unselfish approach to the game and his devotion to the Magpies.

The goal that gave him most satisfaction was the 201st he scored for Newcastle, which took him past Jackie Milburn's record, netted at home against Portsmouth on 4 February 2006.

'I had grown up with the Milburn legend ringing in my ears,' he said. 'My dad was a great fan of his, and I realised just how much my record-breaking goal meant when the Newcastle fans were still chanting my name five minutes after I had put the ball in the net. It sent a shiver down my spine. I consider it a privilege and an honour just to be mentioned in the same breath as Wor Jackie. To have overtaken him in the record books means so much to me. You have to be a Geordie to know what I am talking about.'

Yes, Alan Shearer would bleed black and white. How long down the line will it be before he returns to his beloved St James' Park wearing the manager's hat? He has now got the necessary coaching certificates, and is waiting in the wings. It would just about complete his perfect relationship with the club he should have joined at 15. I wonder who it was who put him in goal. Perhaps the man who turned down The Beatles?

41

Roy Keane

Born: Cork, Republic of Ireland, 10 August 1971

Career span: 1989–2006

Clubs: Cobh Ramblers 1989–90; Nottingham Forest 1990–93 (114 league games, 22 goals); Manchester United 1993–2005 (326 games, 33 goals); Celtic 2005-06 (10 league games, 1 goal)

Republic of Ireland: 66 caps, 9 goals

Club honours: 7 Premiership titles, 4 FA Cups. 1 Scottish Premier League title, 1 Scottish League Cup, 1 Champions League

Footballer of the Year 2000

PFA Player of the Year 2000

I T was round about the summer of 1991 when Brian Clough told me during an off-camera chat, 'You won't believe this, James, but I've discovered the new Duncan Edwards. His name is Roy Keane. Trouble is he's got a head on him bigger than mine!'

Over the next fifteen years I watched from the sidelines as Keane went out and proved that a) he was one of the few players who could be mentioned in the same sentence as the legendary Duncan Edwards, and b) he did have an inflated ego of Clough proportions. Not that I would dare say it to his face. He is one of the fiercest competitors I have ever seen on a football field – right out of the Dave Mackay/Graeme Souness school of hard men. Eleven red cards with United proved that the wild man from Cork often took his competitive zeal into the unacceptable jungle of violence.

Cloughie, of course, was not put off by his intimidating physical presence. Once, after an FA Cup-tie in which Keane had cost Nottingham Forest victory with a clumsy mistake, Cloughie greeted him as he came into the dressing room with a punch in the face that knocked him to the floor.

Keane accepted it as part and parcel of being a professional footballer, and said he might have done the same thing in Cloughie's shoes (Sunderland players be warned!). But the two of them were soon at loggerheads again when contract negotiations led to the Forest boss calling Keane 'a greedy child'.

Keane's contract included an escape clause if Forest were relegated, and when they went down he agreed to join Blackburn Rovers after talks with manager Kenny Dalglish. At the last minute he informed Blackburn that he was signing for Manchester United instead. It was reported that Dalglish's familiar red-cheeked face turned a nasty shade of purple, but Keane shrugged it off with the simple comment, 'I changed my mind.'

Keane was at the heart of United's charge to seven Premiership titles, four FA Cup triumphs and the remarkable 1999 treble that included the Champions League, although he missed that final because of a suspension.

Like all great holding midfield players, he kept things simple. He saw his main job as gathering the ball and giving it to gifted forwards to carry on the move while he followed up in support.

His style was reminiscent of the fifties' push-and-run. There was nobody better in the modern game at winning the ball, sometimes with tackles that made the earth shudder.

Throughout all the successful years with Manchester United, Keane – a driving, demanding captain – was never far from the edge of controversy. I helped log some of his more contentious moments for a television documentary, and here are some of the headline-hogging moments of the always-simmering man from Cork:

1991: Following a friendly against the United States in Boston, the Republic of Ireland players were allowed a night out. The next morning's departure was set for 7.30 but the rest of the team had to sit on the coach for thirty minutes, waiting for Keane to appear. Furious team manager Jack Charlton said, 'Nineteen years old, your first trip, do you have any idea how long we've been waiting?' Jack was speechless as the teenager shrugged and said, 'I didn't ask you to wait, did I?'

1997: Keane suffered a season-ending knee injury while trying to (his description) 'trip' Alf Inge Haaland, who told him as he writhed on the floor, 'Stop faking it.' Fast forward three years, and Keane got his long-awaited chance for revenge and flattened Norwegian Haaland with a vicious, studs-up, knee-high tackle during a Manchester derby. Keane later went on record with a comment that caused even more fuss than his tackle: 'I'd waited long enough. I f****** hit him hard. The ball was there (I think). "Take that you c***," I told him. "And don't ever stand over me again sneering about fake injuries. And tell your pal [David] Wetherall there's some for him as well." I didn't wait for the referee Mr Elleray to show the red card. I turned and walked to the dressing room.'

1999: Keane's well-publicised binge drinking came to a head when he was arrested in Manchester two days after United had won the Premiership on their way to the historic treble of League,

FA Cup and European Champions League. He was accused of assaulting a woman in a pub, and spent the night in a cell until manager Alex Ferguson arrived to get him released without charge. Keane admitted that his drinking needed to be brought under control, and said that he had binged in Cork, Dublin, Nottingham and Manchester. 'It has all added up to aggravation in each city,' he said.

2000: Keane gave a verbal tongue lashing to a section of the United supporters after a Champions League match against Dynamo Kiev, breaking an unwritten rule never to criticise your fans. 'Sometimes you wonder, do they understand the game of football?' he said. 'We're 1–0 up, then there are one or two stray passes and they're getting on players' backs. It's just not on. At the end of the day they need to get behind the team. Away from home our fans are fantastic, I'd call them the hardcore fans. But at home they have a few drinks and probably the prawn sandwiches, and they don't realise what's going on out on the pitch. I don't think some of the people who come to Old Trafford can spell "football", never mind understand it.'

2001: He accused the Republic of Ireland officials of treating the players like second-class citizens. Following a 4–0 victory in Cyprus, Keane complained, 'Where we trained for the match in Ireland was abysmal and it has been for as long as I've known it. I also feel disgusted about our seating arrangements on the flight out here, when the officials were sitting in the first-class seats and the players were sitting behind. For me that's simply not right. The priority has to be the team – and I don't think that has always been the case here.'

2002: Keane had a monumental slanging match with Republic of Ireland boss Mick McCarthy in front of his team-mates in Saipan on the eve of World Cup 2002. Witnesses reported that the Irish skipper said, 'Mick, you're a liar . . . you're a f***ing w****r. I didn't rate you as a player, I don't rate you as a manager, and I don't rate you as a person. You're a f***ing w****r and you can stick your World Cup up your arse. The only reason I have any dealings with you is that somehow you are the manager of my country! You can stick it up your bollocks.' He was sent home without kicking a ball. That incident made such an impact worldwide that they have produced stage plays about it in Ireland.

2004: As United lost their grip on their Premiership title in 2004, Keane criticised unidentified younger players, accusing them of not pulling their weight. 'We have one or two young players who have done very little in the game,' he accused. 'They need to remember that and not slack off. They need to remember just how lucky we all are to play for Manchester United and show that out on the pitch.'

2005: Coming close to the end of his career at Old Trafford, he verbally attacked seven of his team-mates on the club's TV channel, MUTV. Keane's most vicious criticism was reserved for the club's record signing, Rio Ferdinand. 'Just because you are paid £120,000 a week and play well for twenty minutes against Tottenham, you think you are a superstar,' he said. 'The younger players have been let down by some of the more experienced players. They are just not leading. There is a shortage of characters in this team. It seems to be in this club that you have to play badly to be rewarded.'

When Keane became manager of Sunderland and steered them to the Premiership at the first time of asking, I remembered what Cloughie had told me all those years ago about him being the 'new' Duncan Edwards, and having an ever bigger head than Clough had.

Could Keane, as a manager, develop into the 'new' Brian Clough? Could he become the 'next' Alex Ferguson at Old Trafford?

I wouldn't bet against it. And that would make a few at the Theatre of Dreams choke on their prawn sarnies.

42

Zinedine Zidane

Born: Marseille, France, 23 June 1972

Career span: 1988–2006

Clubs: Cannes 1988–92 (61 league games, 6 goals); Bordeaux 1992–96 (135 league games, 28 goals); Juventus 1996–2001 (151 league games, 24 goals); Real Madrid 2001–06 (155 league games, 37 goals)

France: 108 caps, 31 goals

Club honours: 2 Italian league championships, 1 Spanish league championship, 1 Champions League

World Cup 1998, runner-up 2006

European Championship 2000

Italian Footballer of the Year 1997 and 2001

European Footballer of the Year 1998

Best Player of Tournament Euro 2000

Uefa Best Player of the Last 50 Years 2004

World Player of the Year 1998, 2000 and 2003

Golden Ball winner World Cup 2006

THERE has never been a footballer quite like Zinedine Zidane. In all my years playing and watching the game I have not seen anybody play with his style and technique. He shielded the ball in a unique way, dribbled as if the ball was glued to his feet, and made it all seem as easy and effortless as a walk in the park. There was just one weakness – a short-fuse temper that was likely to explode at any second.

How sad that one of the few footballers who can challenge even Pelé and Maradona for the 'Greatest of All Time' accolade will be best remembered for his anger rather than his artistry. It was famously said of him that he 'smiles like Saint Teresa and grimaces like a serial killer'.

One of the theories about Zidane (known in France by his nickname 'Zizou') is that he was driven throughout his football career by an inner rage, and was always sensitive to racist comments about his Algerian ancestry.

He was sent off fourteen times, and often the trigger that made him lose his temper could be traced to an opponent making a remark about his family background. It became common knowledge in the game that he could be easily wound up, and players with a quarter of his ability would make him lose his concentration – and often his rag – by verbally insulting him.

When in the right restrained mood, he would punish them with football that was almost supernatural, but on the bad days a red mist would descend and he would answer the taunts with physical retribution.

There was no more telling or sadder evidence of this than in the last game of his career when the eyes of the world were on him. A billion television viewers saw him explode with anger during extra time in the 2006 World Cup final between France and Italy. Suddenly he charged at Italian defender Marco Materazzi and butted him in the chest like a billy goat with its balls on fire.

Materazzi went down and Zidane went off, apparently after the referee had been told in his earpiece what the fourth official had seen on the television action replays. Lip-reading experts claimed that what Materazzi said to detonate the Zidane temper was, 'You're the son of a terrorist whore, so just f*** off.'

It was well known that Zidane was ultra sensitive to any mention of terrorism, because his father had been falsely accused by French fascists of being a Harki (an Algerian who fought for the French during the War of Independence).

Zidane's version was that Materazzi kept tugging his shirt, and he claimed, 'I told him if he wanted my shirt that much he could have it after the game, but he said he would rather have my sister.'

That hardly justified the moment of madness that brought sudden shame to Zidane, who had been head and shoulders above any player in the tournament as he held his passing-out parade in front of the biggest audience in sport.

It was nothing new for Zidane to self-destruct in a major match. He was red-carded for head-butting Hamburg's Jochen Kientz during a Champions League match when he was at Juventus, and he was in trouble for stomping on Faoud Amin of Saudi Arabia during the 1998 World Cup finals.

He used his head much more intelligently in the 1998 World Cup final against Brazil, nodding in two superb goals from corner kicks to put France on the way to a stunning 3–0 victory over Brazil.

Many football followers throughout France, Italy and Spain will tell you that he was the greatest playmaker of them all. We might have got to see more of him in England because Kenny Dalglish had him on his wish-list of players when he took over at Blackburn, but Jack Walker, the chairman bankrolling Kenny's ambitions, looked at the list and asked, 'Why do we want this fella Zidane when we have Tim Sherwood?'

Those who witnessed his early performances for Bordeaux claim he played better football while he was there than he did anywhere else in the future, because he performed without pressure and was always making the impossible look possible.

Heavy responsibility at Juventus robbed him of some of his adventurous spirit. The Italian media, who had previously fallen in love with the charming, outgoing Frenchman Michel Platini, were unhappy that Zidane was so reclusive off the pitch. He avoided the celebrity roundabout, and was happiest at home with his Spanish dancer wife, Véronique, and their four sons.

But this basically shy man still produced enough magic on the pitch for Juventus to persuade Real Madrid to part with a world record £47.2 million for him in 2001. He repaid a lot of the huge fee with the winning goal – a spectacular volley – in the 2002 Champions League final against Bayer Leverkusen at Hampden Park.

David Beckham got to play in the same Real attack (they became close friends), and described him simply as 'the greatest footballer in the world'.

In 2004 a Uefa jubilee poll put him ahead of all the footballers who had performed with European clubs throughout the previous fifty years. That meant Johan Cruyff, Eusebio, Di Stefano, Puskas and George Best trailed in his wake. Another poll in France had him voted the most popular of all Frenchmen. It seemed that everybody loved Zizou, but he had still not conquered those inner demons.

Zidane ended his last game with Real in tears as the capacity crowd at the Bernabeu continually chanted 'Merci' throughout the final club match of his career.

Then it was on to Germany for World Cup 2006 and his final shots. He managed to get himself booked and suspended in the second match for petulantly pushing a South Korean defender, but after missing one game he returned to steer France through to the final with a series of match-winning performances against Spain, Brazil and Portugal.

He put France into a 1–0 lead against Italy in the final with a penalty that crashed against the underside of the bar and crossed the line by inches. That goal made him only the fourth player (along with Pelé, Paul Breitner and Vavá) to have scored in two World Cup finals.

Everything was set for him to make a glorious exit from the world stage. Then came the red mist and a head-butt that over-shadowed all that had gone before.

As I said at the start, there has never been a footballer quite like him – whether you are measuring him by his talent or his temperament. I don't think Tim Sherwood can quite be mentioned in the same breath.

43

Ryan Giggs

Born: Cardiff, 29 November 1973

Career span: 1991–

Club: Manchester United (504 league games, 98 goals; 716 games in total, 141 goals, so far)

Wales: 64 caps, 12 goals

Club honours: 9 Premiership titles, 4 FA Cups, 2 League Cups, 1 Champions League

Awarded an OBE 2007

IT is not often that you are a witness to the start of a legend, but I was there when the Ryan Giggs fairytale began. I was with Gary Newbon's talented Central Television team in the mid-1980s when we put together a short feature on the England schoolboys' team. We were concentrating on local lads, but my eye was taken by the Manchester-based captain of the team, a left-winger called Ryan Wilson.

From the second I saw him with a ball at his feet I knew he had quality, and was convinced I was watching an England international footballer of the future. Then I was told there was no chance of that because he was Welsh, and that he was on the books of Manchester City.

The next time he came to my attention he was calling himself Ryan Giggs – and he was being unveiled by Alex Ferguson as a future star with Manchester United!

Crafty Alex had nipped in and signed him from under the noses of Manchester City, where he had spent his days on associated schoolboy terms. It was one of Fergie's greatest ever signings. He knew how important it was to get Ryan under contract, and went personally to his house to clinch the deal.

Ryan was born in Cardiff, the son of black rugby league player Danny Wilson. He elected to take the maiden name of his white mother Lynne Giggs when the marriage broke up. 'I want the world to know that I am my mother's son,' he said in a rare interview, having described his father as 'a bit of a rogue'.

There was never any truth in the myth that Ryan could have played for England along with the other Fergie Fledglings David Beckham, Paul Scholes and the Neville brothers. He lived for the first seven years of his life in Cardiff, and both his parents and all his grandparents were Welsh. He played for England schoolboys because teams were chosen according to districts rather than nationalities. I hope that clears it up, because it is a recurring topic when I travel the country with my road show. Ryan did not *choose* to play for Wales rather than England. He had no option. End of argument.

He represented Wales in 64 international matches, and could easily have topped the century mark but for preferring not to play in meaningless friendlies.

What a shame for football fans that he has in common with George Best, Alfredo Di Stefano and Jim Baxter the fact that he never played on the World Cup finals stage. He deserved to be seen performing at the highest level by a worldwide audience.

His success story with Manchester United has been phenomenal. He has a record nine Premiership titles under his belt, four FA Cup winner's medals and was, of course, a key member of the United team that pulled off the 'Impossible Treble' in 1999, culminating with the Champions League trophy.

Ryan's behaviour on the pitch has been exemplary, and fairly scandal free away from football, give or take a few kiss-and-tell stories by ladies claiming they have been bedded by him. Alex Ferguson must take much of the credit for helping Ryan avoid the traps into which George Best fell. He protected him like a mother hen early in his career, and refused to let him give any interviews to the media until he was past 20. In many ways I thought he was over-protective, but he was putting Ryan's welfare first at all times.

Few British-born left-wingers have been in his class. Before he developed hamstring problems, he could run like the wind and keep control of the ball while in full stride. And even when slowing down in the autumn of his career, he has managed to dismantle defences with clever dribbling and wise positioning that can come only from experience.

While mainly a creator of goals, he has also put together a gallery of memorable solo efforts. One will always crop up when great goals are recalled. Flashback to the 1999 FA Cup semi-final replay between Manchester United and Arsenal at Villa Park. Regardless of the result it was going to be an historic match because it would be the last replay of a semi-final. In future, deadlocked matches would be decided by the dreaded penalty shoot-out.

But Giggs made sure the match would go down in the history books for containing what has been voted the greatest FA Cup goal ever scored. The game was into extra time and United were down to ten men when Giggs gathered a rare misplaced pass by Arsenal captain Patrick Vieira. He was 40 yards from the Gunners goal and there seemed little imminent danger. Less than ten seconds later the ball was in the back of the net, and a queue of Arsenal defenders were on their arses wondering how the heck that had happened.

With the ball at his educated feet, Giggs had set off on a zigzagging run that had the most disciplined defence in the country at sixes and sevens. Vieira, racing in front of him to try to atone for his mistake, was the first to be dispatched as the Welsh whirlwind went past Arsenal defenders as if they were Madame Tussaud dummies. Class tacklers Lee Dixon, Martin Keown and Tony Adams were left kicking thin air as Giggs raced into the penalty area and beat goalkeeper David Seaman with a rising drive that whooshed into the roof of the net from a tight angle.

Rarely one to show off on the football pitch, Giggs realised he had achieved something special and he whipped off his shirt as he did a lap of honour, chased by his celebrating team-mates. They knew that his astonishing goal had kept United en route for the Treble.

What is often forgotten in assessments of Giggs is his unselfish work for the team. With his individual skill, it would be easy for him to sit out on the wing and wait for the ball to be delivered to him. But, even when an established fixture in the side, he was always prepared to run himself into the ground, helping out in defence, collecting the ball and trying to bring fellow forwards into the game. Like Gianfranco Zola, he is hugely respected by rival fans, and you always find him being appreciated and applauded at away grounds.

He puts in a lot of unsung effort for charities, and is outspoken against racism in sport. 'A lot of people don't realise that my father is black,' he has said. 'But when I went to school, I used to get racist taunts. Half my family is black and I feel close to their culture and their colour. I am proud of my black roots. I do not wish to hide my origins, nor do I seek to make it a subject of conversation. I am what I am.'

It has been a sheer joy watching him progress from schoolboy to superstar. Dare I say it – what a pity he was not English. Every England manager since the early 1990s has, I promise, had exactly the same thought.

44

David Beckham

Born: Leytonstone, East London, 2 May 1975

Career span: 1992–

Clubs: Manchester United 1992–2003 (265 league games, 62 goals); Preston, loan 1995 (5 league games, 2 goals); Real Madrid 2003–07 (115 league games, 13 goals); Los Angeles Galaxy 2007–

England: 97 caps, 17 goals (58 games as captain)

Club honours: 6 Premiership titles, 2 FA Cups, 1 Spanish championship, 1 Champions League

BBC Sports Personality of the Year 2001

World Footballer of the Year runner-up 1999 and 2001

GOLDEN Balls David Beckham always brings out the Jekyll and Hyde in me. As a footballer I rate him up there among the best we have produced, even if he is more one-footed than Long John Silver. The thing that irritates me is the circus that surrounds him, and I wonder just how much more he might have achieved in the game had he not generated so many off-the-field distractions.

Maybe I am a jealous old git because of the millions he has made, both out of football and – more so – from his commercial activities. Financial experts tell me he turns over more than £35 million a year from outside interests. That's more than the entire Spurs double team earned collectively in their entire lives.

I have to be fair and admit he has performed wonders for a kid from East London, who was not exactly scholarly. Becks was typical of that breed (and I suppose I have to include myself among them) described as having their brains in their feet. He grew up learning the game on the same playing fields in the Leyton and Leytonstone area where a generation earlier a young Bobby Moore had taken his first kicks.

I often get involved in arguments about who has been the best passer of a ball in English football. Beckham has huge support from the under-40s, and Glenn Hoddle quite rightly gets into the frame. But those of us who were around in the 1950s and 1960s will tell you that Johnny Haynes could match Becks for accuracy over long distances. And, as I've said in my chapter on Haynsie, the big difference was that Johnny could do it with either foot.

But there have been few players in the history of the game with a right foot to compare with Beckham's. Like most people, I first became aware of just what he could do with that golden boot of his when he scored an awesome goal from the halfway line against Wimbledon at Selhurst Park in August 1996.

His crosses from the right have created dozens of goals for Manchester United, Real Madrid and England, and his swerving free-kicks from just outside the box strike fear into any goalkeepers facing him. It is a mystery to me why, with his deadly accuracy, he has not scored many more goals with his right foot in open play.

You have to hand it to Becks for having character and courage. He was crucified for stupidly getting himself sent off in the World Cup finals match against Argentina in France '98. For much of the next domestic season he had to run a gauntlet of hate from knuckle-headed fans who booed and jeered him at every away match. They even burned an effigy of him, and one newspaper wasted ink filling a double-page spread with Beckham's head as a dartboard.

This, in my view, was way over the top and I wondered if Beckham would ever be able to hold up his head again. But he refused to let it affect his concentration and in the season after his World Cup disgrace he produced some of the best football of his career as he helped United to their historic treble of Premiership, FA Cup and European Champions League.

It was about this time that his romance and subsequent marriage to Victoria Adams, the far-from-Posh one of the Spice Girls, started getting the headlines rather than what he achieved on the football field. Becks had we old pros cringing with embarrassment as he became involved in modelling, outrageous hairstyles, and all the trappings of a false celebrity world. And there was Posh sitting on the Parkinson Show telling the nation that Becks wore her knickers. I could hear the ghosts of great footballers past, such as Sir Stanley Matthews, Billy Wright and Danny Blanchflower, wailing in disbelief.

Thank goodness for David's sake that he could play the game better than most. He gave one of the most determined individual displays ever by an England player when they needed to avoid defeat against Greece to qualify outright for the 2002 World Cup. He capped a magnificent one-man display by scoring with one of his signature free-kicks in the last minute. He was voted BBC TV Sports Personality of the Year on the back of that stunning performance, an amazing turnaround for somebody who had been a hated figure of fun after France '98.

He was lucky to have an England manager in Sven-Goran Eriksson who gave him unqualified support regardless of his form, and there were times when we wondered whether it was skipper Becks and some of the senior players running the team rather than the slippery Swede.

David's strong character shone through again in the spring of 2002 when a broken metatarsal bone in his left foot threatened to put him out of the World Cup finals. He battled back to fitness in time to take his place in the team, and provided one of the highlights of the tournament against the old enemy Argentina. His sweetly struck penalty gave England in general and Beckham in particular a revenge win four years after Argentina had provided him with the lowest point of his career.

We heard on the grapevine that all was not sunshine and flowers between Becks and his mentor Sir Alex Ferguson, who continually had to bite his tongue as the Becks–Posh Empire grew to monster size and overshadowed his football.

The Becks–Ferguson relationship hit rock bottom when, in one of his famous dressing-room furies after a defeat by Arsenal in February 2003, Sir Alex kicked a football boot that smashed into Beckham's pretty-boy face and cut him over an eye. You could not make it up.

United and Beckham had been good for each other – six Premiership titles, two FA Cups and the Champions League crown – but a parting of the ways was inevitable.

While Manchester United were busy negotiating to sell him to Barcelona, Beckham's advisers opened talks with Real Madrid and it was at the Bernabeu where the Becks circus next pitched its tent.

Raul, the Prince of Real, had it in his contract that he had to wear the No. 7 shirt that Beckham had made his own with United and England. Cleverly, Becks (no doubt with the help of financial advisers) elected to wear No. 23, because it was the number associated with basketball legend Michael Jordan. It is an indication of his worldwide popularity that thousands of the shirts sold, paying off a huge chunk of his £25 million fee.

Despite never really setting the Bernabeu alight, Beckham became hugely popular with the Real fans, and friends with star players Zinedine Zidane, Ronaldo and Roberto Carlos. He was also very popular with the ladies, and a spate of kiss-and-tell stories in the tabloids dented the image of the 'golden couple' Posh and Becks.

Beckham quit as England captain after a disappointing challenge for the World Cup in 2006. With tears in his eyes, he told a packed press conference:

Peter Taylor gave me the greatest honour of my career six years ago in making me the captain of England, fulfilling my childhood dream. It has been an honour and a privilege to have captained our country and I want to stress that I wish to continue to play for England and look forward to helping both the new captain and Steve McClaren in any way I can. I came to this decision some time ago but I had hoped to announce it on the back of a successful World Cup. Sadly, that wasn't to be.

This decision has been the most difficult of my career to date. But after discussing it with my family and those closest to me I feel the time is right.

Our performance during this World Cup has not been enough to progress further, and both myself and all the players regret it and are hurt more than people realise.

I wish to thank all the players for their support during my time as captain, as well as Peter Taylor, Sven and all the coaches.

I would also like to thank the press and, of course, all the England supporters who have been great to me and my team-mates. I want them to know for me it has been an absolute honour.

Finally, I have lived the dream, I am extremely proud to have

*worn the armband and been captain of England and for that I
will always be grateful.*

One thing went wrong in the Beckham master plan. Steve
McClaren announced that he didn't want him for his new-look
England team. But Not-So-Super Mac made such a mess of his
early games in charge of England that he had to recall one of the
few footballers who could at least be counted on to pass the ball
to a player wearing the same colour shirt.

Beckham ended his hot-and-cold association with Real by
playing a walk-on part in their regaining of the *La Liga* championship in 2007 before taking the Posh-and-Becks circus to the perfect
setting of California. Perhaps it would have been more fitting if
they had pitched the tent in Disneyland. Dropping Beckham and
his artistic right foot into the world of American football – where
'soccer is a kick in the grass' – was the equivalent of asking Constable
to paint by numbers.

If he sees through his five-year contract with Los Angeles Galaxy,
it's estimated that he will earn more than (pass the sick bag, Alice)
$250 million. Yes, he's come a long way from Leytonstone down
in East London to the American West Coast.

Far be it from me to try to give Becks any advice, but I just
happen to know the area where he is based quite well. If he drives
his Hummer about an hour south to Blythe in Riverside County,
California, in the Palo Verde Valley, he will find at the crossroads
with Lake Havasu State Park a traditional American diner that
serves the best cheeseburger and deep-fried chips in the whole of
the United States.

David, take your lovely wife there and let her gorge herself. Get
some flesh on those ribs of hers. I think you can afford it.

Oh yes, and from one East Londoner to another – good luck,
mate. You've done the East End and yourself proud.

45

Ronaldo

Born: Rio de Janeiro, 22 September 1976

Career span: 1993–

Clubs: Cruzeiro 1993–94 (14 league games, 12 goals); PSV Eindhoven 1994–96 (45 league games, 42 goals); Barcelona 1996–97 (37 league games, 34 goals); Inter Milan 1997–2002 (68 league games, 49 goals); Real Madrid 2002–07 (146 league games, 104 goals); AC Milan 2007– (13 games, 10 goals, so far)

Brazil: 97 caps, 62 goals

Club honours: 1 Brazilian Cup, 1 Dutch Cup, 1 Spanish League, 1 Spanish Cup, 1 European Cup-Winners' Cup, 1 Uefa Cup

World Cup 2002, (non-playing squad member 1994)

World Cup runner-up 1998

Fifa World Footballer of the Year 1996, 1997 and 2002

European Footballer of the Year 1997 and 2002

European Golden Boot 1997

World Cup Golden Ball 1998

World Cup Golden Boot 2002

No player in my all-star selection has had more of a roller-coaster ride of a career than Ronaldo. He has somersaulted between being hailed as the greatest footballer on the planet to being assailed as a big fat flop.

We watched in astonishment in the 1998 World Cup final when he played for Brazil against France like a man in a trance. The player saddled with the title of the 'new' Pelé performed as if his boots were rooted in shifting sands.

Horrendous after-match stories suggested that Ronaldo had suffered a convulsive fit, and Brazil tried to play down the story that he had taken part only because of pressure put on them by their kit sponsors. Football was now in the throttling hands of the commercial companies.

In the previous two seasons Ronaldo had been elected Fifa World Footballer of the Year, but suddenly his career was on the floor. There seemed no way he could regain his standing as the world's number one player.

Things went from bad to worse for Ronaldo. An injured knee forced him out of the game for most of the following season. In his comeback match for Inter Milan against Lazio he damaged the same knee again and was stretchered off in tears. Doctors feared he would never be able to play again.

While off the sports pages Ronaldo was a frequent visitor to the gossip columns with his nightclubbing and sizzling romances. He had a short marriage to the beautiful model and leading European ladies footballer Milene Domingues, and then returned to his womanising ways. I wonder what all the ladies saw in the bald, buck-toothed fat boy? As Mrs Merton once famously said to Debbie McGee, 'Tell me, what is it that attracted you to the bald, short millionaire Paul Daniels?'

I had been tipped off about Ronaldo's potential early in his career by my old mate Bobby Robson. The Brazilian – then considered a boy wonder – came under Bobby's wing when he was coaching at PSV Eindhoven. 'Ronaldo was the most naturally talented footballer I ever worked with,' said Bobby. 'He was the nearest thing I had ever seen to Pelé. His major problem was that he was always having to watch his waistline. If he ate the wrong food he could quickly put on the pounds.'

When Bobby moved on to Barcelona he convinced the Spaniards that they should invest in Ronaldo. He made a tremendous impact in one season with Barca, scoring 34 goals in just 37 games. Most of his goals were of the spectacular type – he'd make his trademark runs from the halfway line before thumping in long-range shots. He netted the winning goal in the 1997 European Cup-Winners' Cup final against Paris Saint-Germain.

Ronaldo then sickened Barcelona when – still only 20 – he negotiated a controversial transfer to Inter Milan for a fee of £18 million, money that he used to buy out his contract with the Spanish club. It took a series of meetings by the top brass of Fifa before they rubber-stamped the unique deal, which was surely the work of his agents rather than the shy boy from Brazil.

His double knee injury wrecked his adventure at Inter Milan. He travelled to the United States and Paris for emergency treatment while missing an entire season. The 2002 World Cup finals seemed a dream too far, but he showed he had tremendous character to go with his talent. He worked off unwanted pounds and got himself fit to prove he should still be recognised as the world's number one footballer.

From being written off as finished, he came roaring back to capture the Golden Boot with eight goals as he fired Brazil to their fifth World Cup. This meant – added to the four he had scored in France '98 – he had equalled Pelé's Brazilian record of 12 goals in World Cup finals.

For an amazing third time he was elected Fifa World Footballer of the Year, and transferred to Real Madrid for a then record £33 million. He did not receive any good-luck messages from Barcelona as he returned to Spain.

His debut with Real was delayed because of injury until October 2002, but he quickly made up for lost time with 23 *La Liga* goals in his shortened season. He was given a standing ovation at Old Trafford after scoring a hat-trick in a Champions League match.

Despite his 104 goals in 146 *La Liga* games for Real, a section of the supporters continually jeered him if his standards dropped. He became disillusioned after another series of injuries, and upset the Real fans with a brutally honest assessment of them: 'I have never understood the Bernabeu fans, which are not the same people who show me their affection and support in the streets. I have never felt at home; they have never treated me with affection and care. What we need is the fans to be behind the team not against us. I am used to being whistled at in disapproval. I get picked on after a single mistake. It is very discouraging. Nevertheless, I will keep on doing my best for the team's benefit.'

Spectators looked on in disbelief when he turned up for the 2006 World Cup finals looking fat and unfit. Brazilian fans heckled him as he struggled to show any of his old pace and power, yet he still managed to score two goals against Japan to equal, with 14 goals, the all-time aggregate World Cup finals scoring record held by *Der Bomber* Gerd Muller.

It was embarrassing to watch Ronaldo haul his overweight frame around the pitch, but his natural goalscoring instinct showed against Ghana when he celebrated his record-breaking fifteenth World Cup finals goal. He became only the second player ever to score at least three goals in three World Cup finals (Jürgen Klinsmann was the first).

Ronaldo never forgot his Brazilian roots, and often talked about how he had been brought up in a poverty-stricken family. He showed his compassionate side by joining a United Nations team committed to fighting world poverty, but he got little thanks for it when, on a return to Rio, he was beaten up by three thugs and had his car stolen.

It was obvious that Ronaldo's days at Real were numbered when coach Fabio Capello publicly criticised him for being overweight. He preferred to select the slimmer, fitter Ruud van Nistelrooy ahead of him. 'It breaks my heart,' Ronaldo said. 'The coach has made it clear that he does not want me, and so I must find another solution. I am a professional and I want to keep playing.'

In January 2007 the 30-year-old Ronaldo bought out his contract and moved back to Milan – this time with Inter's bitter rivals AC, where he hooked up with Kaka, the Brazilian who has been called the 'new' Ronaldo.

At his absolute peak, Ronaldo was, in my opinion, up there with Pelé, but his continual battle with a spreading waistline and a sequence of horrible injuries means that in the final analysis he has to be rated outside the top six.

46
Thierry Henry

Born: Paris, 17 August 1977

Career span: 1995–

Clubs: Monaco 1995–98 (110 league games, 20 goals); Juventus 1998–99 (16 league games, 3 goals); Arsenal 1999–2007 (254 league games, 174 goals); Barcelona 2007–

France: 91 caps, 39 goals

Club honours: 1 French league title, 2 Premiership titles, 3 FA Cups

World Cup 1998

World Cup runner-up 2006

European Championship 2000

European Golden Boot 2004 and 2005
Footballer of the Year 2003, 2004 and 2006
PFA Player of the Year 2003 and 2004
Fifa World Footballer of the Year runner-up 2003 and 2004

T does not seem that long ago since the many Arsenal fans among my friends – the Groaning Gooners I call them – were moaning and groaning about what a waste of money Thierry Henry had been. This is when he failed to find the back of the net in his first ten games with what was then the Highbury-based club.

Now, va-va-voom, these same Arsenal supporters are in mourning, and moaning because he has taken his God-given gifts to Barcelona. Even after his defection they worship him as the greatest footballer ever to pull on the famous red-and-white shirt. It was, after all, his record haul of goals that played a big part in helping put the deposit down on their magnificent new Emirates stadium.

Before his switch to Spain, there was a common denominator in Henry's success at two clubs – Monaco and Arsenal – and that was manager Arsene Wenger, who can read Henry like a French book.

When he first took Henry under his wing as a kid at Monaco, Wenger realised that Thierry had the pace to unsettle any defence. He is one of the few players in my list who could give Paco Gento a run for his money over 100 metres.

Wenger moulded Henry into a left-sided attacking player, making the most of his sprint speed and encouraging and educating the impressionable youngster. He loaded him with advice not only on developing his football skills but also on how to live an athlete's life with the right diet, discipline and attitude.

Master and pupil were parted when Wenger moved to Japan and Henry – after helping Monaco become French champions – switched to *Serie A* with Juventus.

Without Wenger to show the way, Henry was like a little boy lost in the suffocating world of Italian football. He scored just three goals in 16 appearances for Juventus, where – continually warming the substitute's bench – his confidence hit an all-time low.

Meantime his mentor Arsene Wenger had taken over as the 'Professor of football' at Highbury, where his refreshing ideas on tactics, diet and training were having a revolutionary effect. When Wenger decided he needed a replacement for the magnificent but moody Nicolas Anelka, he rescued Henry from his miserable existence at Juventus in return for a £10.5 million fee.

It took Henry those goalless opening ten matches to find his feet, and then he grew into one of the giants of the game. He overtook the ebullient Ian Wright and golden-oldie Cliff Bastin as the most prolific goalscorer in Arsenal's history, and he was the main motivator of the team that won two Premiership titles, including the astonishing 2003–04 season when the Gunners were unbeaten.

It was not only Henry's devastating finishing that took the eye, but also his unselfish contribution to the team effort as Arsenal sliced open defences like skilled surgeons with some of the best passing-movement football I have ever seen at club level. His understanding with Dennis Bergkamp and Robert Pires seemed almost telepathic, and he had an assist in nearly as many goals as he scored. With my Spurs blood it was hard to admit, but Arsenal were looking as good if not better than the exceptional Tottenham 'double' side of 1960–61. And it was that man Henry who was at the centre of it all, and making me wonder if perhaps he – rather than Bergkamp – was the best foreign footballer ever to take the English pound.

Most of his goals are things of rare beauty, and two in particular stick in the memory. Playing against Manchester United at Highbury in 2000, he collected a pass when standing 22 yards out, with his back to goal, which was guarded by his old French team-mate Fabien Barthez. He almost nonchalantly flicked the ball into the air, spun on a sixpence and fired a dipping volley past the fingertips of Barthez who was beaten all ends up.

He worked harder for the second goal that I remember above all his others. It was against my old Tottenham team in the North London derby at Highbury in 2002. He controlled the ball on his thigh just outside his own penalty area, brought it down and tamed it before starting off on a trademark sprint. Spurs defenders backed off to cover all exits as he raced towards them. Two made challenges and he swept past them imperiously before making a pretence at a shot that completely disoriented another defender. He then shaped to shoot and this time he meant it, unleashing an unstoppable shot for what was possibly the greatest of his record haul of goals for the Gunners.

Stories of his stunning goals and his consistent form spread around the football world and Real Madrid and Barcelona put in record bids to try to lure him away from Arsenal, but Henry stayed faithful – evidence of the respect he had for his old teacher, Wenger.

Henry had mixed fortunes on the international stage. He top scored for France with three goals on the way to the 1998 World Cup final, but had to watch from the substitutes' bench as they beat Brazil 3–0. Two years later he was again the main marksman as France captured the European Championship.

The 2002 World Cup was a disaster for France in general and Henry in particular. He was red-carded for a reckless, studs-up challenge against Uruguay as France were eliminated at the group stage. What a different story four years later when he scored three times on the way to the Zidane-incident final, in which Italy dramatically beat France on penalties.

For all his high football profile, Henry has usually managed to keep his private life private. But soon after leaving Arsenal he made tabloid headlines when his marriage to English model Nicole Merry was reported to be on the rocks. Just two years earlier he celebrated the arrival of their daughter, Tea, in May 2005 by holding his fingers in a 'T' shape and kissing them after scoring a typical Henry goal against Newcastle.

An intelligent, sensitive man, Henry has made it clear he wants to play his part in changing the world. His best friend is Tony Parker, the American-based French basketball idol, who supported his campaign against racism with this statement:

It's no secret that European soccer is fighting a racism problem, in the crowd and on the field, and no player has done more to exorcise it than Thierry. After cameras caught Spain's national coach using a racist slur to describe Thierry in 2004 [the phrase he used was 'black shit'], he could have lost his cool. Instead, Thierry recruited a host of fellow soccer stars to launch his Stand Up Speak Up *campaign, which raised millions of dollars and unprecedented awareness to fight racism. We talk about the problem all the time. Racism bothers him so much, but he wanted to attack it in a measured, professional manner. Given his upbringing in the ethnically diverse housing projects south-west of Paris, no one can speak out against intolerance better than Thierry. His impact has been immense. Sure, racism hasn't entirely disappeared from the soccer landscape, but you can sense it fading a bit. You've got to give Thierry some credit for this change.*

So, on and off the pitch, Thierry Henry has made his presence felt, and he is one of those players whom you can say has truly played a big part in making it the Beautiful Game. And he has done it with lots of va-va-voom.

It will be fascinating to see what he achieves with Barcelona. He made the surprise move because he sensed that his guru, Arsene Wenger, was becoming unsettled at Highbury, where boardroom politics were suddenly poisoning the atmosphere.

Gooners will look back on his reign as that of King Henry, the football ruler with the Midas touch who brought them their golden years.

47

Michael Owen

Born: Chester, Cheshire, 14 December 1979

Career span: 1996–

Clubs: Liverpool 1996–2004 (216 league games, 118 goals); Real
  Madrid 2004–05 (36 league games, 13 goals); Newcastle United
  2005– (14 league games, 7 goals)

England: 84 caps, 40 goals

Club honours: 1 FA Cup, 2 League Cups, 1 Uefa Cup

BBC Sports Personality of the Year 1998

European Footballer of the Year 2001

THIS will not, I hope, sound too arrogant, but since retiring from
playing the game I've continually seen young footballers described
as the 'new' Jimmy Greaves. The only time I have considered that close
to a fair description was when Michael Owen first emerged at Liverpool.

I could see a mirror image of myself at the same age. We both
made our first-team debuts at 17, Michael for Liverpool and me
for Chelsea. We were of a similar build, stocky and with the same
low centre of gravity. I was strongly reminded of myself by his ball
control and his ability to wrong foot defenders with his acceleration and sudden changes of direction.

When it kept being put to me that he was the 'new' me, I always made a point of saying, 'No, he is the one and only Michael Owen, his own man.'

I have watched his career with close interest, and only a succession of awful injuries has prevented him from becoming arguably England's finest ever striker. Because of restrictions on the number of home-grown players in my list, I had to decide between Michael and Gary Lineker for the top spot. I came down on Owen's side because he is the more natural finisher, while Lineker was manufactured. The architect of goals beat the poacher.

Michael, a bright young man who collected ten GCSEs at school, has never had any doubt about his job in football. 'Some players create, some players score,' he says. 'My role is to put the ball in the net. Sometimes you need to be selfish to do that, but in a crowded penalty area you have no time to stop and ask questions about which is the right option. For me, there is no greater satisfaction than scoring. As much as I know that I have responsibilities to the team effort, I'm always on the look out for the chance to score. It's what I do best.'

At his peak – before injuries robbed him of a yard of pace – Owen was truly world class. Just cast your mind back to the 1998 World Cup finals when he conjured a goal against Argentina that was as good as any ever scored by an England player. He took possession in the halfway circle, and set off on a glory run in which he tricked and powered his way past two Argentinian defenders before finishing his 40-yard surge with a blistering right-foot shot that bulged the net. It was the goal of a born marksman.

It made him just about the most popular person in the country. While David Beckham was getting pilloried for being red-carded in that match against Argentina, Owen was praised to the hilt, and five months after his golden goal, he landed the coveted BBC TV Sports Personality of the Year award.

As well as the 1998 World Cup finals, Owen has played in Euro

2000 and Euro 2004, and in the 2002 and 2006 World Cup finals. He is the only player to have scored in four major tournaments for England. His hat-trick against Germany in Munich in 2001 was as good a threesome as you could ever wish to see, and it was the highlight of a season in which he was elected European Footballer of the Year.

This was all the good news for Owen, but the bad news came in the shape of a series of painful, career-interrupting injuries. He badly damaged a hamstring against Leeds United in 1999, and was sidelined for three months. His comeback was disrupted by another hamstring injury, and from then on he lost a little of the necessary confidence to go flat out when in possession. Once you have suffered a bad hamstring pull, it is always psychologically there in the basement of your mind.

I thought Owen would remain a red-blooded Liverpool player throughout his career, continuing an association that went all the way back to his schooldays. Long before he made headlines as a league player my old partner Ian St John (who knew a thing or three about what was going on at his former Liverpool club) told me, 'We've got a kid at Anfield who is going to score even more goals than you did, Greavsie. His name is Michael Owen, and he's dynamite.'

Owen had been Liverpool's leading goalscorer every year since 1998 when he was tempted by the bait to join the exodus to Real Madrid in 2004. It seemed to me to be the wrong move at the wrong time, and he spent a far from satisfying year with the Spanish giants, often decorating the touchline bench. He got enough action to gather 13 goals in 36 *La Liga* appearances, a strike rate that proved he still had a nose for goal.

There was another surprise from Michael when he returned to England, where he belonged. The belief was that he would go back to his favourite hunting ground at Anfield, but he turned up on the opposite side of the country with Newcastle United.

Owen had hardly settled in with the Magpies when disaster struck. He 'did a Beckham' and fractured his fifth metatarsal during Newcastle's 2–0 defeat at Tottenham on New Year's Eve 2005.

You would not have thought his luck could get worse, but after battling back to fitness and claiming a place in England's 2006 World Cup squad the injury jinx struck again. Playing against Sweden, he suddenly sank to the ground with nobody near him after just two minutes of the group match. Obviously in pain, he was carted off the pitch and out of the World Cup.

The damage was diagnosed as a ruptured anterior cruciate ligament, and led to two major operations in the United States and another long spell out of football.

I know a lot of footballers who would have waved the white flag at this point, taken the insurance money and got out of the game. But Michael is an intelligent, determined man who does not know the meaning of the word surrender.

He fought his way back to fitness yet again, and was swiftly recalled to the England attack in the summer of 2007 by manager Steve McClaren, who was desperate for a finisher of his quality and commitment.

There were all sorts of rumours in the village world of football that he was on his way back to Anfield, where his eventful career had started. The then Newcastle chairman Freddy Shepherd said for public consumption, 'Michael owes us some loyalty and we want him to stay.'

A few days later Shepherd was driving away from Newcastle's training ground when a couple of Scousers with a palm-sized camera asked him if they could have Owen back at Liverpool for a fee of £9 million.

Completely unaware that he was being filmed, Freddy told the supporters, 'For nine million I would f*****g carry him there!'

Within a few hours the hilarious film clip was on the internet on YouTube as evidence that 'Fearless Freddy' had put his foot in his mouth yet again.

It's worth repeating Owen's comments at the press conference when he was welcomed to Newcastle, because it gives an insight into the way modern transfers are conducted:

I've obviously had a bit of a head-spinning couple of days. But to start with, that's not a complaint, as I've had three great clubs in the frame – Newcastle, Liverpool and Real Madrid. The nearer it got to the deadline, the more and more it started becoming clear that Newcastle was going to be my destination. I met with Real's president, directors and managers and then with Rick Parry of Liverpool and manager Rafa Benitez and I came up here and met the Newcastle contingent as well. At the end of it all, I thought it was best for my future and everything to move to Newcastle.

I've been honest all along, right from the start when it was becoming clear Real had bought a couple of new strikers. When it was looking like I wasn't going to be in the starting eleven automatically, I knew it was time to move on. Everyone who knows me knows I want to be playing, not sitting on the bench watching. If Real had said I would start every week, I'm sure I'd still be there now. They made it clear to me there were other strikers in front of me and that meant I wanted to talk to the clubs showing an interest in me in England.

The two teams who were keenest to sign me were Newcastle and Liverpool; and for various reasons I've chosen Newcastle.

Alan Shearer's been a good friend for a long time. Everyone knows it's his last season here and it'll be an honour to play with him for his farewell year. Apart from that, he shares a lot of the same interests as I do – golf, horse racing, football, family life. The chairman's and manager's sincere desire for me to sign and Alan's wise words in my ear were three reasons why I decided it was the best option.

I don't think Liverpool need too much comfort. They're the reigning European champions and had some great success with a new manager.

Obviously I'd been at Liverpool for a long time, I still have friends there and they will continue to be a part of my life because I played there so long. But it's a new chapter now and I'm really looking forward to it. Seeing the reception I've got from the Newcastle fans, I just wish there was a game tomorrow.

I had chats with a lot of teams before settling on a shortlist of two. Obviously Liverpool were interested. You don't become one of England's best clubs by not having great strikers. I'd like to think other teams think I'm a good player but when you've got Ruud van Nistelrooy, Wayne Rooney, Thierry Henry and Dennis Bergkamp, and people like that, the way of the world is that some teams don't need your services at that time.

But I was grateful that two massive clubs were interested in me, and I am delighted to be signing for Newcastle. There is, I am sure, a lot we can achieve together.

As I write, Michael Owen has scored 40 goals in 84 England games and his two goals against Russia at Wembley in a Euro 2008 qualifier showed he had regained his world-class status. History will judge him as one of the pluckiest and also unluckiest strikers. Without the injury hoodoo, he might well already have overtaken Bobby Charlton's all-time record of 49 England goals. The 'old' Jimmy Greaves would have been delighted for him.

48

Ronaldinho

Born: Porto Alegre, Brazil, 21 March 1980
Career span: 1998–
Clubs: Gremio 1998–2001 (110 league games, 37 goals); Paris Saint-Germain 2001–03 (55 league games, 17 goals); Barcelona 2003– (128 league games, 61 goals)
Brazil: 74 caps, 29 goals
Club honours: 1 Rio Grande title (Brazil), 2 Spanish league titles, 1 Champions League
World Cup winner 2002
European Footballer of the Year 2005
World Footballer of the Year 2004 and 2005

E VERY time I watch Ronaldinho play he performs something magical
that convinces me he is the greatest thing on two feet. But then,
when I'm not watching him, he often slips down a gear and finds
himself the centre of criticism for lack of effort and enthusiasm.

Rarely has a player of his quality so split the football public
and alleged experts with his performances. Even in Barcelona,
where he has been worshipped as one of the gods of football, many
supporters have turned against him because they feel he does not
always pull his weight.

And 'weight' is the operative word. It was a slimline Ronaldinho who was a World Cup winner in 2002 and World Footballer of the Year in both 2004 and 2005. He glided through defences like a ballet dancer in football boots, and scored goals with a stunning simplicity that made it all look so ridiculously easy.

How can any English football follower forget his miracle goal for Brazil against England in the 2002 World Cup in Japan. Paul Scholes conceded a free-kick 40 yards out, and there seemed little danger as Ronaldinho placed the ball far out on the right, with the entire England defence packing the penalty area and goalkeeper David Seaman on guard at the back.

Ronaldinho sent the ball on a high, swirling circular tour of the penalty area, and Seaman looked on like a tourist on a sight-seeing trip as the ball sailed into the top corner of the net. It was an astonishing goal, which I thought at first was a fluke. But Ronaldinho insisted that he meant it, and there was plenty of evidence during the next few seasons to prove he had the skill to do exactly what he wanted to with the ball.

Six minutes later we saw the unacceptable face of Ronaldinho. He went into a tackle on Danny Mills with his studs showing, was red-carded, and then took forever to leave the field as he revealed a suspect temperament.

He blew hot and cold in *La Liga* with Barcelona, and there were rumours that he was not training properly. The whippet of the glory years with Brazil was suddenly being whipped for dropping below the skyscraping standards he had set for himself.

The controversy about his increasing weight boiled over when he was pictured exchanging his shirt at the end of Barcelona's Champions League defeat by Liverpool at the Nou Camp in February 2007.

Not to put too fine a point on it, Ronaldinho appeared to be carrying what could be described as a beer belly. Or, perhaps more politely, he was carrying love handles. The Spanish press used the photograph as evidence that he had not been training properly. They reached for the biggest insult they could find, accusing him of becoming 'as fat as Ronaldo'.

Even more buck-toothed than his countryman, Ronaldinho gave a goofy grin and admitted, 'I am not as fit as I should be, and I am going to work at it. There are many reasons why I appear to have put on weight, but I am going on a special diet and will make every effort to regain my old fitness.'

A warning shot came from Brazil coach Dunga. 'It is imperative that Ronaldinho trains properly,' he said as the weight story gathered momentum. 'When he is well physically there is nothing that can stop him. But with the extra weight, he lacks that vital speed, the initial burst that allowed him to get away from his rivals. I would say that Kaka has now overtaken him as our best player. It is up to Ronaldinho to regain his old fitness.'

Before taking a pounding from the press (sorry), Ronaldinho had done enough to be categorised as one of the all-time greats. He had come a long, long way from the beaches of Brazil where he first perfected his ball control.

Arsenal were the first major club to move for him when he began to make a name for himself with his local club Gremio, but there were work permit problems. While negotiations stalled Paris Saint-Germain moved in for him and Ronaldinho surprisingly agreed to sign for them rather than the cluster of major clubs who were now on his trail.

He was not the first – and will not be the last – footballer to be sucked in by Paris nightlife, and PSG manager Luis Fernandez was soon complaining that Ronaldinho was too interested in the wrong sort of clubs. There were lots of legs on show, but not of the footballing variety. Ronaldinho quietened down after becoming engaged to top French model Alexandra Paressant.

All the clubs who had been chasing him while he was in Brazil kept a close watch on his progress in Paris, and when he announced in 2003 that he was disillusioned about PSG's lack of success they came rushing in for him.

Barcelona won the race for his signature, just ahead of Manchester United. He cost £21 million, the price dictated by his performances for Brazil in the 2002 World Cup rather than club form with Paris Saint-Germain.

He established himself as a player who could make as well as take goals, steering Barcelona to the *La Liga* crown with a string of outstanding individual performances that earned him the first of two successive World Player of the Year awards.

His worldwide popularity could be measured in monetary terms. A survey showed that he was challenging even David 'Golden Balls' Beckham as the highest earner from sponsorship and commercial deals, pulling in more than £30 million a year.

Chelsea tried to lure him to Stamford Bridge with a reported offer of £60 million, but Barcelona turned it down because they knew Ronaldinho had unfinished business at the Nou Camp.

He played a key role in putting Chelsea out of the Champions League in 2006, and went on to help Barcelona conquer Arsenal in the final. Ironically, both London clubs had been desperate to sign him. It was reported that it would take a mind-blowing (unless you're Roman Abramovich) £85 million to persuade Barcelona to part with the Brazilian – but then came his slump in form.

Ronaldinho had set the standards by which he was to be judged, and when he failed to produce anything like his best in the 2006 World Cup, disappointed fans smashed a 23-foot high fibre-glass statue that had been raised in his honour in Brazil after the 2002 World Cup. They were upset when reports appeared about Ronaldinho partying with team-mates in a nightclub after their exit from the tournament in Germany.

His popularity in Barcelona dipped even more in June 2007 when Real Madrid pipped them for the *La Liga* title, and the fans started to question whether it had been Ronaldinho's lack of commitment earlier in the season that had cost them the championship.

One of the finest footballers ever suddenly had a weight on his mind.

49

Steven Gerrard

Born: Whiston, Merseyside, 30 May 1980
Career span: 1997–
Clubs: Liverpool 1997– (268 league games, 44 goals)
England: 58 caps, 12 goals
Club honours: 2 FA Cups, 2 League Cups, 1 Uefa Cup, 1 Champions
League
PFA Player of the Year 2006

THERE are not many players worthy or capable of carrying the accolade of the 'new' Duncan Edwards. Brian Clough hung the title on Roy Keane, and now I bestow it on Steven Gerrard as he builds an impressive career at Anfield.

He has developed into the sort of player Duncan had already become when he was cut down before his prime in the 1958 Munich air crash. That tragedy decimated the Busby Babes long before they had reached their full potential.

Gerrard is stamping his authority on the midfield for Liverpool and England and charging through to score spectacular goals in true Edwards style. The human dynamo is there to support his forwards and pops up from nowhere to help out in defence.

I tossed up between Gerrard, the swashbuckling but injury-prone Bryan Robson and Frank Lampard for this spot in my élite list, and came down on Steven's side because he has the better all-round game. If I had decided purely on attacking qualities, then Lampard, son of my old West Ham team-mate Frank Lampard Senior, would have got the nod.

One of the big puzzles for the England management team is why Gerrard and Lampard do not function properly together on the international stage. On paper, they appear to be the perfect partners, but they rarely spark each other off on the pitch. This is possibly because they are too similar, both of them mixing aggression with a desire to make breaks from a central-midfield position.

If they could only find a way to play in harness, England would have their most potent midfield for years. All the ingredients seemed to be there when Beckham was at his peak wide on the right, but the final mix was often disappointing. As I write, Gerrard and Lampard have played together for England in 33 internationals, of which 20 have been won, seven drawn and six lost. Unfortunately, several of the defeats have come in the major tournaments when their twin-engines have spluttered. I don't claim to be the world's greatest tactician (when I was a player I thought tactics were a sort of mint), but surely it is as simple as when Gerrard goes forward Lampard should sit back, and vice versa. But too often they seem to want to fill the same hole.

Off the pitch, they are strong in support of each other. Many of the spectators booed when Lampard's name was announced in the starting line-up against Brazil as international football returned to Wembley in the summer of 2007. His hit-and-miss season with Chelsea and sudden lack of goals for England turned a lot of fickle fans against him.

'It was a shock to hear that reaction,' said Gerrard. 'You hear it on the Tannoy as they go through the names. The majority of the team got a cheer but not Frank. He got a few jeers.

'As a football player it can affect you in two ways. You either go into a shell or you puff out your chest, take it on the chin and get on with it. I definitely know the way Frank will go – he will beat his critics. He'll score a wonder goal in the next few games or put in a wonderful performance.

'Let's get this right – Frank is a world-class player. We're lucky to have him in an England shirt and I have no problems whatsoever playing alongside him.'

Lampard is equally admiring of Gerrard. 'We are very disciplined together and work hard for each other,' he said. 'I think people have to understand that when we play together for England you won't always get the same performances we produce for our clubs, where we have a freer rein to get forward.

'When we play for England, we have to be more disciplined. It's a different sort of responsibility. We have a good understanding, and communicate well. Neither of us is a selfish player wanting to go running all over the pitch. The team comes first. I really enjoy playing with Steven. He is as good a midfield player as they come.'

England are lucky to have the pair of them together at their peak. I just hope they find the right balance to bring the best out of each other.

A player who nearly knocked them both out of my list was Paul Scholes, who has been one of my favourite players with Manchester United for years. He has a raw competitive edge to go with his skill, and his tackles have got him in trouble with referees. But what a player to have on your side, whether supporting the forwards or making himself available to relieve pressure on the defence. Flashing on to my memory screen came powerhouses, such as Alan Ball, Billy Bremner, Alan Mullery, Chopper Harris (ouch!), Nobby Stiles and Bryan Robson, and gentle executioners, such as Colin Bell, Martin Peters and Jimmy McIlroy.

But I was restricted to just one more midfield player, and after plenty of agonising I decided it had to be Steven Gerrard simply because he is the complete package and is more versatile than any of the other candidates. Box to box, Gerrard is the guvnor.

Yet early on in his career the Liverpool backroom team had serious doubts about whether their brilliant young prospect would have the physical strength to last a full season. He was continually suffering from back problems, which were eventually diagnosed as growing pains following a sudden acceleration from a 5ft 8in frame to a strapping six footer. Then, just as he was on the verge of breaking through to a regular first-team place, he was hit by a series of groin injuries, and it took four operations before they were sorted out.

My Liverpool spy, Ian St John, told me as long ago as the mid-nineties that the club were about to launch a midfield player who would set Anfield alight. Gerrard's recurring injury problems meant it took a couple of seasons before he proved the Saint right, and then in 2000–01 he suddenly came of age. He played 50 first-team games and piled in with 10 goals as his contribution to Liverpool's remarkable treble of League Cup, FA Cup and Uefa Cup.

Stung by criticism from manager Gerard Houllier that he was not properly focused on his football during a dry spell in 2002–03, he responded with a series of barnstorming performances that convinced Houllier he was purposeful enough to warrant taking over the captaincy.

Continually the subject of transfer speculation, Gerrard elected to stay at Anfield when Rafael Benitez arrived as successor to Houllier.

The game for which he will always be remembered on Merseyside is the 2005 Champions League final against AC Milan in Istanbul. The Italians were 3–0 clear at half-time and seemingly coasting to a comfortable victory when Gerrard suddenly became a man inspired. One Italian reporter described him as being 'like an avenging devil on horseback'. He powered in a goal in the 54th minute and rallied the Liverpool players and supporters with waving fists and increased effort.

Over the next manic six minutes Liverpool scored two more goals to draw level, the equaliser coming after the almost demented Gerrard had won a penalty with one of his typical charging runs through the middle.

Liverpool eventually won on penalties to complete one of the most amazing comebacks in sporting history, and man-of-the-match Gerrard became the second youngest captain ever to collect the European Cup. His had been one of the supreme examples of leading from the front.

It was an open secret that Gerrard was wanted by money-no-object Chelsea, but he was so moved by the Liverpool spirit in Istanbul – of the players and the fans – that he said, 'How can I leave after a night like this?'

Chelsea would not give up and tabled a British record bid of £32 million. They saw Gerrard and Frank Lampard as the dream team in midfield.

At one stage Gerrard weakened and said that he would be leaving Anfield, but there was such a backlash from devastated Liverpool fans that within forty-eight hours he had apologised to the supporters, changed his mind and signed a new contract.

A year later the transfer rumours started again, and Gerrard stated firmly, 'I'm not going to get involved in all that wild speculation again.

I'm settled and happy at Anfield, and I'll be staying here until the day someone tells me they don't want me.'

In 2007 he led Liverpool to another Champions League final, magnificently conquering favourites Barcelona and Chelsea on the way. Again the opponents were AC Milan. His reward for inspiring the Reds to reach the pinnacle for the second time in three years was a new contract that tied him to Anfield until 2011 on the tasty wages of £120,000 a week.

This time AC Milan made no mistake, and even Gerrard – the 'new' Duncan Edwards – could not turn things around as the Italians eased to a deserved 2–1 victory.

Liverpool are planning a grand new stadium. In the red-blooded Steven Gerrard they have the corner stone on which they can build the foundations.

50

Cristiano Ronaldo

Born: Funchal, Madeira, 5 February 1985
Career span: 1999–
Clubs: Sporting Lisbon 1999–2003 (28 league games, 3 goals); Manchester United 2003– (129 league games, 35 goals)
Portugal: 46 caps, 17 goals
Club honours: 1 Premiership title, 1 FA Cup, 1 League Cup

Footballer of the Year 2007
PFA Player of the Year and Young Player of the Year 2007

THE best is yet to come from Cristiano Ronaldo, the boy from the tiny mid-Atlantic treasure island of Madeira, who makes football seem as easy as a piece of cake. He has all the tricks that we used to see in the George Best locker, and several more of his own concoction.

In the blinking of an eye he has established himself not only as a favourite at Old Trafford but as, potentially, one of the greatest wingers ever to play on the world stage.

It takes a lot for this grizzled old pro to get excited, but Ronaldo – Cristiano Ronaldo dos Santos Aveiro to give him his glorious full name – always brings me to the edge of my seat whenever he is in possession.

I liken him to George Best. He can also be compared to the 'Wizard of Dribble' Stanley Matthews, except that he plays at three times the speed of the old shuffler.

Equally at home on the left or right wing, there are times when Ronaldo is too clever by half and is in danger of disappearing with a flash and a bang up his own exhaust pipe. He was becoming a show pony who decorated rather than decided matches, and he made theatrical productions of falling and claiming unwarranted penalties.

But this is all the flashiness of youth. As he started to mature we could see him developing into the complete winger, able to take apart even the tightest defences.

He has already crammed a fairytale of adventure, excitement and controversy into his young life.

It will make Liverpool fans spit Anfield-red blood when they realise he could have been wearing their shirt rather than that of the old enemy down the road in Manchester.

Their then manager Gerard Houllier spotted him playing for

Portugal in the Under-17 championships when he was 16 and still raw. After much debate, Liverpool decided to pass on him because it was felt he was too young to settle at Anfield.

Two years later Ronaldo made a mess of the Manchester United defence when he played against them for Sporting Lisbon in a friendly match to inaugurate the new Alvalade XXI stadium. The United players were buzzing about his ability, and it confirmed Sir Alex Ferguson's belief that he was worth investing in for the future.

Sir Alex had already been monitoring his progress, and moved in with a £12.24 million bid even though he had played just 28 Portuguese league games for Sporting Lisbon.

The plan was to bring him along slowly at the Theatre of Dreams, but he made such rapid progress that by the close of the 2003–04 season he had scored eight goals in 39 first-team appearances and was voted the Sir Matt Busby young player of the year.

He had to grow up fast from the teenager who, at Sporting Lisbon, was banished from a youth tournament for throwing a chair at a teacher. Emotional outbursts were common in a sensitive boy who left his family in Madeira at the age of just 11 for the Portuguese capital. 'He rang me many times crying and telling me he wanted to give it all up,' recalls his mother, Maria Dolores.

By the time he arrived at Old Trafford Sir Alex Ferguson was torn between treating him with kid gloves and boxing gloves.

In modern language that I struggle to understand, the tall (6ft 1in), handsome Ronaldo, with his dark Latin looks and flashy ear diamond, is described in celebrity magazines as 'a babe magnet'. There was a heart-stopping moment for the United management in October 2005 when he was arrested and questioned about an alleged rape in the penthouse of a five-star London hotel. The whoosh of relief when all charges were dropped could be heard the length of the M6.

But less than a year later he was engulfed in a controversy that led to him becoming English public enemy number one, and lumbered with a nickname that he struggles to lose – 'The Winker'.

Ronaldo was seen stirring it up for his Manchester United team-mate Wayne Rooney when Rooney was red-carded for appearing to stamp on Ricardo Carvalho's family jewellery during the 2006 England–Portugal World Cup finals clash in Germany.

The television cameras picked up Ronaldo clearly winking at Portugal's coaching staff as Rooney made his sad exit. It was a gesture that seemed to say 'Gotcha!' and confirm that the plan had been to wind up the temperamental English boy.

The rage of the country at England's dismissal from the World Cup was turned on Ronaldo, who was hardly at fault for Rooney's sending-off or for England's missed penalties in the shoot-out that meant Portugal progressed after a goalless draw.

But he got the full in-the-stocks tabloid treatment usually reserved for failing England managers or scandal-hit politicians. *Sun* readers were invited to take aim at a dartboard covered in his face, and there was an avalanche of criticism on television, radio, the internet and in every form of the media.

Alan Shearer reckoned Rooney should 'stick one on him' and radio phone-ins were jammed with callers demanding that Ronaldo should never be allowed to step foot in England again let alone on the Old Trafford pitch.

There were firm stories that Ronaldo had arrived at the same conclusion, and that he was secretly negotiating to join Real Madrid rather than risk the anger of England fans in the Premiership.

Enter stage right Sir Alex Ferguson, the arch diplomat, who had talked Eric Cantona out of quitting, steered Roy Keane through his indiscretions and kept faith with Ruud van Nistelrooy when the Dutchman's serious knee injury – while still at PSV Eindhoven – had threatened his future with Manchester United. He used all his powers of persuasion to convince Ronaldo that it was in his best interests to remain at Old Trafford, even though thousands of football fans up and down the country were baying for his blood.

Ronaldo looked on Sir Alex as a father figure, and had been touched and grateful at how he had helped him through the emotional wringer of losing his dad in September 2005 followed soon after by the false rape accusations.

The turn-round in Ronaldo's fortunes from the moment he agreed to pledge his future to United was just sensational. He won over even the most hateful fans with a procession of devastating performances in which he showed breathtaking skill, speed and off-the-wall trickery.

He and Wayne Rooney made nonsense of the predictions that they would never be able to play together again after the World Cup fiasco. 'Terrible things were said about my team-mate and friend Wayne,' Ronaldo explained. 'How can they say that I helped to get him sent off? He wasn't angry with me, or anything like it. He told me to ignore what was written about it in the English press, that they only want to cause trouble. As usual. As if he didn't want to play with me at United again. Of course he wanted to. Both he and I are used to these things in the newspapers. I guarantee that they won't take my dreams away.

'I stayed because of the way the United manager and the chairman spoke with me. They gave me their support and that way we returned to normality. Manchester United are the ideal club for me. I want to leave my mark here.'

By the end of the following season Ronaldo had made such an impact with his fellow professionals that he was voted both the PFA Young Player of the Year and *the* Player of the Year, a double achieved only once before by Andy Gray back in the 1970s.

United rewarded him with a new contract worth £120,000 a week. He was one of the world's richest young men.

And the 'Best' is yet to come!

51

Wayne Rooney

Born: Liverpool, 24 October 1985

Career span: 2000–

Clubs: Everton 2000–04 (67 league games, 15 goals); Manchester
United 2004– (100 league games, 41 goals)

England: 38 caps, 12 goals

Club honours: 1 Premiership title, 2 FA Cup runner-up, 1 League
Cup

PFA Young Player of the Year 2005 and 2006

THE 'baby' of my list has the potential to become as good as
any of the fifty other players featured in this book when he
grows up. There is no doubt whatsoever about his talent – that
has been given to him by the footballing gods. The question is,
does he have the temperament to fulfil all his rich promise?

Rooney plays his football on the edge, and you always sense
that he is an earthquake waiting to happen. Rival defenders know
that he has a tinderbox temper, and it is easy to imagine managers
giving pre-match instructions: 'Wind up Rooney.'

This certainly happened when he was sent off while playing
for England against Portugal at World Cup 2006, and Ronaldo's
wink to the touchline bench proved that the plan had worked.

Rooney is the most naturally gifted footballer to emerge on the English scene for years. You cannot teach him the gifts with which he has been blessed. He is an instinctive genius, who produces magical moments without really knowing himself how he has done it.

A succession of incredible goals from rocket-shot volleys, scored in his early appearances for Everton and then Manchester United, caused explosions of excitement.

Starved of being able to rave about English-born superstars, the media went overboard and started to call him 'the white Pelé' and such like. Just remember that Pelé scored more than 1,200 goals in his career. Let Rooney reach, say, 500 goals and then we can re-open the debate about whether he can be placed on the same pedestal as the Brazilian 'King' of football.

But there is no doubt that Rooney is massively talented, and I just hope he can live up to his early promise.

At least he is not handicapped by the good looks that played a part in the downfall of some, including George Best. Yet he still manages to make appearances in the salacious news and gossip columns, first while a teenager at Everton. He was reported to be spending a lot of time at a notorious massage parlour, and signing autographs while seeking his pleasure.

His fiancée Coleen McLoughlin is one of the leading members of the WAGS club (Wives and Girlfriends), and her 'shopping-until-dropping' lifestyle has made her almost as famous as her ball-juggling husband-to-be, who was alleged to have run up gambling debts of more than £700,000. This will make a slight dent in his five-book publishing contract that guarantees him a £5 million advance. I must have a word with my editor about that.

Rooney owns a £4.25 million mansion in an exclusive Cheshire location, and also has homes in Marbella and Florida. His fleet of cars have included a huge Cadillac Escalade, a Mercedes, BMW, Chrysler, Audi, a ten-miles-to-the-gallon Hummer and a Porsche 911 for Coleen. Clearly an environmentalist!

I hate to do the 'in my time' whinge, but here are just a few facts to show how football today is on another planet from the one I inhabited at Rooney's age: I was earning £20 a week at Chelsea before joining Milan, was one of the few players at the club who owned a motor car, lived in a rented flat at Wimbledon's Plough Lane football ground with my wife, Irene ... and got kicked from behind in every match, a challenge that is now outlawed.

Before this develops into a 'we-were-so-poor' Monty Python sketch, let me say, hand on heart, that I do not begrudge Rooney and his team-mates their riches, just as long as they produce the goods on the pitch.

Not for nothing did Wayne become England's youngest ever player (at 17 years 111 days) against Australia in February 2003. He was head and shoulders above other players his age, and they knew at Everton they had discovered a real gem.

But Rooney's advisers were soon convincing him that he belonged on a bigger stage than Goodison, and when he handed in a written transfer request at the age of 18, he triggered a bidding war between two of football's most respected elder statesmen.

It was a battle of the footballing knights as Sir Alex Ferguson at Manchester United and Sir Bobby Robson at Newcastle set out to try to sign the Everton prodigy (who, so it was claimed, had two brothers at home who were equally talented). Sir Alex and Sir Bobby have been around in the game long enough to know that Rooney was the real deal, and both were prepared to dig deep into their club coffers to get him.

These two wise old men of football were both ready and willing to put all footballing and financial logic to one side and make Rooney the most expensive teenager in British football history.

All those of us in and close to the game knew that Rooney was something special. His exceptional talent had been whispered about while he was still in the youth team at Everton.

Everton legend Colin Harvey, once a supreme midfielder, later manager of the club and then in charge of the Goodison youth team, said, 'This is the greatest kid I have ever seen. He can make the ball talk.'

Rooney signed his first contract on the pitch at Goodison Park before he had made his first-team debut after he had almost single-handedly guided Everton to the 2002 FA Youth Cup final. He scored a fantastic goal and then revealed a 'Once A Blue Always A Blue' T-shirt to show that he was a blue-blooded Everton player through and through. That would come back to haunt him whenever he re-visited Goodison after his transfer.

His fame spread beyond the Merseyside borders on 19 October 2002 when television action-replayed to death his scorching 25-yard winner in the last minute as Everton ended Arsenal's 30-match unbeaten run with a 2–1 victory.

There were question marks about his weight and his fitness, but manager David Moyes explained that this was how the boy wonder was built.

He looked as good as any player in the Euro 2004 finals until a broken foot against Portugal put him on the sidelines.

This did not lessen the interest of Sir Alex Ferguson, and he was biding his time to make a move when suddenly Newcastle came into the frame. United had to go to £27 million to sign a player whose experience of first-team football with Everton stretched to just 67 league games and 15 goals.

Rooney settled quickly into the 'Old Trafford way', starting with a hat-trick against Fenerbahce in his debut game. It took some time to find his most potent position after experiments playing wide, but once he settled into a central supporting role he became a handful for the best Premiership defences.

I thought I detected a lack of focus and total commitment from Rooney during the 2006–07 season, following a ten-match spell without a goal. But just as I started to whine about him in my *Sun* newspaper column he got back on track and played a major role in United's regaining of the Premiership title.

Perhaps we got a glimpse of the future in October 2006 when Rooney wore the United captain's armband for the European Champions League match against FC Copenhagen. He is the type who just might mature quicker the more responsibility he is given.

Sir Alex Ferguson said after the 3–0 victory, 'Wayne is quite possibly the youngest player to captain United. You look for someone who could respond to it – Paul Scholes, for example, doesn't want to be captain again. So it was an easy choice, giving it to someone that it would give a lift to. He did a fantastic job and his form is back, as we expected.'

But I still worry about Wayne's temperament. The establishment will not stand for him slow-handclapping the referee, continually arguing with officials and thinking that every decision against him is an injustice.

He is walking a tightrope with his indiscipline, and I am sure that Sir Alex and the Old Trafford backroom team are doing their best to get him to channel his nervous energy into other areas, beneficial to his game. There will also be a never-ending debate about his weight. He seems to carry more pounds than is good for a thoroughbred footballer, but he insists he is comfortable with it.

The problem is, how do you tell a multi-millionaire how to behave and what to eat? Fines are just loose change to him, and from his outside interests alone he is earning more than a thousand people in the land put together. Then there is the little matter of his £100,000-plus weekly wages.

The riches have come all too easily, but you cannot blame Wayne for that.

In return he must be seen to be at least trying to play to his peak at all times, otherwise I fear his Theatre of Dreams could become a place of nightmares.

Even in his early 20s, Wayne Rooney can be said to be at the crossroads of his career. He can either continue to act like a spoilt child when the pressure is on, or knuckle down and show that he really is what I believe him to be – the greatest English-born football discovery of the last thirty years.

Epilogue
WHO WILL MANAGE TO MANAGE?

MY final challenge is to select a manager for the squad of super-star superstars. Who would have the man-management skills, the authority, the patience, the diplomacy and the tactical intelli-gence to bring the best out my top fifty-one footballers?

My choice is confined to managers who have enjoyed success in the English League, which rules out the great Scot Jock Stein, who had only a brief flirtation with the Football League. As with my player selection, I present my Top Ten contenders in the order of their birth:

SIR MATT BUSBY
Born: Orbiston, Scotland, 26 May 1909

The Master of Old Trafford built the foundation for all the glory years under his fellow-Scot Sir Alex Ferguson. He proved he could get the best out of Best, when other managers failed to control George. He won five old First Division championships, two FA Cups and, memorably in 1968, the European Cup. The Father of the Busby Babes, Sir Matt had the patience of Job and believed in sending out sides to play attractive Scottish-style, on-the-floor football.

BILL SHANKLY
Born: Glenbuck, Scotland, 2 September 1913

A legend of Liverpool, Bill Shankly's fame transcends football. Shanks started the Red revolution at Anfield that continues to this day. Liverpool were in the bottom half of the old Second Division when he took over in 1959, and over the next fifteen years he established them as one of the outstanding club sides in Europe. Bill's only problem managing my élite squad would be finding a place for his all-time hero Tom Finney.

STAN CULLIS

Born: Ellesmere Port, England, 25 October 1916

Stan Cullis could be called the founder of European football because it was his insistence on Wolves playing floodlit matches against the top continental clubs that inspired the introduction of the European Cup. Wolves were magnificent under the martinet management of Cullis in the 1950s, but how would he have handled wild spirits such as Garrincha, Cantona and Best? And his Route One approach would hardly have suited precision players such as Di Stefano, Zola and Platini.

BOB PAISLEY

Born: Hetton-le-Hole, England, 23 January 1919

Taking over the baton from Bill Shankly, he became the most successful manager in English football until the emergence of Alex Ferguson. In nine glorious years in charge at Anfield he captured six league titles, three European Cups, one Uefa Cup and three League Cups. 'Uncle Bob', always cheerful and optimistic, would have got the best out of my squad by giving the individualists free rein within a disciplined team system.

BILL NICHOLSON

Born: Scarborough, England, 26 January 1919

One of my all-time favourites, Bill Nicholson was the architect of the Super Spurs. Being modest and honest, Bill would have given a lot of credit for his success to his mentor Arthur Rowe, who created the push-and-run Spurs. Bill, firm but fair with off-the-wall players, managed the first team of the twentieth century to win the League and Cup double. I was proud to be part of his team that was the first English side to win a major European trophy – the Cup-Winners' Cup in 1963.

SIR ALF RAMSEY

Born: Dagenham, England, 22 January 1920

Despite what people may think, I had a lot of affection and respect for Alf. He had one of the most flexible minds in football and what he achieved in winning back-to-back Second and First Division titles with unsung Ipswich was little short of miraculous. Alf was not sure of his best England formation going into the 1966 World Cup. Don't forget that he tried three wingers (John Connelly, Ian Callaghan and Terry Paine) and dropped Alan Ball. But using his great football tactical brain, he got it spot on in the end, and leaving me out of the final was the right decision at the right time. Alf's nickname as a player at Spurs was 'The General' and that captured him perfectly. Mind you, he was rubbish at PR.

BRIAN CLOUGH

Born: Middlesbrough, England, 21 March 1935

Can you imagine the fun 'Old Big 'Ead' would have in charge of this squad! He proved with Derby and then Nottingham Forest that he could mould contrasting players together into a winning combination, and winning two successive European Cups with unfashionable Forest was one of the great managerial feats of the twentieth century. It was criminal that he was never given the chance to manage England by an establishment frightened of his egoism.

SIR ALEX FERGUSON

Born: Glasgow, Scotland, 31 December 1941

Sir Alex Ferguson conquered Europe on a shoestring with Aberdeen and then spent boldly but wisely to make Manchester United one of the world's great clubs, building on the foundation laid by his fellow Scot and great hero, Sir Matt Busby. Fergie has proved he can handle the wild players and make the shy, introspective men walk tall. The only manager to win five FA Cup finals and three successive Premierships, Sir Alex is a genius of a leader.

ARSENE WENGER

Born: Strasbourg, France, 22 October 1949

Everything about Arsene is stylish – the teams he produces, his attention to detail, and the way he conducts himself. George Graham did an exceptional job in charge at Highbury, but George's sides were mean and tight, while Arsene's Arsenal always plays with flair and a flourish. Who will ever forget the way he guided Arsenal through their historic 2003–04 Premiership season wthout a single defeat? A master manager.

JOSE MOURINHO

Born: Setubal, Portugal, 26 January 1963

Love him or loathe him, you cannot help but admit that Jose really *is* a Special One. Four successive titles – two at Porto and then two at Chelsea – are proof positive that he puts action where his mouth is. Could he have achieved it without Russian billionaire Roman Abramovich's chequeskis? We will never know, but one thing's for sure, Jose would be entertaining if put in charge of my élite squad and would no doubt be telling them how good he is!

THE VERDICT

There can only be one manager for my squad of superstar super-stars. Take a bow Sir Alex Ferguson. He, in my opinion, has been the best manager in English football by a street, and has the advantage over the older giants in my shortlist of handling players in the modern game, which is a world away from when the Beautiful Game was truly a game of the people, rather than the idle rich.

Finally, just for argument's sake, this is the team (in 4-2-4 formation) I would select for the first match of Greavsie's '51 All Stars':

Lev Yashin

| Franz
Beckenbauer | John
Charles | Bobby
Moore (capt) | Duncan
Edwards |

Alfredo Di Stefano   Dave Mackay

Stanley Matthews   Pelé   Maradona   George Best

Heroes and entertainers every one of them. Thank you for your company. Now let the arguments begin! It's a wonderful old game.